Childhood in World Histor

Praise for the first edition:

> "Those seeking a primer on the field ... might well begin here." *H-Childhood, H-Net Reviews.*

> "a succinct and deft survey ... Undoubtedly this book will be a godsend to teachers ... In the assured hands of Stearns, with his readily accessible style, readers will come away much better informed ... " *Social History of Medicine*

> "Stearns's treatment is characteristically learned, conceptually sleek, and sensitive to societal and temporal variation." *Journal of Social History*

> "an engaging, well-written, and thoughtful resource for readers who seek a solid understanding of the subject." *History of Education Quarterly*

Childhood exists in all societies, though there is huge variation in the way it is socially constructed across time and place. Studying childhood in history greatly advances our understanding of what childhood is about, and a world focus permits some of the broadest questions to be asked.

This new edition of *Childhood in World History* has been completely updated, including:

- an expanded discussion of the theory and methodology involved in a global history of childhood
- expanded coverage of childhood in Africa and South Asia
- extra material on religious change, including more discussion of Judaism and Islam
- new material on the role of the state
- a brand new comparative chapter on happiness and childhood

Now fully up to date, this second edition of *Childhood in World History* highlights the gains, but also the divisions and losses, for children across the millennia.

Peter N. Stearns is Provost and Professor of History at George Mason University. He is co-author of *Premodern Travel in World History* (2008), and author of *Globalization in World History* (2009), *Sexuality in World History* (2009), *Gender in World History* (2nd edition 2006), *Consumerism in World History* (2nd edition 2006), and *Western Civilization in World History* (2003), all in this series. His other recent publications include *The Global Experience* (2005) and *World History in Brief* (2007).

Themes in World History
Series editor: Peter N. Stearns

The *Themes in World History* series offers focused treatment of a range of human experiences and institutions in the world history context. The purpose is to provide serious, if brief, discussions of important topics as additions to textbook coverage and document collections. The treatments will allow students to probe particular facets of the human story in greater depth than textbook coverage allows, and in the process to gain a fuller sense of historians' analytical methods and debates. Each topic is handled over time – allowing discussions of changes and continuities. Each topic is assessed in terms of a range of different societies and religions – allowing comparisons of relevant similarities and differences. Each book in the series helps readers deal with world history in action and to evaluate global contexts as they work through some of the key components of human society and human life.

Childhood in World History

Second edition

Peter N. Stearns

Routledge
Taylor & Francis Group

LONDON AND NEW YORK

First published 2006
by Routledge

This edition published 2011
by Routledge
2 Park Square, Milton Park, Abingdon, Oxon, OX14 4RN

Simultaneously published in the USA and Canada
by Routledge
270 Madison Ave., New York, NY 10016

Routledge is an imprint of the Taylor & Francis Group, an informa business

Typeset in Times New Roman by Taylor & Francis Books
Printed and bound in Great Britain by CPI Antony Rowe, Chippenham,
Wiltshire

British Library Cataloguing in Publication Data
A catalogue record for this book is available from the British Library

Library of Congress Catalog-in-Publication Data
Stearns, Peter N.
Childhood in world history / Peter N. Stearns. -- 2nd ed.
p. cm. -- (Themes in world history)
Includes bibliographical references and index.
1. Children--History. 2. Children--Social conditions. I. Title.
HQ767.87.S73 2010
305.2309--dc22
2010018691

ISBN13: 978-0-415-59808-8 (hbk)
ISBN13: 978-0-415-59809-5 (pbk)
ISBN13: 978-0-203-83975-1 (ebk)

Contents

Preface

It is a pleasure to offer a revised preface for this new edition, while retaining some of the comments that accompanied the book in the first place. I am of course delighted that the book has done well enough to warrant this new effort. The history of children and childhood is expanding rapidly, but linking it directly to a world history context remains somewhat unusual. In my view, the relationship helps an understanding of world history and childhood alike, and I am pleased that growing efforts in teaching and research reflect the connection at least to some extent. The hope is that the new edition will contribute further to this expansion of range and perspective.

I discussed the possibility of a contribution on childhood to the Themes in World History series several years ago, but the challenge initially loomed large. The subject is huge, and there remain big gaps in available historical knowledge. While the situation has improved somewhat in the past four years, particularly with new works on China and on child labor as a global theme, a substantial challenge remains. The importance of childhood as part of the human experience, and therefore of history, made it impossible, however, to abandon the goal. I owe huge debts to many scholars, most of whom I don't know personally, for the pioneering work that ultimately made this book possible. In terms of people I do know, Bruce Mazlish, Raymond Grew, Ben Carton, Paula Fass, and Brian Platt, and the work they have encouraged on childhood and globalization, have contributed very directly; I also thank the several other historians and anthropologists who participated in a related conference here at George Mason University. Three readers, Paula Fass, Heidi Morrison, and Colin Heywood, provided very helpful suggestions for the new edition. Joan Fragaszy, Clio Stearns, and Earnie Porta generated extensive research assistance, and their efforts were both diligent and imaginative. Laura Bell, as usual, went beyond the call of duty in preparing the manuscript for the second edition. My thanks also to Vicky Peters of Routledge, who has done so much for this book and for the Routledge series.

I had a deep desire for children of my own at least as early as high school (though I didn't start the process immediately). I have never been disappointed in the experience, so I thank my four children for what they have contributed to my life and, in various ways, to this book; and three grandchildren (two new ones since the first edition) remind me again of how interesting all the stages of childhood can be.

Chapter 1

Introduction

Childhood in world history

The practice of swaddling infants – wrapping their bodies and limbs tightly with bands or in a cloth – seems to have originated in Central Asia about 4000 years ago. Quite probably, the practice made sense for people who were converting to a nomadic herding economy and needed to be able to move children easily. Gradually – for Central Asian nomads had many trading contacts with other societies in Eurasia – the practice spread, and it was devised independently in the Americas. Many parents believed it was beneficial to children – encouraging good posture, for example – and it had the huge advantage of keeping infants safe while parents worked nearby. On the other hand, some societies – particularly those located in tropical climates – could not use swaddling for fear of overheating the child. In many parts of Africa, mothers carried (and still carry) children in loose slings on their bodies, while they went about their tasks; many people believe that this method provides particular comfort to a young child. In Western Europe, attacks on swaddling mounted from the seventeenth century onward, around arguments that it unduly restricted a child and inhibited creative, individual development. (We will also see that, compared with many swaddling societies, the West European version had become particularly harsh.) The practice was increasingly abandoned, and Westerners began attacking swaddling practices in other societies and in their own lower social classes as a sign of lack of modern concern for the child.

Today, swaddling is still widely practiced in places such as China, Turkey and other parts of the Middle East, and Russia, in many cases with over 90 percent of all parents using the technique at least for a few months. And it is still attacked. Some doctors believe that swaddling, by limiting motion, promotes deaths from respiratory disease. Critics have also argued that swaddling creates dependent, but also highly emotional personalities, and they sometimes generalize about the deficiencies of whole populations on that basis. Yet swaddling also has its modern defenders. The practice has gained acceptance in places such as the Netherlands, where some parents have reintroduced it on grounds that it comforts children and reduces crying (and therefore adverse adult reactions to crying).

Swaddling is one of many possible introductions to the importance of world history in the study of childhood. It shows the significance, but also the complexity, of global historical comparisons – different societies have behaved very differently in the past, some accepting and some actively rejecting swaddling, and the variations defined quite different childhood experiences. Swaddling obviously connects the present to the past – here is an active practice now many centuries old. It shows the importance of links among different regions – nomads helped spread swaddling to other parts of Asia and Europe, but more modern linkages have also promoted criticisms of one society's practices by others who claim more advanced knowledge of what children need. Swaddling, a very basic method of caring for young children by adults who have to work, locates childhood squarely in global processes of change, variety, and interconnection. Raising children and being a child are intensely personal experiences, but they operate in a wider geographical and historical context than we sometimes realize.

All societies throughout human history, and most families, have dealt extensively with childhood and children. There are many standard features, regardless of time or place. Always and everywhere, children must be given some training to prepare for adulthood. They must learn to deal with certain emotions, such as anger or fear, in ways that are socially acceptable. Always and everywhere, given the long period of helplessness of the human species in infancy, young children require arrangements for feeding and physical care. Childhood diseases, or trying to prevent them, as well as possible accidents, are preoccupations of parents from the earliest times to the present. Some kind of socialization for gender roles seems an inescapable part of the process of dealing with childhood, even in the most egalitarian contemporary settings. The list of common basic features is a long one.

Biologists note the special childrearing needs of the human species. Young chimpanzees and other great apes, when they wean from their mothers' milk around age three, immediately grow adult teeth. For food-gathering and processing purposes, they are adults. Human children, in contrast, do not get adult teeth until age seven or later, long after weaning. They require extra years of adult care in obtaining food. Here is an important feature of childhood in human societies, at all times and in all places.

Childhoods can vary amazingly from one society or one time period to the next, as the example of swaddling suggests. Some societies assume that it is normal for most young children to work, often fairly hard. Other societies are shocked at this kind of violation of childhood innocence and vulnerability. Some societies think that children should be happy. Others, while not advocating unhappy childhoods, would find this notion quite strange. Some societies assume that a large percentage of young children will die, and organize much of their approach to childhood, including the way they discuss death with children, around this fact. Others work very hard to prevent children's deaths. Some societies find babies cute; others emphasize how animal-like they are. Some societies routinely use physical discipline on children; others are shocked by such methods: American Indians, in the seventeenth century, were appalled at the spankings European immigrants gave their children. Some societies assume that childhood ends around puberty, and there are many examples of great kings and conquerors who begin their careers in their mid-teens, such as Alexander the Great. But other societies define adulthood much later, and invent categories such as adolescence specifically to insist that post-puberty people are still children of a sort. The list of major variations and changes in basic features of childhood is a long one.

Puberty represents a specific way to focus the tensions between commonalities and differences in childhood around the world. Virtually all children who survive into their teens go through puberty, achieving the capacity to reproduce. All societies and families, by the same token, have to recognize puberty and provide some guidance (or regulation) about post-puberty behaviors, and while this guidance may be prepared before puberty, it makes post-puberty different from prepuberty childhood. Almost all societies have some way to mark off the age period in which puberty is usually achieved. (In the United States, the separate status of middle school is one way puberty is set apart both from earlier childhood and from full adolescence; middle schools are designed to recognize, among other things, that children have some distinctive experiences and issues as they go through puberty.) So there is much that is shared around the common experience of puberty. But think also of the differences: in the first place, the average age of puberty varies greatly from one society to the next (it is lower in hot climates, and also where food is abundant). By the same token, it can change over time; puberty today, in the United States and Western Europe, occurs four years earlier (or more) than it did on average 200 years ago. Some societies view people as adults, or virtually so, when they have completed puberty. In many societies marriage at the age of puberty, particularly for girls, is quite common. Other societies, like our own in the contemporary West, still mark off an extensive period of childhood. Some societies have elaborate rituals around puberty; others, like our own (aside from religious confirmation markers), tend to downplay the ceremonial aspects, partly perhaps because they worry about the consequences of puberty for people still regarded as children. The variations, and potential changes over time, are striking.

Childhood in historical study

Key features of childhood, including puberty, thus involve a complex interplay between basic, biological aspects of the human experience – such as sexual maturation – and the fact that different societies handle these aspects quite variably. This is where the history comes in: figuring out why different societies have developed distinctive approaches, while also charting how societies change over time, constitute vital component of figuring out what childhood is all about.

The history of childhood opens important windows into past experience: for children, for adults who deal with children, and for broader social institutions. It provides active insights into childhood today, by showing how it has moved from earlier formulations to current patterns – and this is particularly crucial when, as during the past two centuries, the rate of change in childhood has measurably accelerated. Casting the subject in a global framework, finally, allows comparative analysis of both past and present, and a vital perspective on the connections between present and past. Contemporary societies grapple with some common forms of change – for example, in adjusting to new schooling demands – but amid varied traditions and opportunities.

At the same time, serious histories of childhood face several important constraints. Children leave relatively few direct records. People recall their childhoods, adults write about children, and there are material artifacts – cradles, toys and the like, though these too are usually arranged by adult intermediaries. Childhood, by the same token, is easier to deal with historically than children are, because childhood is in part defined by adults and adult institutions. Actual children in the past, however, are elusive. It's hard to know how they experience work or schooling even today, much less in previous years. What's the difference between children who normally encounter the death of several brothers and sisters, and children whose contact with death rarely goes beyond losing a grandparent? The question is historically clear and significant, but the answer is not obvious at all. And even adult ideas about childhood are not always easy to come by, if only because actually managing childhood can be so personal. We usually know what society officially thinks about childhood – laws reflect this thinking, among other things – but it's harder to know what actual clusters of parents believe or how they act on their beliefs. For one example of the latter: in the 1960s over 80 percent of all polled German mothers believed that women should not work when their children were under the age of five, but in fact the majority of them did – so what did they actually think about maternal responsibility for childhood?

The history of children and childhood has fascinated many contemporary historians, and the field right now is gaining ground once again. Historians of childhood admit that there are aspects of children's experience for which we lack direct evidence, but they argue that we can gain important knowledge about children's situations in the past and about changes in the nature of childhood. Children's roles and functions, discipline, gender differentiation, health, material culture, relationships to family structure, even some aspects of emotional life are open to investigation. Though frustrating gaps remain, historians are making steady progress in exploring the various facets of past childhoods and their significance for the societies involved.

Analytical challenges

The history of childhood involves combining and admitting two core tensions in the field. Historians of childhood acknowledge that it's harder to find good evidence about past children than that concerning past adults – there are some topics we just can't know as much about as we would like. But at the same time, most important topics can at least be approached, and overall there's a vast amount of material available for historical work. The significance of knowing about childhood in history, to understand the past more fully and to provide historical perspective on the present, makes it important to work on the topic despite the unusual problems of sources. And historians are making steady progress in unearthing evidence about children directly, by using recollections, or surviving evidence about toys and games, or other direct expressions.

The second tension is at least as important as the imbalance of the evidence: there are crucial aspects of children and childhood that don't vary or change significantly from one place or time to another, including the biological aspects, but also the obvious fact that all societies have some way to designate childhood as different from adulthood, at least in part. (Historians used to argue about this one quite a bit, as we will see, but there's now reasonable agreement that some designation is a historical constant.) At the same time, however, there are real, sometimes truly fundamental variations and changes, which is where the serious historical work comes in. Indeed, the history of childhood forces a confrontation between what is "natural" in the experience of children, and what is constructed by specific historical forces, and this confrontation is both stimulating and informative.

A few examples of both kinds of tension, and how they can be creatively worked out, will illustrate these general points. On information: we know that in some past societies children were physically disciplined much more often than they are in the contemporary West. You only have to remember stories of teachers or preachers wandering around classrooms or churches, ready to whack unruly or sleepy children across the knuckles, to make this obvious. But it's a lot harder to know what children made of this physical discipline, or even what adults intended by it. Contemporary American children would be deeply offended, and they and their parents would rush to claim child abuse. But in a different setting, where punishments were normal and there was no assumption that childhood should be free from pain, reactions may have differed. Adults were quite capable of loving children deeply while punishing them (by our standards) harshly. We can speculate about these different meanings, and we can get some evidence, for example from autobiographies, but we will never have a fully precise rendering, and we might as well admit it.

The line moves further toward ignorance when it involves deliberately secret things that children do. Children's humor is inconsistently recorded, even in fairly recent times. Games are a bit easier, because some last a surprisingly long time; students of folklore make important contributions here. Other topics are even more problematic. It's easy to talk about adult attitudes toward children's masturbation, for example, and historians have found out a great deal about changes in these attitudes over time. But there's literally no way to know how often children masturbate, even today, when sexual frankness is more common than it was in the past, much less 200 years ago, when adults were saying that the practice was evil or sick. Happily, other aspects of the history of children's sexuality, as well as adult attitudes and practices concerning children's sexuality, produce much clearer evidence – premarital sexual intercourse, for example. But there are some unshakable limitations.

The tension between invariant aspects of childhood and areas of differentiation and change is not always much easier to handle than the question of the sheer availability of information. Take, for example, the issue of birth order. Contemporary researchers (working mainly on Western evidence) believe they know quite a lot about the effects of birth order on personality. First-borns receive the most parental attention, and as a result they are likely (so the argument goes) either to be particularly adept people-pleasers or to be unusually aggressive and achievement-oriented. Second-borns and last-borns have their own typical formulas. But do these generalizations apply as firmly to past as to present (and there's debate even about the present)? Are they as marked in societies when seven or eight children were the normal brood per family as they may be today when one to three are more normal? When lots of children (including first-borns) died? When gender cultures dictated much sharper differences in the treatment of boys and girls than apply in at least some societies today? The questions are important, but obviously hard to answer. Frequently, historians of childhood butt against the question of how much variation different cultural assumptions and material realities cause, as against invariably natural features of the childhood experience.

A related point is obvious: some aspects of modern Western childhood (indeed, modern childhood in any advanced industrial society) seem so normal and significant that it is difficult to empathize with key features of the past. Who would go back to a situation when a third or more of all children died before age two, in which some parents did not even bother naming children before that time because the kids were so likely to die? How can we understand an earlier tradition that saw parents reusing the name of a child who had died, almost seeming to imply that the child had never existed while simultaneously reducing the individuality of the newcomer? What of teachers who shouted at their students and loudly proclaimed their ignorance in front of others, not only ignoring self-esteem but almost deliberately undermining it? An extension of the issue of what's natural in childhood thus involves some really difficult challenges to historical empathy, when we realize that aspects of childhood we take for granted did not apply so clearly in the past (and do not apply in some other societies even today).

Yet historical and cultural empathy is necessary, not only to understand the past accurately, but to avoid silly self-congratulation about the present. Children had advantages in the past that have been lost or challenged today. Gains are real, but so are some distinctive problems. It is hard not to feel smug about what has been achieved – until we remember how many things worry us about children and childhood today.

In sum, several challenges are inescapable in dealing with any extensive history of childhood. The subject is difficult but not impossible; there will be conclusions that are not entirely certain, but there is considerable knowledge even so. The subject mixes some standard human features with real variety and change. And while some of the changes seem clearly good (if only because, quite understandably, we judge by contemporary standards), it is neither fruitful nor accurate simply to bemoan the past, and it is really important to recognize that some of the new features of childhood have not turned out very well. What's called for is analytical agility, and the exercise, while challenging, can be enlightening and even enjoyable.

After all, the topic has one distinctive allure: we have all been children, so we all know the topics involved at least to some extent; and the chance to improve our grasp of childhood through historical perspective is correspondingly more meaningful than is true with some more standard historical subject matter. We're dealing with some fundamental features of the human experience.

The global approach

This book seeks to discuss not just the history of childhood, but the world history of childhood, and this adds some additional spice. Obviously, looking at childhood in the world history context adds complexities: the vastness of the subject is one complexity, and any brief inquiry can focus only on certain highlights. Variability of existing historical work is another complexity. While the history of childhood is gaining ground, for example as part of Latin American history, some major societies offer a richer literature than others, and while these differentials will be repaired over time, they certainly affect any current analysis.

The fact is that we know more about the history of childhood in the West and in China than about developments in Africa or India, and the imbalance remains frustrating. Leading historians of childhood are increasingly interested in a global context – in a field that had long been West-focused – but there is much still to be learned, even at basic levels.

But the world history context for childhood offers opportunities as well as challenges, and this book emphasizes these vantage points. World history is commonly approached through some combination of several methods.

Major societies or cultures are usually identified and compared, and while uneven scholarly treatment complicates this approach for childhood, it is an obvious and important entry point. A second mode emphasizes the importance of contacts among different societies – for example, when Chinese traders and students began interacting more regularly with India at the end of the classical period, and among other things helped import Buddhism to China in the process. We know less, systematically, about the impact of contacts on childhood than we do about intercultural comparison, but there are some findings and, for the modern period when contacts accelerate, the evidence deepens substantially. Shared patterns, across many societies, in reactions to disease, or immigration, or new trade also provide insights on childhood, particularly again in the modern period right up to the network of interactions often called globalization.

World history also generates a fairly standard periodization, in which shared themes can be identified across a number of societies. The classical period, for example, running from about 1000 BCE to about 500 CE, saw the formation of several large civilizations, based on use of iron for tools and weapons. Large culture zones, around the dissemination of systems such as Confucianism or Hinduism, and substantial empires were key results. The postclassical period, from 500 to about 1450, emphasized the spread of major religions, including the rise of Islam, and more extensive patterns of inter-regional trade. It is not always clear that the history of childhood fits all the major world history periods, but there is a close relationship in most cases, and this book will actively inter-relate changes and continuities in childhood to these major chronological clusters.

The comparative aspect of world history shines through most clearly, at least from the classical period onward. What differences, if any, for example, did the major religions make to the conceptualization and experience of childhood? How can modern distinctions be traced and explained? We know, for example, that Japanese and American emphases in school differ considerably today – the Japanese place much more value on making sure children get on well with their peers when they start school, whereas Americans pay more attention to trying to establish the authority of teachers. When and why did differences of this sort emerge? Comparison not only links civilizations in ways that make world history more manageable and interesting, it also highlights distinctive patterns within a single society. Shading off from comparison is contact between different societies.

The results of contact, though not unrelated to comparison, are often more challenging. Childhood is, after all, in some ways a relatively personal experience, and many societies and families will seek to shield it from outside influences even when contact is being accepted in other, adult areas. We don't know much, for example, at least as yet, about the results of Chinese–Indian contacts in the late classical period on childhood, even though we can trace influences in formal, adult culture and trade. Even more recent examples can be elusive. What happened to childhood in India or Africa (if anything) as a result of new contacts with Europeans through imperialism? What does "Americanization" do to childhoods in other parts of the world? As a simple but intriguing example of this latter: almost every major language now has a version of "happy birthday to you," sung at children's celebrations in very different cultures. What's the significance, and have birthdays (a modern invention even in the United States) come to mean the same thing around the world as a result of American example?

World history also focuses attention on major changes in the ideas and experiences of childhood. Some world historians use the term "big history" to define their topic, because obviously, given the vastness of the field, it's the really significant and general changes that most invite analysis on a global scale. The clearest transformation in childhood's world history involves the replacement of agricultural with industrial societies (and the imitation of industrial patterns, like mass schooling, even in societies still striving to complete the industrialization process). Not everything changed, of course – again, some aspects of childhood are simply natural, and so persist across time – but the basic purpose of childhood was redefined, and from this a number of intriguing consequences followed. Even advanced industrial societies are still working out the implications of these alterations.

But this is not the only big change to focus on: the shift from hunting and gathering to agriculture also had huge implications for childhood, even though (because of remoteness in time) we know less about them. And there are a few other markers in world history, like the spread of world religions, which encourage assessment in terms of big changes as well. At the most recent end, the phenomenon of globalization, accelerating the interactions among major societies, has impacts on childhood, introducing some further changes within the larger patterns of the modern experience. Most obviously, the spread of consumerism for children provides interesting challenges for established ideas about childhood, and provokes some resistance as well (from adults, almost surely, more than children themselves). Again, world history encourages us to address the big picture, where children are concerned.

Analyses of comparisons and big changes intertwine. While major changes, like the tendency to universalize schooling for children, apply across many political and cultural borders, they interact with different traditional beliefs and practices, which means that the general shift – to schooling – must in fact be treated comparatively, as in the Japan–United States example. Even children's consumerism is not uniform. Children in both the United States and Egypt are exposed to some of the same television shows, like *Sesame Street*; but many Egyptian children watch *Sesame Street* into their teens, which suggests they are getting some meaning from it that differs from what American children get, who usually outgrow this show by early primary school.

Theoretical frameworks

Sketching a global history of childhood involves the encounter with standard problems in the field, including the limitations of evidence from actual children and the tension between natural features and cultural determinants. It involves applying world history categories, including periodization. But it involves as well the need to recognize and grapple with two overlapping analytical problems, which must be identified in advance. Both problems link to the wider features of this historical field and the world history context, but they have more specific dimensions as well. The problems involve the lenses through which childhood can be viewed, and the extent to which these lenses are shaped or distorted by the modern and the Western.

The traditional–modern contrast

Problem number one, which is really a version of nature or biology versus cultural change, focuses on the relationships between modern childhoods and childhoods in the past. Here, some of the first historians to undertake serious research on childhood made a major, though understandable, mistake. Many of them, working on Western Europe and to some extent colonial America, were overimpressed with the huge differences between the childhood they saw around them and what they were uncovering about the past. Children at work, often disciplined severely, frequently dying young, sometimes actually sent away to labor under harsh strangers – what could be more distant from contemporary ideals? So some historians wrote about how traditional parents, in contrast to modern ones, did not love their children – as one historian of England put it, one would not expect to find any more love in a premodern family than one would in a bird's nest. Another argued that only in the twentieth century (at least in the Western world) did children begin to be treated properly for the first time in human history.

Debate focused particularly around the views of a pioneering French historian, Philippe Ariès, and it went beyond the most general claims about a traditional–modern contrast. It was in 1962 that Ariès issued his book, *Centuries of Childhood*, on the history of childhood in medieval and early modern Europe, based both on demographic and on cultural data. The book essentially opened childhood to serious historical inquiry for the first time.

Ariès' take on the past convinced him that the relationship between modern and premodern childhood had been widely misunderstood. Using evidence rather skewed toward elites, including family portraits, he argued that traditional Europeans did not have a very distinct conception of childhood as a separate stage of life, and tended to relegate children to the margins of family activity. Paintings, for example, revealed children either hovering on the edges of the main family group, or dressed up as adults, or both. Ariès did not mean that parents had no affection for children – he was prepared to grant that this is a natural manifestation – but that they simply did not devote much time or special attention to them. In his view, this situation began to change in the seventeenth and eighteenth centuries, first among the upper classes. Childhood became more central, with growing recognition of special needs for nurture and guidance; a focus on schooling increased; birth rates began to drop in order to permit more attention to individual children; and a more formal distinction between childhood and major stages within it, and adulthood, marked this transformation as well.

Ariès himself believed that the premodern approach to children had many advantages over the modern. His argument is worth attention still: he claimed that lesser focus on childhood in the past, though seemingly a drawback, actually gave children more latitude than they would have amid the careful monitoring of modern societies. This was a conservative outlook with a special twist. Most historians who took up Ariès' claim, however, simplified it to read that premodern folks tended to neglect childhood and children, often misusing them in the process, and that the modern rise of child consciousness supported a host of specific gains. It was this argument, in turn, that soon drew revisionist fire.

For attacks on what we might call the bleak-traditionalist school were not slow in coming. Historians began to look at different kinds of evidence, while dismissing some of Ariès' data as too limited. A number of scholars working on early medieval England, for example, discovered law codes that clearly stipulated the need to protect children, recognizing childhood as a distinct and important phase of life. A number of medievalists, deeply convinced of the human qualities of their subjects in a time period they loved, also reacted viscerally to the notion that these subjects were nasty and cruel to children.

Revisionists, objecting to the bleak-traditionalist interpretation and its strong contrast between present and past, emphasize two points most strongly. First, as the legal studies suggest, they dispute the idea that traditional Europeans lacked a conception of childhood as a stage of life, with some special needs. Second, they vigorously reject the notion that most parents were not affectionate with their children. In contrast, they argue that when personal kinds of evidence are examined, such as letters and diaries, it becomes obvious that parental love was normal, expected, and natural. Fathers in premodern England were often so pleased at the birth of their children that they sent out congratulatory letters.

The upshot of this often heated debate was that Ariès and some of the other pioneers in childhood's history got it wrong. They overdid the past–present contrast. There are situations where parents don't love children, and individual parents may hold back their affections in any society. But love for children is not just a modern invention; it exists in most times and places and is, to some extent at least, natural. Indeed, for mothers who breastfeed, a hormone is released that strongly promotes emotional bonding. We should not overdo changes from the premodern to the modern, for some aspects of childhood apply almost everywhere. Nor has the Ariès argument about a lack of traditional recognition of childhood as a separate stage held up: the more recent revisionists have largely put that contention to rest. And no current historian would still contend that the twentieth century magically invented the first acceptable treatment of children – the past was not that bad, the contemporary period not that good, for such a claim to hold water.

Indeed, it is tempting now to dismiss the whole debate around Ariès as over and done with, not worth mentioning any more. And the fact that the debate centered strictly within a Western context risks makes it even less relevant for a brief book dealing with global and not merely Western dimensions. Yet two factors – in addition to showing how major controversy accompanied the first steps to deal with childhood historically – legitimate and even require that the discussion be reviewed, while dismissing some of the initial exaggerations. In the first place, the revisionists themselves sometimes went too far; and in the second place, somewhat surprisingly, some of the research now being devoted to other societies – for example, Japan – replicates some of Ariès' earlier contentions about the absence of a very specific designation of childhood after a period of infancy. The debate, in other words, may end up taking on global dimensions.

First, the revisionist excesses. Just as the first group of childhood historians oversimplified, in their excitement at seeming to find how different premodern childhood was, so their critics sometimes minimized genuine contrasts in their zeal to find premodern parents just as loving and responsible as their contemporary counterparts. Loving parents in two different time periods may significantly vary in the ways they treat children, and even the ways they express love. Modern parenting is often different from premodern patterns – not necessarily better, certainly not necessarily more affectionate, but different. Later chapters in this book discuss some of the huge changes in the unfolding of modern childhood that risk being overlooked or oversimplified if we paint earlier parents as simply alternate versions of modern ones. It remains essential to remember the debate: showing that styles of discipline or the functions of children have changed, as they have, should not lead to hasty conclusions about alterations in the emotional content of children's lives. But there is a distinctive modern childhood in several crucial respects, despite some of the revisionist protests.

The global aspect of the debate is even more surprising. For a time, even as the debate raged, the Western confines of most historical work prevented any wider extension of the subject. Many experts believed, if they thought about comparative issues at all, that the whole issue was a matter of Western culture alone. Many features of premodern childhood in Europe, however, were shared by other agricultural societies, including strict discipline and a lack of some of the more modern forms of affection. More important, historians working on some other societies are themselves finding that, prior to the past two centuries or so, there was a lack of a fully developed concept of childhood – just as, in broad outline, Ariès had argued for medieval Europe. A number of Japanese historians have thus pointed to a fairly weak concept of childhood prior to the nineteenth and twentieth centuries. While some schools existed – and they began to expand rapidly after 1800 – they were private institutions; the state (as was true in most other premodern societies) did not recognize any educational responsibility to children. Child criminals were treated just like adults, with no sense of special sensitivities. The Japanese publishing industry (which in Europe by the late eighteenth century was beginning to crank out some books specifically directed to children) paid essentially no attention to a child market. Rural villages, where the majority of people lived, had little or no recreation specifically directed toward children – they may have done less in this regard than traditional European villages did. According to this line of argument – and there is some debate – a full sense of childhood emerged in Japan only with other aspects of modernity, that is from the later nineteenth century onward. Traditional Japanese society certainly understood that children were different in some respects – indeed, until about age seven Japanese children were often treated with great indulgence, only to fall often rather suddenly under a harsh work regime thereafter. The point is, as with Europe, that the traditional approach was different from what it would become in modern Japan.

No one is eager to make the mistakes of Ariès and his overenthusiastic followers by overdoing claims about a lack of distinct childhood before modern times. But historians working not only on Japan, but also on India, Africa, Russia, and elsewhere do nevertheless conclude that not only traditional conditions, but many traditional concepts about children were quite different from modern ones. Of course, some of the arguments may turn out to be overstated, just as they were with the pioneers of research on the West. Now that we know the importance of not exaggerating contrasts, of understanding that some aspects of childhood and its treatment are both natural and constant, finding words to express sometimes subtle differences in modern times is not always easy. But the tension between a proper appreciation of the positive qualities of premodern childhood, and a realization that modern conditions have brought or are bringing some serious change, turns out to be a global issue, not just a Western one. The debate around Ariès, in other words, has been displaced; but a more nuanced debate about modern change is virtually unavoidable. The still-tentative global expansion of childhood's history makes this point inescapable.

The West and the world

The second key issue, related to the analysis of modernity and tradition, involves putting Western patterns in proper perspective. World history is predicated, among other things, on the importance of delineating Western developments and influence very carefully, to make it clear that several traditions besides that of the West are valid and significant in the global past, and that even in modern times Western models are contested and modified in their interactions with other regions.

The history of childhood may seem to challenge this more global approach, for two reasons. First, as noted, the history of childhood has been more fully developed for Europe and the United States than for most other societies. This means that Western details may seem to predominate simply by default. Before modern centuries, in fact, we already know enough to make it clear that Western patterns were not always very unusual and certainly not unduly significant. European childhood can be put in proper context, even though knowledge of some other regions is not as abundant as might be hoped.

For modern times, however, the gaps in available historical findings are compounded by the facts that the West led, chronologically, in introducing many key modern forms of childhood, and that it was Western influence that helped bring change to many other parts of the world (including, for example, Japan). Even in the twenty-first century, when voices from different regions have greater resonance than they did in the age of Western imperialism, Western standards show up disproportionately – for better or for worse – in international declarations about children's rights. And Western criticism of other societies continues to have particular sting.

All of this raises real challenges for a world history approach to childhood, to make sure that it does not become, in its modern phase, merely a mindless history of what the West did and how the rest of the world reacted – which is precisely the simplification world history seeks to avoid. There are three basic correctives.

- Try to distinguish between Western influence and larger forces that pushed both the West and then other societies toward certain kinds of change. The West, for example, was the first society to introduce modern levels of birth-rate reduction, but many other societies would later follow suit, not really because of Western pressure or example, but because the trend made sense given larger modern conditions. Change, in other words, was often shared by the West and other places because of factors that were also shared.
- Recognize that, even when Western influence combined with modern changes, many societies produced their own reactions based on regional traditions and other elements. Certain types of change are widely current in the modern world, and Western models are undeniably influential, but different types of modern childhood still echo regional differentiations. Swaddling is an obvious case in point: there is no uniform, global reaction to traditions or to criticisms of this age-old practice. The same point applies to distinctive forms of modern consumerism.

- Trace, finally, the extent to which Western activities, and particularly economic exploitation, often inhibit societies from adjusting childhoods as fully as Western advocates urge, for example in the area of reducing child labor. Western impact, in other words, is not simply a force for positive change. It can also add to regional inequalities and variety.

Modern childhood is a complex phenomenon, and must not be reduced to Western patterns alone, or (even worse) to a comparative approach that holds Western achievements as the model on the basis of which other regions must be criticized for failures to reach the Western level. Western standards have gained influence, which is one of the developments that must be explained as part of the global modern history of childhood, but far more is involved.

Many of the chapters that follow grapple with the twin problems of assessing changes and continuities between modern and premodern contexts, in many regions of the world, and with identifying Western roles and diverse reactions in this process. Even the most advanced industrial societies are still adjusting to some of the shifts in childhood that the decline of agriculture and the rise of urban, industrial forms impelled. The implications of modern transformations of children's functions, from work to schooling, and of rates of birth and death are still being worked out, though in different ways, from the United States to sub-Saharan Africa or India.

We begin, however, with the establishment of agricultural society itself. The replacement of hunting and gathering economies with agriculture ushered in its own fundamental transformation in the ways childhood was defined and implemented, even though, because of the remoteness in time, we know less about this shift than about the more modern one. Different regions then produced distinctive variants on agricultural models, in response to subsequent developments such as the advent of civilization as a form of human organization, and then the impact of major religions. Alterations in trade and contact patterns also bridged between agricultural childhoods and some of the forces that would later coalesce into more modern forms.

The advent of industrialization itself was not a final transition. Later additions, such as the rise of global consumerism, brought further changes into modern childhood standards, providing new challenges for widely held ideas about what childhood should involve, and provoking various kinds of resistance as well.

Childhood in world history is a particularly revealing topic precisely because it blends common components from the nature of the human animal with some widely shared big changes headed by agriculture and then industrialization, with a criss-cross of comparative differences. For childhoods mirror the societies that surround them, and they also help produce these same societies through the adults who emerge from children's socialization.

Childhood, in this sense, is a unique key to the larger human experience, from historical past to global present.

Further reading

Few works attempt anything like a global history of childhood. Important works include A.R. Colon, *A History of Children: A Socio-Cultural Survey Across Millennia* (Westport, CT: Greenwood Press, 2001) and Paula Fass, ed., *Encyclopaedia of the History of Childhood*, 3 vols (New York: Macmillan, 2004). The *Journal of the Society for the History of Childhood* provides reliable, current information.

See also Philippe Ariès, *Centuries of Childhood: A Social History of Family Life* (New York: McGraw-Hill, 1962). A recent critique is Willem Koops and Michael Zuckerman, *Beyond the Century of the Child: Cultural History and Developmental Psychology* (Philadelphia: University of Pennsylvania Press, 2003).

Chapter 2

Childhood in agricultural societies
The first big changes

The natural economy for human beings involved hunting and gathering. Most of the history of the species has been wrapped up in a hunting and gathering economy, and this means that the initial ideas and practices directed at childhood were formed in this context as well. Our knowledge about hunting and gathering societies in the past is limited, beyond the fact that hunting and gathering bands, usually with 60–80 people from two or three extended families, featured men specializing in the hunt while women collected seeds, nuts, and berries. Childhood fits into this context, but we have few details; most evidence comes from material remains plus observation of some of the hunting and gathering societies that have persisted into modern times. Assessing childhood in these societies is important nevertheless, because traces of hunting and gathering habits linger today, even in very different economies, and because some of the natural or inherent aspects of childhood shine through as well. People in hunting and gathering societies, for example, were responsible for the fundamental adaptations to prolonged dependency in childhood, which differentiated them from their ancestors and cousins among the other primate species.

This chapter also deals with the first great revolution in human conditions, the replacement of hunting and gathering with agriculture among many of the world's peoples in the millennia after 9000 BCE. Huge adjustments in the treatment of children were involved in this shift, though we lack detailed information about the transition itself, including the extent to which adults were aware of how much they were redefining childhood. Most world history, from the advent of agriculture until a few hundred years ago, has involved agricultural societies, so getting a fix on the ways in which this new economy determined novel but durable qualities in childhood is extremely important. Basic features of the conditions of childhood in agriculture can be drawn from many regions, particularly in Africa, Asia, and Europe, from agriculture's inception about 8000 BCE.

Direct evidence about childhood in hunting and gathering societies is very sparse. The most obvious point involves the tremendous constraints on childhood as a result of frequently limited resources, and the need to travel regularly in search of food. Among other things, it was very difficult to carry more than one fairly small child per family as a small band moved to a new location to find game, which placed definite limits on the permissible birth rate.

Few families, in fact, had more than four children during their entire reproductive span, because of the prolonged burdens each child placed on the available food supply. Children could and did undoubtedly help with women's gathering of seeds, nuts, and berries, but their needs regularly outstripped what they could contribute; and until their early teens, boys were of no real use on the hunt at all. Most hunting societies developed significant rituals for the introduction of boys to hunting, and some cave paintings depict adult men bringing older boys, undoubtedly their sons, on the hunt for training. Demonstrations of hunting prowess are central to coming-of-age rituals in some hunting and gathering societies even today, and they were surely widespread in former times. Their importance was more than symbolic: the point at which boys were old enough to provide for themselves and assist their families was crucial in the demanding conditions under which hunting bands operated.

Evidence from contemporary hunting and gathering societies suggests, similarly, that children often played little role in economic life until they were in their teens. One group, where children did go on foraging trips with women, actually was less productive than when adults worked on their own; children simply got in the way. Other bands did not try to make children consistently useful until age 14 or so. The limitations of children's utility shaped these societies in distinctive ways; this may help account, also, for the relative infrequency of representations of children in primitive art. Hunting and gathering children had rich opportunities for play, for example, mixing different age groups. The most obvious impact of the limitations on children's practical functions, however, was on the numbers born.

Restriction of birth rates occurred through various means, but above all by prolonged lactations – up to four years or beyond – during which time the mother's capacity for conception was limited by her body chemistry. The method was not foolproof, but it had wide effects. Further limitations resulted from deliberate infanticide – there is archeological evidence of this from the Americas, Australia, and India. A few societies, for example some American Indian groups, also experimented with plants that would induce abortion. Many families surely found themselves torn between sexual desire and the need to avoid too many children. Disease and malnutrition played a role in reducing the number of conceptions by limiting women's fertility, and also affected survival rates of those children who were born. Long lactation did not encourage abundant nutrition, and mortality around the weaning period would add to the death rate. Other diseases attacked children, and some, like malaria, could also limit the fertility of adults. Many mothers died in their twenties – life expectancy generally was short – which further limited the per capita birth rate.

Revealingly, on the eve of the introduction of agriculture in Europe, most hunting and gathering bands did not bother to bury children who died before the age of five. This must not be taken to mean that parents did not care about their children's deaths; but there was clear awareness that the survival of too many children was a threat to family and community, and that death was to be expected. In point of fact, given the various measures taken to keep children's numbers down, the populations of hunting and gathering societies grew very slowly, if at all.

The importance of constraints, and the fact that children must have been seen as a burden to some extent, particularly in contrast to what would come with agriculture, should not overshadow the opportunities for children in hunting and gathering societies. In the first place, while work was vital, it was not boundless even for adults. Many hunters and gatherers labor, on average, only a few hours a day. This leaves considerable time for, among other things, play with and among children. In many contemporary hunting groups, children and adults often play together, limiting the space for children by themselves but providing great opportunity for wider inter-actions. On a second point: many hunting and gathering societies began fairly early to provide some extra treats for children in the families of leaders   the first examples of the use of children to express social distinc-tions, a practice that obviously continues, though in quite different ways, to the present day. The graves of some older children in pre-agricultural sites contain decorative jewelry, carved bone weapons, and colored orna-ments. One child skeleton in Europe was found with a flint knife at the waist, and laid on a swan's wing. This kind of preferential treatment most obviously suggested a family's special status, using childhood even in death to demonstrate wealth and importance, but it may also have reflected a real affection for the children involved. Finally, while childhood was undoubtedly a time of play and occasional work assistance, adulthood typi-cally came early: once the hunting rituals were passed, a boy became a man, and many girls were introduced into marriage and adulthood in their early teens as well. The notion of a prolonged waiting period between childhood and maturity, common to subsequent societies both with agri-culture and with industry, was usually absent in this original version of human organization.

Gender distinctions among children in hunting and gathering societies were complex. Young boys and girls were under the care of women and joined in similar games. In later childhood, boys, knowing their destination to the hunt, tended to pull away, forming separate games and groups. But opportunities for division were limited by the fact that hunting bands were small and there were relatively few children in any given group. Furthermore, while the work of women was different from that of men, it was at least as important economically, which reduced opportunities for huge status distinctions between boys and girls in growing up.

Studies of contemporary hunting and gathering societies also reveal tremendous variation from one setting to the next, in the specific kinds of personalities encouraged among children. Because bands were small and fairly isolated, diverse approaches were inevitable. Take anger, for example. Some hunting and gathering groups encourage quite a bit of anger among children, with parents setting the example in their own approach to discipline. Others, for instance the Utku Inuit group in Canada, refuse to acknowledge anger in children beyond the age of two – even lacking a word for it, and assuming that children will avoid direct expression entirely in favor of crying or abusing pets. Various specific patterns of childrearing seem to be functional in hunting and gathering situations, beneath the basic frameworks imposed by resources.

Agriculture began to replace hunting and gathering about 10,000 years ago, providing a dramatically new economic system with major implications for childhood. Agriculture spread slowly across the world, and did not convert all regions. Hunting and gathering pockets have persisted even to the present day, and an alternative economic form, nomadism based on animal herding, developed as well. Agriculture gained ground, however, both by diffusion and by separate creation (there were at least three distinct "inventions" of agriculture, in the Middle East/Black Sea region, in the rice-growing areas in southern China and Southeast Asia, and in Central America). Increasingly, agriculture became the most common framework for the human experience – and therefore for childhood.

The most obvious change that agriculture brought was a reconsideration of children's utility in work. Much more clearly than in hunting and gathering societies, useful work became the core definition of childhood in most agricultural classes – including those devoted to craft production and home manufacturing. Of course, there were still costs associated with young children, particularly before some work could begin at age five or so. Children would not fully earn their keep until their early teens, but by their mid-teens they could actively contribute to the family economy through their labor in the fields and around the home.

We have no idea exactly how quickly agricultural families realized that children provided such an essential labor force. We do know that the birth rate began to go up fairly rapidly, which expressed the expanded food supply agriculture made possible, and also the new realization that children could and should help out beyond casual assistance in food-gathering. Families undoubtedly increased the birth rate primarily by reducing the period of lactation, often to 18 months or so, which (assuming at least consistent sexual activity) automatically increased the number of children born per family to the six or seven that became the common average among ordinary people throughout the agricultural centuries.

It's worth noting, as a vital sidelight, that this new birth rate was hardly the maximum achievable. We know, from the example of the Hutterite religious group in Canada in the late nineteenth and early twentieth centuries, that when a family really wants to breed to the fullest, starting when a woman first becomes fertile and extending to menopause, it will average 12–14 children; few agricultural families ever did this and even fewer wanted to, because the burden on family resources would be too great. So most families continued to use lactation to limit family size; often they also discouraged sexual intercourse immediately after puberty (even in married couples), and typically they slowed sexual activity during the parents' thirties and forties, in part to keep the number of children within bounds. Most agricultural societies also saw the wealthier classes have more children than the masses of the population, because they alone had the means of support. Despite the continued need to balance birth rate and resources, agricultural societies did bring huge change. Childhood became a more important part of society, both economically and quantitatively.

Agricultural villages, as a result, were full of children. Relatively high birth rates and fairly low average life expectancies positioned children and youth as easily half of the total population. The contrast with hunting and gathering societies, and with modern industrial settings, is dramatic: agricultural societies may not always have treated children well, but they were child-centered to a degree we may find hard to imagine. There is some reality to the notion that whole villages raised children – responsibilities were not those of parents alone; and this in turn was partly because there were so many youngsters involved. Children gained notice in wider societies as well: legal codes, such as those in Mesopotamia, mentioned obligations to children. In both Egypt and Mesopotamia, couples who were childless were regarded with suspicion (if one could not have children directly, then a family should adopt, which was another way to spread both labor and property around). A childless Egyptian scribe was denounced: "You are not an honorable man because you have not made your wives pregnant ... As for the man who has no children, let him obtain an orphan and raise him."

Childhood also became more identifiable to children themselves. There were more siblings to interact with, and agricultural villages, with several hundred people rather than the 60–80 of hunting bands, were filled with potential companions as well.

Death remained a constant companion of childhood. While nutrition probably improved for some children over hunting and gathering, famines were frequent. Contagious diseases such as measles and smallpox became a greater problem for agricultural societies than had been the case for hunters, and this disproportionately affected children and the elderly. Sickness, accident, and death loomed large in agricultural childhoods. Few children would fail to see at least two siblings die before reaching adulthood, and overall 30–50 percent of all children perished before age two in the average agricultural society. Here was an obvious source of sorrow, but all agricultural societies had to adjust to the inevitability of children's deaths, and along with grief there was often a considerable amount of fatalism. Even where medical help existed, many families did not bother with it for children, because death seemed so inevitable; and in all agricultural societies, the rate of what modern people might see as preventable accidents – children falling into wells, for instance – was quite high.

Perhaps related to death, most agricultural societies also developed some interesting fears and what we would call superstitions about children. Many African groups believed that twins carried evil spirits, and often put them to death. Children in the early Harappan civilization, along the Indus River, had their ears pierced to keep out evil spirits. European Christians were afraid of children born with the caul (the fetal membrane that might still cover an infant's head at birth), believing this might be a sign of witchcraft. Specifics varied, but anxieties about deviation were widespread.

The presence of death obviously affected children directly – particularly when, as was not uncommon, they directly witnessed the death of a parent while themselves still young. An essayist in Ming China described the impact of his witnessing his mother's death, at age seven: "I worry constantly about people who are still alive, that there may not be enough time to know them fully – all because of that tragic event, which still hurts me very deeply."

The centrality of work deserves particular emphasis. Many agricultural societies saw a sharp break between initial years of infancy and early childhood, when coddling and indulgence could be emphasized, and an often abrupt introduction to stricter controls around age six or seven, when serious work could begin. Premodern Japanese folklore, for example, regarded very young children as close to the gods, not really part of this world, and exempt from normal rules and strictures; but Shinto rituals around age seven introduced them to this world and the need to adhere to detailed restrictions and expectations. Quite generally, in agricultural or artisanal households, young children could help mothers around the home; slightly older children could tend domesticated animals and assist with the lighter work in the fields, including harvesting. Adolescent boys might still hunt, as an ancillary to the main production, but the key point was regular work activity as part of a family labor team. The same concept would be imported into most manufacturing, with children cleaning, preparing materials, and doing the simpler tasks in production while beginning to learn the trade through formal or informal apprenticeship.

Work explains the new extent and importance of childhood, but it also introduced a clearer tension into agricultural childhood than had been present in hunting and gathering. In order to get full value from child labor, families had to retain children's services into their mid- to late teens. Otherwise the investment in younger children would not pay off, and families might find themselves short of labor as parents began to age. In many agricultural societies parents deliberately had a child in their early forties – called a "wished child" or *Wunschkind* in early modern Germany – in order to work for them if they reached old age. It was essential to delay full adulthood for many children, so that they would continue to operate in the family economy. They might be allowed to marry, on the assumption they would still function as part of the extended family; but they would not voluntarily be granted full independence. Not surprisingly, rites of passage changed in agricultural societies. They tended to shift from demonstrations of economic competence, as in hunting, to religious ceremonies that would signal spiritual maturity – confirmation ceremonies such as the Jewish Bar Mitzvah. These were solemn, truly important rituals, but not badges of economic independence of the sort that hunting prowess had established.

Most agricultural societies designated a period of "youth" running between real childhood and clear adulthood, marking years in which labor for the family was still usually assumed, but in which work skills and capacities had advanced to the point of being really productive. This was not necessarily an easy combination. We will see that one way or another, all agricultural societies developed a strong emphasis on the need to instill obedience in children, and one of the reasons for this was the hope that this quality would last into youth, and provide a rationale for dependent labor in the family economy. Agricultural societies all established clear concepts of property, of course, in contrast to hunting and gathering or nomadic societies; and property would be passed down to younger generations through inheritance, another motivation for a period of faithful family labor through which children would want to make sure that parents remained well disposed.

Many agricultural societies, however, also recognized the tensions of youth by tolerating periodic expressions of high spirits, deliberately out of the ordinary pattern of life. Agricultural festivals, around planting, harvesting, and often religious or historical recollections, provided opportunities for young people (particularly, young men) to gain special roles in games and athletic contests, sometimes committing minor acts of vandalism or mocking their elders and social leaders. Crowds of young people often waited at the home of a newly married couple to make sure evidence was provided that the marriage was consummated (and, ideally, that the bride was a virgin). Displaying a bloody sheet to a waiting crowd of rowdy youth was supposed to do the trick. These charivarees were part of village life in agricultural Europe and the Middle East alike, amid otherwise very different religious contexts. In Europe, wrestling matches on festival days sometimes pitted bachelors against recently married men, a clear invitation to let those not yet qualified for adult family status vent their frustrations through competitive victories. Occasional rowdiness or misrule provided a vital means to encourage young people to accept their inferior economic status during the bulk of the year.

Along with the growing emphasis on work and the new, if vague, category of youth, agricultural societies introduced several other changes in the conception and experience of childhood, wherever this form of human organization took root. Because it generated more economic surplus, agriculture enhanced the possibility of expressing differences of status in and through childhood. Distinctions had already surfaced in hunting and gathering settings, but now they became more elaborate. In late Mayan civilization in Central America, for example, the children of elite families were fitted with headbands in infancy, when their skulls were still soft, in order to elongate the head – creating a visible physical testimony to their social position for the whole of life. The later practice of footbinding for women in China, which began with the upper classes, provides another example of using children to express status. In this case, girls' feet were so tightly wrapped that small bones were broken, giving girls and women a shuffling walk throughout their lives. The result was regarded as graceful and attractive, despite the fact that it reduced women's work capacity – which was why it did not spread to the lower, rural classes of the population.

Beyond specific practices of this sort, which of course were not uniform from one society to the next, agricultural societies often introduced other distinctions that affected childhood. The first quite simply involved the nutritional advantages available to children in the upper class, who had better access to adequate food, and particularly to proteins (in meats, most obviously) than did most children. Significant size differences developed between the average children (and subsequent adults) in the upper classes and those in the population at large, and these tended to perpetuate status distinctions. The second differentiation involved training and specialization. Because agricultural economies produced greater food surpluses, on average, than hunting and gathering societies did, they also afforded opportunities for a minority of children to receive special training in order to become skilled craftsmen (in this case, the training was normally associated with work, through apprenticeship arrangements) or for adult roles as warriors, priests or government officials. In some cases, this training would come to involve formal schooling. Childhood for educated elites would not be defined by work, in the sense familiar to most children in these societies. Two quite different paths were created in most agricultural societies, though one was open only to a small minority.

Agricultural societies also generated new opportunities for contacts between children and grandparents. These were not unknown in hunting and gathering economies, where grandparents could, among other things, serve as sources of stories and wisdom that created a sense of identity for children in societies dependent on oral transmission of knowledge; but the short average lifespan of adults limited their frequency. Many adults still died young in agricultural societies, but a significant number would survive into their sixties. They could assist in caring for children while their own adult children worked, and maintain other forms of contact. An evolutionary biologist has recently urged the importance of grandparents in advancing the human species through provision of care and knowledge, compared with other species where this link does not exist; whatever the merits of this interesting claim, the connections definitely increased with agriculture. Along with new social distinctions, this was another key change.

Agriculture, finally, encouraged new kinds of gender differentiation among children. All agricultural societies moved toward patriarchy in gender relations, and in parent–child relations, with disproportionate authority vested in males and in fathers as power authorities in the family. In most agricultural societies, men took over the most productive tasks in the family economy – in farming itself, responsibility for grain growing; women tended to become supplementary workers, vital to the family's operations but not as independently important as they had been in hunting and gathering settings. Their activities as mothers of course increased with the heightened birth rate. These changes translated into definite efforts to differentiate boys and girls, in terms not only of tasks and ultimate functions in life, but also of importance. Girls, despite individual exceptions who gained special parental indulgence, were made to feel inferior. Emphasis on the power of fathers showed up primarily in terms of property control, which gave fathers an instrument in dealing with children that mothers lacked, at least to the same degree; but mothers might compensate by their emotional investment in children and by force of personality, so the distinction between parents, though usually considerable in law and economics, should not be exaggerated.

Gender issues were not always straightforward. In Chinese civilization, for example, boys were unquestionably more esteemed, female infanticide an unquestionable reality. But young girls might be treated more kindly, gain more indulgence, than boys – particularly the oldest boy – precisely because the responsibilities of manhood were so serious. Girls, in contrast, faced fewer expectations and so could gain some unexpected latitude.

Gender distinctions, though always present, could also vary, a point obvious in the earliest agricultural civilizations. Ancient Egypt did not discriminate between boys and girls at birth, to the amazement of Greek visitors accustomed to seeing many girls left to die: as one Greek noted, "They feed all the children born to them." But in Mesopotamia, while boys and girls were entrusted to mothers until weaning (at about three years), fathers then took over the training of boys and strict differentiation was emphasized. As one Sumerian father put it, "I would not be a man if I did not supervise my son." The attention was double-edged: on the one hand, boys were the hope of the family, and the oldest boy would take it over if the father died; on the other, punishments for disobedience could be severe, including home imprisonment, shackling with copper shackles, or branding (on the forehead). Girls had fewer opportunities, but also fewer occasions to incur parental wrath.

As with hunting and gathering societies, agricultural societies shared a number of features across time and place, but they also varied greatly, as was obvious in gender practices. Most agricultural societies emphasized extended families, with strong links among surviving grandparents, adult children and their spouses (usually with wives moving to the extended families of husbands), and children; but more isolated, nuclear families could also develop. Many agricultural societies emphasized parental care for children, except perhaps in the upper classes; but in Polynesia children were often exchanged among families, through informal methods of adoption. Many agricultural societies developed a strong religious orientation, but secular values loomed large in some cases. Some agricultural societies, translating patriarchy, denied property to daughters; others, while firmly patriarchal, granted careful property rights. Some agricultural societies gave special attention to the oldest son, transmitting inherited property and offices through a system of primogeniture that left other sons, and unmarried daughters, without assured support; but other societies spread inheritance more widely, at least among boys. Though it would be good to explore the topic further, considerable variation defined sibling relations in what were relatively large broods of children. Traditional African society distinguished children by age and gender, but promoted open competition for status, whereas Chinese society placed great emphasis on preserving hierarchy among children by careful rules of etiquette. In the following three chapters, I explore key variations that resulted from some of the major developments in world history after the rise of agriculture itself: the impact of particular civilizations and the results of religious change head the list of factors that could significantly influence childhood within the agricultural context, generating especially systematic differentiations among agricultural societies.

It remains important to remember that agriculture itself introduced some of the biggest changes in childhood that the human species has ever experienced. Specific patterns from individual civilizations and religions would work within this framework, generating variations and changes that functioned amid some broadly common patterns. Individual families and whole societies regarded childhood differently, with agriculture, from the ways childhood had been defined in hunting and gathering bands – and the new reliance on children's labor was central to this contrast.

Not surprisingly, we still deal with legacies of agricultural childhoods, even in societies that have developed yet another overarching pattern as agriculture yielded to industry. (And agriculture still directly defines life for almost half the world's people, often in quite traditional terms, even alongside rapidly changing urban conditions in places such as India and Africa.) Even industrial societies still organize the school year in part around assumptions that children should be free in summer – initially, to work in the fields; now, free for vaguer and more varied agendas. We still grapple with some of the distinctions between boys and girls that had been forged with agriculture, even though many of them make less objective sense now. Many modern people continue to believe that a dose of agriculture, or at least of country living, will be beneficial to city kids – this belief may be correct, but it also reflects a nostalgia for types of childhood that prevailed for many centuries under agriculture's aegis. Before turning to the break from agriculture, with its mixture of advantages and disadvantages, we need to explore some of the versions of agricultural childhoods that accompanied some of the more familiar markers of world history.

Further reading

On hunting and gathering: Patricia Phillips, *The Prehistory of Europe* (Bloomington: Indiana University Press, 1980); J.S. Wiener, *Man's Natural History* (London: Weidenfeld & Nicolson, 1971); Robert Braidwood, *Prehistoric Men* (8th edn, Glenview, IL: Scott, Foresman, 1975); Robert Wenke, *Patterns in Prehistory: Humankind's First Three Million Years* (4th edn, Oxford: Oxford University Press, 1999).

On transitions to agriculture, David Christian, *Maps of Time: An Introduction to Big History* (Berkeley: University of California Press, 2004); Joanna Sofaer Derevsnki, ed., *Children and Material Culture* (London: Routledge, 2000).

On early agricultural civilizations, André Burguière, Christiane Klapish-Zuber, Martine Segalen and Françoise Zonabend, eds, *A History of the Family, I: Distant Worlds, Ancient Worlds* (Cambridge, MA: Harvard University Press, 1996); A.R. Colón, with P.A. Colón, *A History of Children: A Socio-cultural Survey Across Millennia* (Westport, CT: Greenwood, 2001); Traci Ardren and Scott R. Hutsom, *The Social Experience of Childhood in Ancient Mesoamerica* (Boulder, CO: University Press of Colorado, 2006); Jane Eva Baxter, *The Archaeology of Childhood: Children, Gender and Material Culture* (Lanham, MD: AltaMira Press, 2005). See also Colin Renfrew, *Prehistory: The Making of the Human Mind* (London: Weidenfeld & Nicolson, 2007); Mario Aguilhar, ed., *The Politics of Age and Gerontocracy in Africa: Ethnographies of the Past & Memories of the Present* (Trenton, NJ: African World Press, 1998); and Susan B. Hanley, *Everyday Things in Premodern Japan: The Hidden Legacy of Material Culture* (Berkeley, CA: University of California Press, 1999).

Chapter 3

Childhood in the classical civilizations

This chapter and the next explore the relationship between very familiar themes in world history and the topic of childhood: first, the impact of civilization, including comparisons among different civilizations; and second, the results of further changes within the major civilizations, particularly those associated with the spread of deeper religious commitments.

All world history surveys note the rise of civilization as a particular form of human organization from about 3500 BCE onward, spurred by technological changes such as the use of metal, though still embedded within agricultural economies: as more complex societies, civilizations involved a greater importance for cities amid rural majorities, the introduction of writing, and more elaborate expressions of high culture. Organized states also introduced more formal legal systems. The question is, how the rise of civilization affected childhood, already considerably transformed through agriculture itself. We know too little about the earliest, river valley civilizations to do much with childhood beyond some basic statements, but the picture changes amid the flowering of the great classical civilizations in China, India, and the Mediterranean/Middle East, from 1000 BCE or so until the collapse of the classical empires by the fifth or sixth centuries CE. The classical civilizations did not embrace all the world's territory – they did not, for example, reach into Russia, Scandinavia or sub-Saharan Africa – but they did increasingly tie large regions together, most notably in China (with influence on other East Asian neighbours), in the Indian subcontinent, and in the Mediterranean. Each of the classical civilizations generated characteristic belief systems and artistic styles, political patterns, and trade and social structures that inevitably involved childhood. Further, even as the classical civilizations themselves drew to a close, all three transmitted legacies that endured well into more recent centuries, with some echoes even today. It's been argued, for example, that children in India are encouraged to have particularly lively imaginations because of vivid traditions of storytelling, and some belief that reality varies with social position – being different for a warrior, for example, than for a merchant – and religious achievement. This is speculative, to be sure, but it suggests connections with

Indian traditions born more than two millennia ago, when characteristic classical patterns were being defined.

The obvious invitation involves comparing how different classical societies created somewhat different childhoods, within the common constraints of agriculture. The Indian example directly suggests some ongoing distinctions of childhood, launched in the classical period, that survive even today. But a more fundamental comparative question looms even larger: is commonality or contrast the best way to approach the patterns of childhood in each of the great classical civilizations?

Even before the classical period, civilization itself, as it first developed in key river valleys, brought several changes to childhood. The first may simply have codified characteristics of earlier agricultural societies: children were legally tied to the social group in which they were born. Early Mesopotamian laws, like the Hammurabic Code, specified most notably that children born of slaves inherited slavery unless explicitly freed. Other social statuses were inherited as well, including nobility. These qualities became characteristic of agricultural civilizations. Roman law would pay detailed attention to the same kinds of questions, specifying, for example, that a child of a slave father but free mother would in fact be free.

The second change involved formal laws themselves, the result of the development of organized states. Law now helped define childhood and children's obligations. Many early civilizations used laws to emphasize the importance of obedience. Not only Mesopotamian but also Jewish law specified the rights of fathers to punish disobedient sons; in Jewish law, this could include execution.

Thus, in Deuteronomy in the Bible: "If a man have a stubborn and rebellious son, which will not obey the voice of his father, or the voice of his mother. ... Then shall his father and his mother lay hold on him, and bring him out to the elders of his city. ... And they shall say unto the elders of his city, This our son is stubborn and rebellious, he will not obey our voice; he is a glutton, and a drunkard. And all the men of his city shall stone him with stones, that he die."

River valley civilizations also recorded many sweet moments with children, in play and as they grew up; but the legal framework was significant as well. There were also a few cases, in early civilizations such as Phoenicia, of child sacrifice as a religious rite.

The law codes of early civilizations also paid a great deal of attention to the issue of inheritance. It was vital to minimize dispute and at the same time assure the intergenerational transfer of property. But inheritance codes also guided different treatments for different kinds of children – older boys versus younger ones in some cases, boys versus girls in almost every instance. Finally, insistence on inheritance codified a key disciplinary tool for children themselves, essential to help keep them near the family and provide labor service into the later teenage years if not beyond. The possibility of withholding inheritance from a child who did not properly serve the family, though not always effective in curbing children's escape or disobedience, formed a central feature of the context with which agricultural civilizations surrounded childhood.

Finally, early civilizations had writing, and this for a small minority of children meant schooling. Mesopotamian clay tablets survive that record the lessons of students, and also parents' admonitions that children study hard. They also record many punishments of laggard students, mainly through caning. The child's experience of early civilization could be harsh. For every story of the child who "delighted" his father with his lessons, there is another of a boy, late to class, "afraid and with pounding heart," who not only is caned, but whose teacher bribes him to induce the parents to invite him to dinner. The advent of schooling and writing also means that we end up knowing far more about the upper-class experience, the only one that normally permitted literacy, than about the majority of children, and also more about boys than girls.

The river valley civilizations did not, for the most part, leave sufficiently elaborate records to make comparisons very meaningful, except around really unusual practices such as Phoenician sacrifice, or the absence of female infanticide in Egypt. There is, however, one exception, developing toward the end of the early civilization period (from 1100 BCE onward) on the shores of the eastern Mediterranean. The Jewish religion, thanks to abundant religious documentation and the ongoing lifespan of the religion itself, allows some glimpses into childhood in one particular early culture, beyond formal law. Jewish practice surrounded childhood with elaborate rituals, from early circumcision for boys (designed in part to set Jewish children apart) to religious confirmation, also for boys, with the Bar Mitzvah at age 13 indicating religious coming of age. Early Jewish practice accepted infanticide through leaving unwanted newborns to die, but the religion surrounded other child deaths with greater sorrow than seems to have been common in other early societies, including the need for empathy for parents who had lost a child. Family responsibility for religious upbringing included considerable emphasis on education, including the ability to read and, for many boys, Talmudic scholarship. In sum, early Jewish tradition incorporated some common features of childhood in early societies, but marked off distinctive paths as well, including an esteem for literacy that would remain distinctive for many centuries.

With this important exception, developing in a transition period between the early civilizations of Mesopotamia and the emerging classical period, it was the classical civilizations themselves that provided richer documentation on the nature of childhood, and a number of specific traditions that – as with Judaism – would shape particular childhoods well beyond the classical period.

The three great classical civilizations differed in many respects as they developed after about 1000 BCE. Contrasts abound: Chinese science, more pragmatic than the more theoretical approaches preferred by Greek philosophers; Indian religiosity, contrasted with the more secular elite cultures of China and the Mediterranean; Chinese political centralization, compared with Indian and, usually, Mediterranean decentralization; India's caste system, contrasted with Mediterranean slavery or the Confucian-based social definitions in China. Of course, many features were shared as well: the classical civilizations were all expansionist; they all worked to provide new integrating mechanisms in cultures and artistic styles, political institutions, and commercial systems; they were all patriarchal; and they all depended on an agricultural economy. Contrast, however, typically trumps similarities in most presentations of the classical societies from a world history perspective.

There is every reason to expect that this would apply to childhoods as well, particularly given the sensitivity of childhood to particular cultural formulations. Explicit comparisons, however, have been rare, so we should begin with a question rather than a set of assumptions. Were there enough basic differences in beliefs and laws to override some of the common requirements for childhood in agricultural economies, to create really significant differences? China offers an initial baseline for comparison, after which the real analytical challenge can be taken up with materials from the Mediterranean and (more briefly, in light of available scholarship), India.

China was the first of the classical civilizations to take reasonably clear shape, from a bit before 1000 BCE onward, and its culture and institutions shaped a number of distinctive features of childhood. Confucianism and Chinese political institutions, particularly as these solidified during the Qin (221–202 BCE) and Han (202 BCE–220 CE) dynasties left a particular mark, clearly tying childhood to broader features of the society. But other factors also entered in, including a complicated marriage pattern and, even more, an intense definition of motherhood, some of which complemented the official approach but some of which coexisted more uneasily.

Confucianism was a secular philosophy that stressed hierarchy and order, prescribing formal manners and ceremonies to curb individual impulse and promote harmony. It deliberately sought to connect childhood and the family to larger political values. The hierarchical thrust, seeing society divided between upper class and lower classes, was largely replicated in childhood through a separation between an elite childhood seen in terms of education and a more standard childhood devoted to work. Confucianism also produced a situation – and this was true of all classical civilizations to a great extent – in which information about the conceptions of the upper class concerning childhood is far more abundant than for the majority. Hierarchy also showed in the practice of wetnursing in many upper-class families, when a lower-class woman who had recently herself given birth was brought into the household to breastfeed a new baby. Many families could become quite attached to a wetnurse, but it was also clear that the practice was an expression of privilege, freeing wealthy mothers from an obligation they might find unpleasant.

Confucianism directly determined a number of characteristics for childhood itself. Elaborate rules specified how children should mourn a parent who died – Confucius himself recommended three years for both father and mother, the same amount of time a child had spent nursing. Etiquette also governed how parents should commemorate a child who died, with considerable emphasis on not displaying much emotion. Little public attention of any sort was due children who died young. Many parents insisted on great formality with their children, who were supposed to greet their elders carefully every morning, and in summer ask if they were cool enough, in winter if they were sufficiently warm. A later Confucian manual extended ceremonialism still further: in a large extended family, each family member took an assigned place in the great hall on a holiday twice a month. "The eldest son goes to the left of the door, and the eldest daughter to the right of the door, both facing south, and all their brothers and sisters bow to them successively. ... All the husbands then go up the western steps and the wives go up the eastern steps, where they receive the bows of all the children ... when this salutation is completed ... the children step up to the east and west sides of the door and receive bows from their younger brothers and sisters."

Confucian culture, with its great concern for family preservation and posterity, also encouraged an unusual amount of commentary on infant and child health. Government support and the practical nature of Chinese science also helped promote a large number of pediatric manuals, dealing with issues such as keeping infants warm, dealing with digestive problems, and nursing. This was a pattern that would continue later in Chinese history, and would involve growing popularization. Whether the results actually promoted better infant health cannot be easily determined. A robust population may suggest some success, but the Chinese did not really break through the high level of mortality common in agricultural civilizations, nor did they abandon infanticide. The production of materials was impressive, nevertheless, and may have contributed to more recent Chinese enthusiasm for children's health gains.

Chinese art and literature offered little by way of appreciating the qualities of individual children. Rather, children were used as symbols and as models for moral lessons, as with a story about a child who insisted on respect for ageing grandparents when his own parents seemed more nonchalant. Children in sculpture or painting were generic idealizations. A child's birthdate was carefully noted, down to the exact time, because this was essential for later astrological calculations, including when would be a good time to marry; but birthdays were not celebrated. Rather, the advent of the New Year was taken to advance everybody's age (even for someone just born the day before), a collective approach obviously designed to minimize individual experience.

Confucianism also complicated the definition of childhood itself. Early childhood was clearly identified, and largely free from harsh discipline. Ceremonies marked the end of childhood in one sense: at 15, girls might start using hairpins; at 20, boys were given caps. But strong extended families and the high valuation on loyalty to parents might delay full adulthood for an indeterminate period.

Both culture and law placed tremendous emphasis on the rights of parents and the duty of obedience. Even talking critically to a parent was, in principle, punishable. A son who struck a parent, even causing them no harm, could be put to death by decapitation. In contrast, fathers could beat children at will, suffering only modest punishment even if they killed them. Parents could punish children for laziness, gambling or drinking, including banning them from the family. Courts of law routinely backed the parents: "When a father or mother prosecutes a son, the authorities will acquiesce without question or trial." A widely quoted saying held that "no parents in the world are wrong." Correspondingly, parents normally arranged marriage for their children, often beginning negotiations soon after birth and signing formal documents by age five or so, with the goal of maximizing property arrangements for the extended family – trying to combine pieces of land, for example, from both the boy's side and the girl's.

Laws protecting children directly were less elaborate. The desire to preserve family harmony extended to some efforts to regulate quarrels between siblings, though punishments here were much less severe. The state did try to protect pregnant women – it was important that children be born. The Qin dynasty allowed for the killing of deformed children, for they would be too costly to raise. In principle, infanticide was banned otherwise, though enforcement was inconsistent and punishments often mild, and it is clear that, in hard economic times, female infants were often put to death. Poor families also sometimes sold children into slavery when times were bad, as a means of helping the family economy while relieving support demands.

Confucianism also encouraged education, though largely for the upper classes. Lower-class families might occasionally try to provide girls with some training in singing or dancing, hoping to sell them as concubines to a rich man. And very occasionally a talented boy might be identified as capable of an education, and then patronized by an upper-class sponsor into the higher schools. Some wealthy families also adopted children, as a means of providing heirs in cases of childlessness, or where no sons had been born.

A host of writings, from the classical period onward, provided recommendations about education, even though only the rare child outside the upper classes had any access. The material could be quite detailed, indicating both the importance of the subject and the formalism of the Confucian approach; it was also clear that moral as well as academic instruction was essential. Writing after the classical period, in 1062 CE, Sima Guang maintained the Confucian spirit: "At six years children should be taught the names of the numbers. ... At eight years when they go in and out of doors and gates, ... they must follow behind their elders. This is the beginning of instruction in deference. At nine, they were taught the numbering of the days. At ten, they go out to an outside master, and stay with him and sleep outside the home. They study writing and calculation." Sima Guang added, more simply, "people who do not study do not know ritual and morality, and those who do not know ritual and morality cannot distinguish good and bad, right and wrong. ... Thus everyone must study."

As with all societies that emphasize education, upper-class parents acquired an obligation as well, to try to make sure that their children did well. Fathers certainly had responsibilities to oversee the performance of sons, but mothers might be even more heavily involved. Writings urged the importance of mothers in early education, even while the fetus was still in the womb. A famous story about the mother of the philosopher Mencius shows her concern. Mencius had turned in some mediocre schoolwork. In response, his mother deliberately ruined a day's worth of her own weaving – one of women's household responsibilities – to show him that lost time could never be regained.

Confucianism was firmly patriarchal but suggested some ambiguous signals about gender, which themselves informed classical Chinese conceptions of childhood. On the one hand, women's roles were different from men's, and girls were inferior. All authorities agreed that, as a result, girls should receive a distinctive kind of education, with emphasis on household skills and submissiveness. But some argued that they did deserve an education, including literacy – again, in elite families. A famous female historian and author of the leading Chinese manual on women, Ban Zhao, argued that girls must be educated in order to learn their inferior place, as well as the skills needed to run a household, a neat twist on Confucian hierarchical reciprocity. But other Confucian authorities were mainly concerned with highlighting the inequality. Thus Confucius' belief that children should mourn their mother's and father's deaths equally was later turned into an insistence on the primacy of fathers: "in the sky there are not two suns, nor in the land two kings ... nor in a family two equally honorable."

Confucianism, backed by law, was not the whole story. Childhood in China was also shaped by additional family characteristics, particularly again in the upper classes, and by some unexpected emotional divisions between the parents. Other factors reflected differences in individual personalities and some changes over time.

Upper-class men often took more than one wife, and even more commonly supported one or more concubines. This could cause huge perturbation within the family, including bitter rivalries between half-brothers, reflecting in turn tensions between their different mothers. "Since the mothers have strong feelings, the sons become separate factions." This was not, of course, a situation compatible with Confucian concerns, which was another reason for all the emphasis on obedience and ceremony; but the disputes could arise even so. If a first wife lacked sons – one of the reasons her husband might take a concubine – she would often try to take over the upbringing of a concubine's son, to solidify her power position within the family even at the expense of confusing the boy's loyalties.

Autobiographies by upper-class adults, from the Han period onward, rarely mention fathers prominently. They emerge as distant authority figures, sometimes credited with some educational encouragement. But emotional ties seem characteristically weak. In contrast, attachments to mothers were unusually vivid, reflecting childhood experience that continued to inform adulthood. Chinese culture emphasized the importance, and also the difficult responsibilities, of mothers. Confucian insistence on the duty of loyalty to parents could obviously reinforce a sense of indebtedness – as one saying put it, "as long as his parents are alive, a son is always a boy." But the extent to which these attachments aimed disproportionately at mothers did not follow logically from doctrine, but rather from a distinctive psychological reality, possibly formed in reaction to Confucian characteristics that so emphasized the hierarchical father. A picture from the Han period showed the resultant ideal: an aged woman is poised to beat her adult son, who is so devoted that his only concern is the possibility that his frail mother might hurt herself while hitting him. Many scholars have argued that this intense bond with mothers created psychological pressures in Chinese children and youth different from those that would develop in other societies.

One historian has recently suggested a complementary line of analysis, while noting that in some families, mothers and fathers did actively consult and collaborate on childrearing issues. Given the pronounced patriarchalism of Chinese culture, a mother was often the only woman a man ever got to know well, or could love unreservedly; and the same held true for mothers concerning their boys, the only males they knew well and loved intensely. From this came the strong emphasis on homage to mothers, with heart-rending stories of men serving mothers who were ill or widowed as a demonstration of their great devotion.

Obviously, Chinese childhoods were neither uniform nor static, despite some general features. Individual families might be less stiff than the Confucian norm, expressing affection more openly. Girls were often valued far more than official doctrine suggested; many fathers seemed to prefer daughters for day-to-day interactions, like the man who commented on how, "in the evening when I come home she would welcome me with a big smile." But it was also in the postclassical period that upper-class families began to introduce the painful and debilitating practice of footbinding for their daughters. Intense grief might emerge on the death of a child, even a young one; one emperor insisted on full public mourning for a daughter who died before age one, even though his advisors urged that this was inappropriate. Comments on grief seemed to be more common after the classical period, under the Tang dynasty. A poet captured the sad trend when he visited his daughter's grave: "As I wept over you I could see your eyes and face. How could I ever forget your words and expressions?" Other changes in post-classical China included some revisionist approaches to education that urged less discipline, more spontaneity, and encouragement to play. Chinese childhood had a definite and distinctive framework, and many aspects proved quite durable; but it could also be modified and challenged.

Classical Mediterranean societies did not offer such a convenient cultural package as Confucianism within which contemporaries could frame childhood, or from which modern historians can derive a point of entry to this often-private subject. Happily, a great deal of historical scholarship on Greece, and particularly on Rome, provides intriguing data that permit a comparative venture.

Using China as point of departure, three features of childhood in the classical Mediterranean stand out. (This is on top of some important differences in the nature of available sources and some significant internal regional variations – for example, in the childhoods of Sparta, where infanticide does not seem to have been practiced, compared with those of Athens.)

- First, classical Mediterranean civilization records far less evidence of intense attachments of children to parents, and more particularly to mothers, than emerges in China in the same period. To be sure, Roman commentators noted that mothers were far more openly loving toward children than fathers were; but the vivid bonding characteristic of China did not shine through. This does not mean that, as part of individual experiences, the attachments never formed; simply that they did not stand out as norms. One reason was the size of the adult community surrounding the children. In many households, especially at the elite level, the number of adults with whom children interacted, often including wetnurses, diffused children's emotional focus, probably to a greater extent than occurred in China. Fathers, though disciplinary figures, were more likely to become involved in early childhood, another distraction from maternal focus. And Mediterranean families were somewhat less stable than their Chinese counterparts, with more frequent divorce or disruption, at least by Roman times. At the same time, there was less internal rivalry between, for example, wife and concubine, of the sort that drove Chinese mothers to their intense focus on their offspring. Emotional standards and interactions were somewhat different.
- The artistic styles developed in Greece and Rome, with their commitment to delineating individual features, spilled over into representations of childhood. (This may, admittedly, reflect an even deeper interest in children's individuality; there is a question here of which came first, the style or the approach to childhood.) Children figure frequently on friezes

and other artistic presentations, and their images are far less stylized than is the case in Chinese art.

- Greek and particularly Roman discussions of childhood involved a far more open concern about youth than occurred in China, where Confucianism may have presented ideals of hierarchy and obedience that were so strict as to limit open discussion. Mediterranean culture involved some admiration for youth, including youthful physique. But youth was also seen as a time of troubling turbulence, an undesirable, even dangerous state that should lead to adult maturity as soon as possible. To be sure, the Athenian philosopher Socrates sought to develop youthful qualities toward a more critical spirit, but he was punished for the effort precisely because his society worried about youthful error that might damage political harmony. The Greek elite (and in practice some Romans as well, though Greek habits here were officially reproved) also formed frequent liaisons between adult and youthful males – another recognition of positive qualities, in this case aesthetic and sexual, in youth, but also an insistence on the need for adult direction and guidance. There was, finally, more open grief upon the death of an adolescent boy in classical Mediterranean culture than in China, combining personal lamentation with elaborate funeral displays mourning both personal loss and the blow to a family when its future support passed prematurely from this earth. Again, the overall point is the complexity of youth as a category in Mediterranean culture, the diverse impulses and evaluations involved, in comparison with China. Did this also link with the greater recognition of children's individuality in art, to form an even more basic distinction in approach?

Against these intriguing differences, deriving from variations both in culture and in family structure, stand a number of similarities all the more striking in that the two societies had no meaningful contact of any sort. Some of the similarities are fairly predictable, but others suggest a deeper commonality in childhood than one would expect from such different cultures and political systems.

Several obvious similarities followed from birth control needs and the high infant death rates characteristic of agricultural societies. Female infanticide was widely used: estimates run as high as 20 percent of all girls born in Athens. Rome may have indulged a bit less, but also disposed of some boys; and the Empire (like its Chinese counterpart) did pass laws against the practice, though with few teeth. Romans also experimented with some contraception and abortion. As in China also, deaths of young children were not given much notice. One author, Epictetus, commented, "When you kiss your child, you say to yourself, 'Perhaps it will be dead in the morning.'" The Roman writer Plutarch noted that when infants died, "people do not stand around long at their funerals or keep watch at their tombs." Ceremonies existed to mark the birth of a child after about eight days, with a necklace, or *bulla*, offered to ward off evil spirits. As in China, classical Mediterranean families also conducted ceremonies to mark boys' maturity, at around 15; in Rome, these involved adopting adult clothing – the toga – and removing the *bulla*. Little literary attention was devoted to young children, and scant interest appeared in medical writings.

Classical Mediterranean culture strongly emphasized distinctions between boys and girls, though again, as in China, these were not in fact absolute. Boys were far more likely to be schooled, but upper-class girls sometimes had tutors, and a few female schools existed. In both classical societies, again unsurprisingly, access to schooling distinguished upper from lower classes, though some interest in schooling as a means of advancing children's future career prospects spread below the elites. The content of schooling differed between China and the Mediterranean – attention to rhetoric and oratory was notable in Greece and Rome – but both societies featured considerable interest in political history and literary classics, and a strong emphasis on memorization. And while the manners imposed on elite children may have been somewhat less elaborate in the Mediterranean than in Confucian China, instruction in "the way to walk, ... the way to eat" was an important part of responsible upbringing.

Discipline and obedience loomed large, a clear but less predictable feature of the two classical civilizations. Both advice literature and the law emphasized parental, and particularly paternal, authority: "Who can bring up sons unless he has the power of a master over them?" or again, "the master and the father are likewise one and the same." Confucian overtones in China were matched by these references to slavery in the Mediterranean: the language differed, but the result was the same. Even elite parents, sending their sons to tutors and then schools, assumed that harsh discipline was essential to keep the boys in line. The atmosphere imposed on children used for work, in other words, carried over even to the minority of privileged offspring provided with education, and there was no assumption that children as a category were likely to enjoy learning.

Both societies also grappled with children who would not knuckle under, who escaped an oppressive family regime to flee to the army or elsewhere. The emphasis on obedience, supplemented by emotional bonds and promises about inheritance, worked in many cases, but it could also backfire, and both classical societies – like agricultural societies more generally – experienced this problem.

No more than in China did Mediterranean culture evidence any particular appreciation of childish qualities. Adults saw some limited value in children's innocence and playfulness – toys were often provided, and children had special functions in religious festivals. But many leading thinkers, including Plato and Aristotle, urged the early regulation of play, and overall the child was most appreciated who showed an adult-like seriousness. The main reason that storks were associated with children and childbirth involved a belief that young storks assisted their parents. Romans often praised the *puer senex*, the "old child"; the author Pliny singled out a girl for her "elderly sense of discretion, her matronly modesty." Children existed to work (or study) and to prepare to carry on the family line, not to express personal ambition or individuality. Laws, aside from enshrining parental authority and promoting goals of family harmony under parental direction, were mainly designed to make sure children had appropriate access to property, which was so crucial to their ability to maintain the family. Considerable Roman legislation was thus aimed at defining property rights for illegitimate children or adoptees, or at defining the social status of children born to mixed parents, one slave and one free. The widespread concern about youth reflected a fundamental interest in promoting acceptance of family authority and as rapid a maturation as possible.

Indeed, both China and the Mediterranean urged an early but dependent adulthood. Early marriage (at 12 for girls in Rome) was possible in both societies, to take one example. Yet Roman writers defined not only a period of youth, but a period of young adulthood, into the mid-thirties, in which people were still not capable of reliable reason – a good basis for continued assertion of mature adult control, similar to patterns recommended in China and reflecting the hope of keeping young people useful to their older parents in the larger context of agricultural society.

Finally, following from this general framework, childhood was rarely singled out as a desirable state by those who had passed through it – another intriguing similarity between the two classical societies. Adult reminiscences in the Mediterranean rarely mentioned childhood, sharing this quality with Chinese comment that was characteristically sparse except occasionally in reference to mothers.

On balance, childhoods in classical China and the Mediterranean presented more common features than contrasts across civilizations, though there were certainly some intriguing nuances – such as Chinese mother-love, or the Mediterranean preoccupation with youth. The different cultures produced surprisingly few distinctions in childhood, as against a common desire to make children as useful as possible while also acknowledging the high death rate, and to limit childish perturbations accordingly.

Even in China and the Mediterranean, individual families might modify the framework with unusual affection or a delight in sharing children's play. In both societies, some sense of greater indulgence for children emerged over time, during the imperial period in Rome or the postclassical Tang dynasty in China, perhaps reflecting new options with enhanced prosperity and political stability. A few later Roman writers, for example, talked about how parents were "spoiling children from the cradle." But this tentative trend merely enhanced the sense of surprising similarity between these two major classical societies, modified only by a few revealing distinctions that followed from different cultures and family structures. Granting the desirability of more extensive comparative analysis, it seems probable that the basic imperatives of agricultural civilizations – the need to rely on the labor, and so the obedience, of older children; the use of legal codes to express and, to a degree, enforce children's inferiority; the obvious basic distinction between elite and ordinary childhoods around the presence or absence of significant education; and of course the emphasis on gender – overrode the impact of different belief systems, different politics, and even some aspects of family structure.

Childhood in classical India was another matter, at least on first impression, offering striking contrasts to both China and the Mediterranean, based particularly on the importance of the religion that evolved into Hinduism during that period. Again, there's a bit of a chicken–egg problem: attitudes toward young children reflected a distinctive maternal approach, clearly aimed at attaching children in a lifelong loyalty; this came to have some relationship to the notion of welcoming a newborn child, as an individual, into a religious community. But the initial relationship between family culture and religious culture is not entirely clear.

In contrast to the two more secular classical societies, Indian religion predictably provided a wider range of rituals involving children, designed to mark the stages of their spiritual advance as well as to ward off disease and evil spirits. The process began at birth, when fathers breathed on the infant three times while invoking the holy Vedas and reciting formulas against illness; a secret religious name was also given at this point. At ten days of age, a public name was disclosed. Additional ceremonies for boys in the priestly Brahman class occurred at the age of three, including a ritual cutting of hair. Inductions of boys in the upper castes to ritual instruction occurred at age 8 (for Brahmans) or 11–12 (for the next two castes). A host of ceremonies marked stages in education. For example, when studies were completed in the merchant caste, usually at 16, the student had his cheeks shaved for the first time and then, with a complex assortment of clothing and jewelry, the young man took a ritual bath and performed an adoration of the sun. He also offered a cow to his guru, or religious teacher. The young man next rubbed himself with ointment and accepted a turban from his guru, which marked his spiritual achievement; the gift of a cane was intended to guard against thieves and human wickedness. Finally, the graduate put a specially chosen log on a sacred fire, and spent the rest of the day meditating in solitude. After a ceremonial meal with his guru, he returned home (being careful to take the first step with his right foot), where his parents and village welcomed him with honor; soon thereafter, he would marry. Similarly elaborate ceremonies, with different specifics, applied to other castes and occasions, as religious markers for childhood and the movement toward maturity.

Along with ritual, Hinduism also encouraged an unusually indulgent approach to young children. Even before a birth, mothers received elaborate attention, to encourage them and to promote a healthy offspring. The child itself was treated as an honored guest: the early rituals gave the child credit as a religiously valid individual with innate individuality, a participant in the divine order, though clearly not yet mature. Breastfeeding on demand was part of a good mother's responsibility, and it might continue, as a treat, even when the child turned to more solid foods. Little discipline was applied by doting parents and other adults in the household. Toilet training was put off until the child spontaneously offered, with members of the household available, to clean up any mess. The family provided toys such as tops and marbles. This was a time to encourage childish fantasy, to keep the child removed from too much contact with adult reality. Mothers devoted tremendous attention to this stage of childhood, and were normally rewarded by intense attachments even as children reached adulthood.

Other aspects of Indian childhood, however, fit the now-familiar norm. While infanticide was not emphasized, it did occur, particularly concerning unwanted female babies. Work was the destiny of most children from an early age, and full indulgence even of early childhood was possible only in the wealthier families, in a society profoundly marked by social divisions. Gender distinctions loomed large. Girls might receive some religious training from their fathers, but there was no sense that schooling was in any way essential even in the higher castes, and a certain value might indeed attach to ignorance in women. Early marriage for girls was the norm, before sexual stirrings might trouble purity; the marriages were negotiated by parents. The Laws of Manu suggested age eight, though with some latitude; but other authorities urged marriage as early as four, and never later than ten. Married girls did not necessarily join their husbands until they were older, but the importance of sexual control was obvious.

Upper-caste boys encountered a different pattern, in some ways more complex. After early years of latitude, they were pulled out for education and the discipline of their fathers, often, as in China, seen as remote figures for sons (if less so for daughters, whom fathers could love more freely). Many boys were sent to gurus for religious training, though with literacy and mathematical skills included as well. Conditions were sparse, so that spiritual goals could rise over bodily needs. This was a disciplined life. It was true that gurus preferred to control their students by example and persuasion, using physical punishment as a last resort; to this extent, later childhood in the upper castes might still differ from its counterparts in China and the Mediterranean. But spankings by fathers and teachers could enter in, and the need to recognize adult authority was obvious. Work duties combined with study, for young men were expected to prepare food and gather wood for the group. And while the subject matter of the lessons differed from the more secular content in the other classical civilizations, the same emphasis applied to the need for extensive memorization. The need to control youth, either through austere education, work or early marriage, clearly applied in India; the most distinctive features of this childhood involved what must have been an extraordinary transition between early years of indulgence and the demands of the subsequent stages prior to adulthood.

The classical civilizations do not yield a clearcut answer on the balance between differentiation and commonality. Cultures and also family structures did vary, and caused important distinctions in ideas and practices concerning childhood. Some patterns, like the Chinese insistence on instilling careful manners, or the Indian delight in encouraging children's imagination, would long outlast the classical period, affecting characteristic approaches to childhood even today. Culture seemed to count particularly when it took the form of a powerful religion, as the Indian case suggests.

Individual variations within the major societies also complicate analysis. Many parents were clearly more loving or grief-stricken than official recommendations might suggest. Advice might seek to restrict fathers' harshness, or urge school reforms toward less discipline and more attention to individual learning styles.

Nevertheless, the power of the basic agricultural model of childhood shines through as well. Similar needs to accommodate the frequent deaths of young children, but also to limit effective birth rates, cut across the classical societies, particularly in the cases of China and the Mediterranean. More interesting still, because less self-evident – the common emphasis on discipline and obedience, even for elite children taking lessons rather than working directly, shows the impulse to make children useful and to instill habits that would continue to tie them to the family even as, physically, they reached adulthood. Even in India, subjection to austere conditions and discipline after early childhood suggested the general need to bend children to a sense of duty. Clearly, while individual parents obviously delighted in children and in children's play, and while Indian culture carved out a special approach to the early years, there was no sense that childhood as a whole was expected to be a particularly happy time, and this carried over into adult recollections about their own early experience. Specific civilizations could introduce a few variants on the basic model, and they certainly could implement it in various ways, but the range was more modest than might have been predicted from the differences among the societies in other respects. Different political forms thus had limited effects on childhood, partly because the state was fairly remote from ordinary family life, and partly because, despite the differences, legal codes tended to emphasize similar concerns about obedience and social hierarchy. Cultures counted for a bit more, as with Confucianism and particularly Hinduism, but they, too, pushed for a fairly utilitarian definition of childhood. Classical children undoubtedly created some spaces for themselves, but childhood in the classical period was a serious business.

Further reading

On Judaism: John Cooper, *The Child in Jewish History* (Northvale, NJ: Jason Aronson, 1996); David Kraemer, "Images of Childhood and Adolescence in Talmudic Literature" in *The Jewish Family: Metaphor and Memory* (New York: Oxford University Press, 1989); Ivan Marcus, *Rituals of Childhood: Jewish Acculturation in Medieval Europe* (New Haven, CT: Yale University press, 1996); O. Larry Yarborough, "Parents and Children in the Jewish Family of Antiquity," in *The Jewish Family of Antiquity* (Atlanta, GA: Scholars Press, 1993).

On China: Patricia Ebrey, *Confucianism and Family Rituals in Imperial China: A Social History of Writing about Rites* (Princeton, NJ: Princeton University Press, 1991) and *Women and the Family in Chinese History* (New York: Routledge, 2003); Alan Chan and Sor-Hoon Tan, eds, *Filial Piety in Chinese Thought and History* (New York: RoutledgeCurzon, 2004); Michael Loewe, *Everyday Life in Early Imperial China during the Han Period 202 BC–AD 220* (New York: G.P. Putnam's Sons, 1968); Hugh D.R. Baker, *Chinese Family and Kinship* (New York: Columbia University Press, 1970); Lisa Raphals, *Sharing the Light: Representations of Women and Virtue in Early China* (Albany: State University of New York Press, 1998). Anne Behnke Kinney, *Chinese Views of Childhood* (Honolulu: University of Hawaii Press, 1995) is exceptionally useful; see also her *Representations of Childhood and Youth in Early China* (Stanford, CA: Stanford University Press, 2004). A recent book, focusing on a later period, is indispensable: Ping-chen Hsiung, *A Tender Voyage: Children and Childhood in Late Imperial China* (Stanford, CA: Stanford University Press, 2005).

On India: Sudhir Kakar, *The Inner World: A Psycho-analytic Study of Childhood and Society in India* (Delhi: Oxford University Press, 1978); S. Vats and Shakuntala Mugdal, eds, *Women and Society in Ancient India* (Faridabad, India: Om Publications, 1999); Harmut Scharfe, *Education in Ancient India* (Boston, MA: Brill Academic Publishers, 2002).

On the Mediterranean: Ada Cohen and Jeremy Rutter, *Constructions of Childhood in Ancient Greece and Italy* (Princeton, NJ: The American School of Classical Studies at Athens, 2007); Beryl Rawson, *Children and Childhood in Roman Italy* (Oxford, UK: Oxford University Press, 2006); Suzanne Dixon, *The Roman Family* (Baltimore, MD: Johns Hopkins University Press, 1992) and ed., *Childhood, Class and Kin in the Roman World* (New York: Routledge, 2001); Cynthia Patterson, *The Family in Greek History* (Cambridge, MA: Harvard University Press, 1998); Sarah Pomeroy, *Families in Classical and Hellenistic Greece: Representations and Realities* (Oxford: Clarendon Press, 1997); Beryl Rawson, *Marriage, Divorce, and Children in Ancient Rome* (Oxford: Oxford University Press, 1991) and *Children and Childhood in Roman Italy* (Oxford: Oxford University Press, 2003); Emil Eyben, *Restless Youth in Ancient Rome* (London: Routledge, 1993). See also Geoffrey Nathan, *The Family in Late Antiquity: The Rise of Christianity and the Endurance of Tradition* (New York: Routledge, 2000).

Chapter 4

Childhood in postclassical world history

The impact of religious change

All world historians note several key changes during the centuries between 500 and 1450, after the fall of the classical empires. We do not know how, if at all, some of the key developments affected children and childhood. The decline of the classical empires themselves involved growing instability, raids by nomadic peoples, and significant increase in epidemic disease. We can assume that children suffered in many cases – they were, along with the elderly, the group most vulnerable to death and disease. But we lack details. Late in the postclassical period, Mongol invaders conquered many areas, from China to Russia to part of the Middle East, but it is not clear – beyond the bloodshed associated with Mongol warfare – that there was any distinctive Mongol impact on childhood.

Three related themes that shaped these centuries unquestionably affected childhood. The spread of missionary religions – religions that came to believe in an obligation to convert peoples across political and cultural boundaries – had the clearest effect. This chapter focuses on the changes the expanding religions introduced, particularly Buddhism and Islam, but with attention also to Christianity. These were the three religions whose expansion helped shape the whole postclassical period, with Islam actually established for the first time in this period. The religions resembled faiths like Hinduism and Judaism in many ways, but they introduced important innovations (collectively, but also through separate features) as well.

The following chapter picks up more clearly on the two other dominant themes of the postclassical period, while continuing the discussion of religious change. First, the areas organized as complex societies or civilizations expanded, which meant that new regions gained formal states, law codes, and growing cities, all of which could affect how childhood was defined and managed. Several new areas also began deliberately to imitate more established centers, as with Japanese efforts to import Chinese forms; this, too, could measurably affect childhood. Finally, trade accelerated, including inter-regional trade. This promoted further urban growth, in new centers but also in established regions such as China, which meant that a larger minority of children were involved with manufacturing and apprenticeship, even though agricultural activities continued to predominate for the majority. Islamic merchants reached out in trade from bases in the Middle East and North Africa, interacting with Europe, central Asia, the whole Indian Ocean basin, and several parts of sub-Saharan Africa. Mongol conquests accelerated trade contacts as well, and the end of the period saw great Chinese commercial voyages for several decades. The spread of civilization, imitation, and mounting trade contributed to a changing framework for childhood in several areas, particularly between the tenth and the fifteenth centuries.

It was the rapid advance of the missionary religions, however, that introduced the clearest and earliest set of changes for this period, generating several significant alterations in childhood away from classical patterns. The religions also require a new set of mutual comparisons, for each of the three expanding belief systems had its own conception of what childhood was and how children's religious responsibilities should be defined. We have already seen that some of the implications of Hinduism shaped aspects of childhood in the classical period rather differently from patterns in societies where an overarching religious emphasis was lacking. The spread of major religions to other societies picked up some of the same interests that Hinduism had developed in treating the child as a spiritual being.

Yet the major religions were not alike, which suggests the new comparative assignment along with attention to more general forces of change. Religious comparison is admittedly delicate, for each major religion had certain emphases that may strike contemporary readers as better or worse than others, casting light on the religion more generally and on current religious affiliations. In this chapter, we consider the implications of more extensive religious commitments for childhood, and the approaches of Buddhism and Islam more particularly. Comparisons with Christianity will be extended in Chapter 5, as a central element in the mix of factors shaping childhood in Western Europe.

The nature of the expanding world religions, and their obvious applicability to childhood, partially modified the patterns that had predominated in the classical period. Childhoods in classical China and the Mediterranean, as we have seen, resembled each other more than they differed. They were more shaped by the needs of agricultural society, including the insistence on obedience and on managed transitions to adult seriousness, by the institutional backing that new legal and political arrangements gave to children's inferiority, and by the basic distinction between elite (schooled) and ordinary (working) childhoods, than by particular cultural or political components. As a result, childhoods in the classical period had varied less, across societies, than had been the case for hunting and gathering groups, where the lower reliance on child labor created more options.

The new commitment to missionary religions altered this equation, producing more distinctions in ideas about childhood and approaches to children than had characterized the classical centuries. At the same time, the religions introduced some common patterns of change and continuity from the classical period, which was another important development.

The expanding religions shared some significant ideas about childhood, which marked them off, collectively, from the approaches that had predominated in the classical period, particularly in China and the Mediterranean. Writings in most of the major religions emphasized the importance of children. Christianity, with its stories and ubiquitous artistic representations of the Christ child, gave more symbolic attention to a young child than any cultural system had ever offered before. All three of the religions that sprang from the Middle East – Christianity and Islam, like their earlier antecedent, Judaism   also highlighted the pride and responsibility of parenthood, and particularly fatherhood (though Christianity, uniquely, also had the strong image of the loving mother of Jesus). These religions also stressed the importance of obedience to parents – "honor thy father and mother" – which in turn could support a number of disciplinary devices. This was carried further still in Christianity, with references to God the Father in the Trinity, which could be taken as an archetype for the father in the family. (It was true that some Christian writers noted that, for children, love of parents should be secondary to devotion to God, which could introduce a discordant note if taken literally; but the obedience theme more commonly predominated.) Here, of course, religions offered new words to maintain a well established emphasis for childhoods in the context of an agricultural economy. Early Christianity even frowned on the emotional grieving some Romans displayed on the death of adolescent sons, urging a more "internal mourning" and a recognition that God's will must be done and that too much grief might displace proper devotion to the Almighty. Though again in different language, this in many ways constituted a return to the more muted reactions to children's deaths, at least in official rhetoric, characteristic of agricultural societies more generally.

In addition to praise for children and parenting, the world religions brought two other elements to childhood, capable of generating significant change. All, in one way or another, stressed a divine element in every human being – a soul, or some participation in the divine essence. This belief – with many specific variants – in turn enhanced the sense of responsibility for protecting children as God's creatures or participants in a divine connection. Most particularly, the major religions vigorously opposed infanticide, which had been widely practiced in many areas dominated either by secular or polytheistic beliefs. Judiasm also turned more decisively in this direction, partly in association with Christianity or Islam. One of Christianity's early results as it gained ground in the later Roman Empire, for example, was to generate new edicts outlawing infanticide. Thus a Christian Emperor in 374 CE had decreed, "If anyone, man or woman, should commit the sin of killing an infant, that crime should be punishable by death." Laws to protect children proliferated, including efforts to ban the sale of children.

Early Christians even tried to discourage wetnursing, in order to protect children and increase the bonds between mother and child. Islam, similarly, quickly developed protective recommendations. Muhammad specifically renounced the Arab tradition of infanticide, and here too there were attempts to prevent the sale of children. While adherence to the various protective measures was surely imperfect, and there were many ways to jeopardize children without admitting outright infanticide, the rate of killing of infants as a means of birth control almost certainly declined under the aegis of the world religions; the practice continued most clearly in areas such as China, where the religions had a less complete foothold. Children were part of the religious community from birth, and this had important implications for real behaviors.

The world religions all paid attention to the need for religious training for children (as Hinduism and Judaism had long done), providing particular rituals soon after birth, to launch the connection between children and the religion, and then, at least for some children, to provide opportunities for more formal religious education. This was the second general impact of the new religious surge. The result was twofold: a redefinition of what education was about – an early goal of Christian educators, attacking the classical curriculum in the Mediterranean in favor of spiritual edification; and, on the whole, an impulse to spread elements of education more widely than had been the case in the classical centuries. Sometimes, for busy peasant or worker families, where children's labor remained essential, religious training consisted of little more than inculcation of certain memorized passages that would serve as prayers and qualify for more formal entry into religious maturity; there is no reason to exaggerate the change. For a minority, however, all the major religions provided rich doctrines and moral and legal codes that could inspire serious scholarship and the kind of schooling that this scholarship in turn required. Many parents, particularly in elite families, were interested in identifying children who seemed to have an aptitude for this kind of education. Two of the great world religions (again along with Judaism) were specifically religions of a book, and this could motivate wider exposure to literacy to provide access to the Bible or the *Quran* even without profound commitment to the higher reaches of religious scholarship. The world religions, in other words, both encouraged schooling and gave it a particular bent, affecting many children to some degree and, for a few, providing access to spiritual and scholarly vocations. By 1000 CE, and outside East Asia, where Confucianism motivated much of the available education, almost all schooling occurred under religious guidance and, at least officially, for primarily religious purposes. Strictness and physical discipline often persisted – this was not always a thorough overhaul of earlier educational traditions – but there was real change.

Beyond the two basic impacts, the major world religions introduced some new tensions into the gendering of childhood. On the one hand, they all emphasized – and this was part of the idea of souls or participation in the divine essence – that girls as well as boys shared in religious life and opportunities. They reduced the assertions of gender inequality that had been present in earlier Judaism or in Hinduism (where, in the classical period, some religious scholars discussed whether women had to be reincarnated as men before they could contemplate any further spiritual advancement). Both Christianity and Buddhism provided explicit religious outlets for women, in the convents, and some girls could be sent there for training and for longer-term vocations. Individual girls also might receive religious education – this was not uncommon in Islam, sometimes at the hands of loving fathers who realized their daughters' talents. But the religions were also patriarchal, clearly judging that advanced religious training was far more important for boys than for girls. While some rituals, like Christian baptism, were common to both sexes, others aimed particularly at connecting boys with the religious experience. Any formal religious education available included far more boys than girls.

The spread of religion in the postclassical centuries involved one other common feature relevant to childhood: wide diversity in the impact of religious beliefs about children. Despite extensive conversions to Islam, Christianity or Buddhism, people varied in how much they knew about doctrines bearing on issues like childhood, and they varied also in how much they cared. Different economic circumstances affected responses as well. The very poor might be influenced by the encouragement toward protecting children, for example, but their circumstances might still seem to require that a child be abandoned, or left on the doorstep of a religious institution (a new recourse, that might, however, often lead to the child's death because of inadequate care before or after the separation). As we turn to consider some of the particular flavor of individual world religions, it is important to remember the obvious: actual practices toward children may have differed less, from one society to the next, than the beliefs implied. In addition, religious authorities themselves argued over some key concerns, which could add to the complexity.

Buddhism, the oldest of the world religions, but spreading in the postclassical period to various parts of East and Southeast Asia, had rather diffuse implications for childhood, certainly compared with Islam and even Christianity. This was partly because the religion was unusually flexible, often blending with local patterns (including Confucianism in China) in ways that might leave childhood relatively untouched. Buddhism also emphasized spiritual goals over detailed, legalistic prescriptions for daily life, defining criteria for family practice with less precision, certainly in comparison with Islam. And while there were many Buddhist writings, there was no single, canonical book, as with Islam and Christianity – another reason for more latitude where childhood was concerned.

Because of its intense otherworldliness, Buddhism could generate some concern about attachments to children. The Buddha himself was said to have told a story about a holy man who had left his wife and child, and was then indifferent to their visits. "He feels no pleasure when she comes, no sorrow when she goes; him, I call a true saint released from passion." Add to this a strong belief that celibacy was the holiest possible state, and that childbirth was a polluting act, and Buddhism could become a religion with little concern for children save that they not consume too much attention. Similar strands, including the organization of celibate communities, by definition without recognized children, cropped up in Christianity.

But Buddhism, as a major religion rather than a limited sect, embraced a large majority of followers who had children, and it did offer some guidance and protection. Most obviously, it helped organize a variety of rituals for children, to ward off harm and prepare for a religious life – in this, it resembled Hinduism and indeed all the major religions. Many Buddhist children attended religious schools, and even more heard inspiring stories of holy lives.

Buddhists also reacted to some earlier practices applicable to children that had developed in India and elsewhere. They opposed the marriage of girls during childhood, believing that marriage was a contract that required mature assent.

In certain cases, Buddhist devotion could also provide children, by adolescence, with a religious vocation in defiance of their parents' wishes, a spiritual alternative to the standard arrangements in the transitions from childhood to adulthood. This was an important tension for Buddhism in China, where Confucianists often attacked religion as undermining family loyalties. A Chinese Buddhist story involved Miao-shan, youngest daughter of a king, who defied her father by entering a convent, which her father (who had wanted the girl to accept an arranged marriage) then tried to burn. The story had a family-friendly twist, however: later, Miao-shan cut off her arm to use for magic medicine that restored her blind father's sight. Other moral stories told of Buddhist children whose prayers for their parents saved them from hell. Some accounts overlapped with Confucianism outright, as when a young man praised his mother for pushing him to study in Buddhist schools: "that I am an official today is due to my mother's daily training." Certain Buddhist concepts for children were translated into Confucian terms to make the religion more acceptable in China: thus a Buddhist (Sanskrit) word for morality became "filial submission and obedience."

Buddhism obviously influenced childhood, particularly through the new set of religious lessons and rituals; but the otherworldly orientation, and the compromises with existing beliefs about children, constrained a more sweeping impact.

Islamic childhood proved to be far more fully defined than its Buddhist counterpart, offering important distinctions as well from Christianity. The fastest-growing religion during the postclassical period, Islam evinced several special interests concerning childhood, some of which blended with other aspects of Middle Eastern civilization. The Prophet Muhammad himself deliberately intended to introduce some changes in the way childhood was defined and guided among Arabs, and his approach encouraged wider initiatives. There was no question that the advent of this new religion had significant implications for childhood. Muhammed noted, "when a man has children, he has fulfilled half his religion, so let him fear God for the remaining half."

Many Muslim writers, both religious and medical, stressed the need for considerable attention to babies. Islam itself – and this was a contrast with Christianity, at least at the doctrinal level – stressed the innocence of new-borns. These infants had not had time to sin, and they were potential believers; further, Allah himself was merciful. So there was no debate about what happened to infants if they died: they would ascend to paradise. Scholars did discuss the fates of children born to infidel – non-Muslim – families, but most agreed that they too were innocent; Christian theologians had similar debates with, on the whole, different conclusions about babies, tainted with original sin, born to non-Christian families. The Prophet Muhammad, whose own kindness to children was often cited, in specifically condemning the practice of infanticide in Arab tradition, offered another indication that early childhood commanded real and sympathetic attention in this new religion. The *Quran* also emphasized care for children if a marriage dissolved, and insisted on the property rights of orphans: "meddle not with the substance of an orphan," "clothe them, and speak kindly unto them." An adult who adopted a child was responsible for providing suitable training, so the child could have some security for its future; Islamic law in this sense provided a number of "rights" for children in potentially vulnerable situations. (The concept of rights is in some respects modern, but it has been applied retroactively to the careful provision for children in Islamic legal codes.) Religious concern for the very young was heightened by the strong medical tradition in the region, which had been enhanced during the Hellenistic period when scientists in places such as Egypt adapted the Greek scientific achievement toward more practical application. There was a great deal of pediatric advice available on children's health needs, which complemented the religious emphasis. An influential childrearing manual by Ibn Qayyim, in the fourteenth century, discussed infant crying (caused by physical stimuli plus a "poke" by the devil), feeding, and teething, but also the importance of children's individual interests and aptitudes that adults should take into account.

Many aspects of Middle Eastern childhood reflected older family practices that had little to do with religion, though they did not contradict it. Sons were clearly identified in terms of their kin relationships, their names chosen largely in advance to indicate what family group they belonged to. Infants were swaddled – wrapped in cloth – to protect them from accidents and in the belief that their limbs would grow better. As we have seen, this tradition persists in the region to the present day. Young children bonded tightly with their mother; weaning occurred relatively late for an agricultural society, from age two to four, and most children would stay close to their mother until age seven. This created intense emotional ties that would outlast early childhood, carrying on into adulthood, and contrasted with the more distant position of fathers. But at age seven, fathers would take over the upbringing of boys. Paternal authority was strongly emphasized in principle, with children enjoined to respect the father or older male, who in turn had the duty to provide for the family. Children's family life was also conditioned by the active role of the other family members, such as aunts and uncles. Training in manners, including hospitality, received much attention.

At the same time, religion was constantly present in a proper home. A prayer was whispered into the ears of newborns to assure that they would be faithful to Islam, while premasticated dates were rubbed on the infants' palates to transfer blessings. When first-born sons were seven days old, their hair was cut and a sheep sacrificed, constituting fathers' official recognition of the children. If the father identified particular gifts, and the family had sufficient means, he might place a four- or five-year-old boy in a religious training program, beginning a commitment to education; religion, in this case, interrupted the normal maternal oversight for young boys. Fathers' responsibility for the religious training of children was widely stressed – "at this age learning is like engraving on a stone" – that is, it will last a lifetime.

Indeed, the religiously inspired commitment to education constituted one of Islam's great contributions to changing patterns of childhood, bridging between the more limited, elite-focused efforts of the classical period and the still more extensive schooling characteristic of modern societies. Even poor families tried to give boys some religious training in the mosque or in a Quranic school or *kuttab*. Girls might attend a Quranic school also, though usually for shorter periods. In elite families, tutors instructed girls in the home. As a thirteenth-century text put it, for a pious Muslim "learning is prescribed for us all." Rates of school formation in the major cities of the Middle East and North Africa began to soar from the ninth century onward, and in some cases the number of major schools rose by over 1000 percent during the next 400 years. A new movement for schools called *maktabs*, aimed at younger children, dated back to the tenth century. The idea was that children learned better when taught as a group than when tutored individually, mainly because of competition, but also because of group discussions. *Maktab* education, widely defined by a Persian philosopher named Ibn Sina, harked back in part to earlier Greek and Persian traditions, but involved far more extensive outreach. Education might begin at age 6 and extend to 14, when elite children were expected to choose a career (including Islamic study and law) and select any further education accordingly. *Maktab* schools taught not only religion and ethics, but literacy, literature, and broader philosophy. One of the earliest handbooks for elementary educators emanated from this general interest, written by Ibn Sahnud in 870 and discussing basic reading, writing, and arithmetic training along with worship and good manners, and some sports and games. Girls had less access to the formal schools, though there were many women teachers and considerable praise for a female tradition of scholarship; one male Sunni scholar, Ibn Asakir, wrote of having had more than 80 women teachers, many of whom were quite erudite. Even aside from the issue of gender, it is not easy to determine the full extent of Islamic education. Some training, particularly in the countryside, aimed more at memorizing passages from the *Quran* than at actual reading, and Islamic education tended to narrow in scope to a more purely religious focus, toward the end of the postclassical period. Still, it's been estimated that about 30 percent of the adult population was literate, undoubtedly the highest in the world up to that point. After 1500, Islamic educators wrote glowingly about books as "indispensable tools for learning," arguing that it was "more important to spend your time studying books rather than copying them." All in all, expansion of education was a vital part of Islam's impact on childhood, with potential influence even on other regions – though without yet making schooling, rather than work, the core obligation of childhood.

Islam also offered less formal features for children and for adults who dealt with them. Young children were greatly indulged, which may have reflected the religious belief in their innocence and certainly expressed parental pleasure. As the family economy permitted, there were special foods and entertainments. There are indications that teenagers were less valued, with little delight taken in their special energy; indeed, childhood itself was seen as ending with puberty. Apprenticeships were often brief, and there was every encouragement to move quickly from childhood to adulthood. Children arranged their own play, with little sense here of parental responsibility, which focused more on the serious business of preparing for adulthood both economically and religiously. Careful arrangements, including considerable seclusion, aimed at maintaining the virginity of girls before marriage. Islam had no special commitment to lifelong celibacy, however, in contrast to strong strains in both Christianity and Buddhism; this may have linked to the belief in childish innocence. Children were given chores at an early age, and this, along with the religious education, gave childhood a tone of seriousness, at least in adult perceptions.

Religious authorities widely debated the role of physical discipline, a debate frankly unusual in this period in world history and perhaps reflecting the religious valuation of children. It was widely assumed that parents, particularly fathers, should punish children who misbehaved, and the practice was common in schools as well. A number of writers, however, urged restraint here. The great North African historian Ibn Khaldun noted that undue punishment for students "makes them feel oppressed, causes them to lose their energy." Islamic law also regulated how children could be beaten – how many blows for what kinds of offenses, and on what parts of the body (the head and hands should never be struck at all); the goal was to avoid excess and to assure a dispassionate rather than angry administration of discipline.

Late in the postclassical period, Islamic writers also produced an extraordinary array of condolence books, designed to comfort parents in their grief at the loss of a child. More than 20 bereavement books appeared in Egypt and Syria between the thirteenth and sixteenth centuries, in interesting contrast to Western Europe at the same period, where the genre was virtually unknown. Titles such as *Book of Anxiety about Children's Death* or *Consolation for Those in Distress on the Death of Children* show the intent. Almost certainly, the series reflected the results of increased disease – bubonic plague hit the Middle East in the mid-fourteenth century, before reaching Europe. Did it also show a growing level of emotional attachment to children? There's a bit of a puzzle here, though the outpouring was consistent with the kind of attention Islam more generally encouraged toward young children.

The implications of religion reached more deeply into childhood, and into ideas about children, than classical cultures had done, particularly in China and the Mediterranean. This is why the spread of world religions promoted significant change, particularly in the common rethinking of infanticide, but also in the new approaches to education. This is why new differences in discussions of childhood opened up, depending on which specific religion was involved. At the same time, a more religious period in world history hardly overturned the basic features of childhood in agricultural economies. Religion provided new reasons for urging obedience, to take the most important continuity. It might permit some new discussion of physical discipline, as with Islam, but it could also impose new psychological pressures – the onus of disobedience against parents translated into disobedience to God's will – which powerfully reinforced the themes that agricultural civilizations had already developed. Even attitudes toward the frequent deaths of children, though again open to new discussion about possible receptions in the hereafter, were hardly revolutionized, for the very good reason that the religions generated no real change in this aspect of traditional childhood. Religion mattered to childhood, but its powers to change, even its desire to change, were hardly unlimited.

Further reading

A good overview is Don S. Browning, Martha Christian Green and John Witte, eds, *Sex, Marriage and Family in World Religions* (New York: Columbia University Press, 2006).

On Islam: Cyril Glasse, *The New Encyclopedia of Islam* (Lanham, MD: AltaMira Press, 2008); Elizabeth Warnock Fernea, ed., *Children in the*

Muslim Middle East (Austin: University of Texas Press, 1995); Avner Gil'adi, *Children of Islam: Concepts of Childhood in Medieval Muslim Society* (New York: St Martin's, 1992); Abdesslam Abadi, "Youth in the Islamic World and the Challenges of Globalisation," *Islam Today*, No. 26, 2009. On Islamic education: Jonathan P. Berkey, *The Transmission of Knowledge in Medieval Cairo* (Princeton, NJ: Princeton University Press, 1992); Medhi K. Nakosteen, *History of Islamic Origins of Western Education, A.D. 800–1350* (Bethesda, MD: IBEX Publishers, 1984); Timothy Reagan, *Non-western Educational Traditions* (New York: Routledge, 2000). See also Munir Ahmed, "Islamic Education Prior to the Establishment of Madrassa," *Journal of Islamic Studies*, 26:4 (1987), 321–49; and Husain Haqqani, "Islam's Medieval Outposts," *Foreign Policy Magazine*, 1 November 2002.

On Buddhism: T. W. Rhys Davids, *Buddhism: Its History and Literature*, 2nd edn (New York and London: G.P. Putnam's Sons, 2009); Arthur Wright, *Buddhism in Chinese History* (Stanford, CA: Stanford University Press, 1971); Jacques Gernet, *Buddhism in Chinese Society: An Economic History from the Fifth to the Tenth Century* (New York: Columbia University Press, 1995); Uma Chakravarti, *Social Dimensions of Early Buddhism* (New York: Oxford University Press, 1987); José Ignacio Cabezón, ed., *Buddhism, Sexuality, and Gender* (Albany: State University of New York Press, 1992).

Chapter 5

Contacts and contrasts in the postclassical world

Significant developments occurred in childhood in some of the newer civilization areas emerging in the postclassical world. The changes provide additional illustrations of the impact of expanding world religions in several cases, but also some wider results of new contacts and imitations and the additional acceleration of inter-regional trade. This chapter deals with patterns in sub-Saharan Africa, Japan, Russia, and Western Europe, where new contacts and influences often combined with economic change. A brief note about the Americas adds one further region. Overall, these societies remind us of some of the starker features of childhood in agricultural societies generally, though inquiry on some points is seriously constrained by lack of easily available evidence or focused historical work. Comparison remains important, around various regional factors now including religious culture.

The Americas

Childhood in the civilizations in the Americas, during the centuries before European arrival, was shaped primarily by work demands supplemented in some cases by strong military values. Here was a unique case where significant internal development and expansion occurred in the range of complex societies, particularly in Central America and the Andes, but in real isolation from other parts of the world. Mayan society, flourishing from before 500 CE until the eleventh century, placed great value on children's contributions to the family. From five or six years of age, girls were expected not only to help, but to exercise considerable responsibility in the domestic sphere, and the same applied to boys for farming. As was typical in agricultural societies, mothers oversaw childrearing in general, but fathers took a hand in educating boys for work and for moral conduct. Respect for elders was strongly enforced. Discipline featured verbal cues more than physical punishments, with positive reinforcements in teaching situations. Aztec civilization, rising a bit later in a broader span of Central America, had a harsher tone. Physical punishments were common, including cactus spines pushed into the skin. Military training for boys supplemented work obligations, though there were some schools (called *calmecac*) for a minority, emphasizing both religious and academic subjects. Childbirth itself was described in military terms, with children seen either as potential warriors or as creators of warriors. Incan civilization, in the Andes, also featured a military framework. Severe treatment began early, with newborns dunked in cold water and then wrapped in a quilt, and with more regular discipline applying by age one. Boys gained manhood through elaborate ceremonies when they reached 14, at which point they were given a weapon. Girls, trained informally in domestic skills, usually married before age 16. Against the picture of rigor – which may have been exaggerated by later Spanish observers eager to make the colonial regime look good – considerable attention also went into the production of toys for children. Central American societies, for example, crafted toys with wheels – which were not used for adult transportation. Not surprisingly, pre-Columbian cultures, like agricultural societies generally, balanced several approaches as they dealt with children.

Africa

Childhood in Africa was also strongly shaped by work demands and, in some cases, military or hunting training for some boys. Here, however, more abundant evidence creates a fuller, more rounded picture; and unlike the Americas, African childhood was also affected by contacts with other parts of the world.

Work demands gained emphasis as agriculture and the use of iron spread through much of the continent, and with this came an increasing premium placed on obedience. Status and age were closely linked, which placed children low on the spectrum, and gender divisions applied strongly as well. At the same time, interestingly, folk tales sometimes painted imaginary pictures of children's vengeance against their elders, undoubtedly reflecting tensions within the age hierarchy; a Chewa legend had children quite simply massacring adults. Responsibilities (particularly for girls) for helping to care for younger siblings again mirrored patterns common in agricultural society.

Along with this came considerable attention to protection of children's health, in regions that saw high rates of disease and infant mortality. Elaborate rituals and ceremonies applied to infants up to age three, which was normally when they were weaned from breastfeeding. Distinctive African family traditions also aimed at protecting children in another way: if a father died, one of his brothers was encouraged to marry the widow to help assure her support and that of any children. Children's play was widely indulged as well, with boys often doing a lot of warrior-play, girls focusing more on games with a domestic twist.

Premodern Africa also offered another important feature in community–childhood relations, common in agricultural societies but unusually well defined in the African case. Villages (and also other units, like royal courts) developed a caste of poets, often called *griots*, whose task it was to teach traditional songs, to use song and rhyme to teach the community about major events, and also to promote the memorization of kinship networks. The *griot* tradition in West Africa presumably took shape in the fourteenth century, initially around the powerful empire of Mali; but it dispersed widely in the countryside. The storytelling was not directed to children alone, but children clearly participated, and the activity constituted a major form of learning in a society based on oral communication. African stories also emphasized various parables, often using animals as protagonists, designed to teach moral lessons – some of these would later be carried to the Americas by Africans seized as slaves.

African childhood was also affected by increasing influence from Islamic missionaries and conversions within the ruling class – even though most Africans at this point remained polytheists. Muslim travelers by the fourteenth century noted how deeply Islam was shaping African childhood in parts of West Africa – though not in all respects. The tireless Moroccan traveler Ibn Battuta thus wrote that one of several "good properties" in the Empire of Mali was parental insistence that boys, at least, commit large parts of the *Quran* to memory, "for if a man finds his son defective in this, he will confine him till he is quite perfect, nor will he allow him his liberty until he is so." But children's adherence to Battuta's idea of Islam was imperfect, for he also criticized – "as to their bad practices" – how parents let their daughters run naked and also allowed daughters easy entry into the presence of the king. Islam, in other words, helped define new obligations for some children, including more formal education, but it was blended with other African practices to shape the larger patterns of childhood.

Several key regions in sub-Saharan Africa participated strongly in growing levels of inter-regional trade, both across the Sahara desert and along the Indian Ocean coast. Commerce often linked to the new religious connections to Islam; it also contributed to changing political and artistic forms. Did it also affect childhood? We lack the evidence to be sure, but it has been speculated that by the end of the postclassical period, children's work obligations were increasing for some groups and in some regions, to help keep agricultural and mineral production apace with opportunities for sales.

Japan

Just as Africa built on new contacts with the Islamic world, so Japan, even more systematically, cultivated relationships with China through most of the postclassical period. Over time, Chinese influence would help promote more extensive education, both in Buddhist and in secular Confucian schools. Ultimately, indeed, the Japanese version of Confucianism would lead to far more extensive education, in terms of percentages of children, than the

Chinese original ever did. But this effect stretched over several centuries, with the clearest results well after the postclassical period itself. Japanese approaches to childhood also strongly emphasized collective loyalties, with children encouraged to play and learn together and form close bonds with their peers. Most villages thus had semi-organized children's groups. Japanese tradition was doubtless at the core of this characteristic, which persists even today, though in more modern forms; but imported Confucian values may have contributed as well.

Russia

Changes in Russian childhood during the postclassical period reflected the impact of widespread conversions to Orthodox Christianity above all, from the tenth century onward – and these followed from wider contacts with the established Byzantine Empire to the south. Christian values pushed Russians toward more sympathetic treatment of children, including stricter definitions of what constituted child abuse. The killing of a child was now definitively considered murder, though it was rarely punished, and though killing of illegitimate children occurred with some regularity into the nineteenth century. Many upper-class families sent children to monasteries or convents to be raised, or at least educated. This aside, many parents took increasing interest in children in order to shape their moral character. There was little overall conception of childhood as a separate stage or an object of any particular inquiry – Russian patterns here echo some of the findings about premodern Japan and the debated evaluation of premodern Western Europe. Only in the eighteenth century, in Russia, would materials begin to be written for and about children and childrearing. Many Russian families, in various social classes, took in children from other families, helping to provide care and support, but also benefiting from children's labor. Into more modern times as well, many upper-class parents turned over much childrearing to servants and wetnurses, limiting their own contacts at least until later childhood. And of course, for most families, particularly that vast majority who were peasants, children were above all a source of labor, vital in an often difficult struggle for survival.

Western Europe

Conditions for children in postclassical Western Europe raise a number of issues, some of which have been central to the debate between supporters and critics of Philippe Ariès' pioneering study (see Chapter 1). As one result, we know more about patterns in this region than in most. Several factors intertwined in shaping Western European childhood at this point. The spread of Christianity had important consequences. It encouraged new interest in religious schooling; though in contrast to Islam, if only because of a less advanced economy, European gains here were gradual and incomplete, particularly before 1500. Christianity also brought some emphasis on a doctrine of original sin, and this in turn could justify a punitive approach to children and considerable use of fear as a disciplinary tool, with threats of damnation if children did not toe the mark. Christianity also, however, promoted new efforts to reduce infanticide and to offer institutions to care for orphaned or abandoned children. The religious factor, in other words, had some mixed implications. Along with this, Europe reflected some standard features of agricultural societies, including strong social class differences and wide reliance on child labor. As the European economy developed during the postclassical period, with more emphasis on commerce and some urban growth, new pressures on child labor may have developed – as has been speculated regarding Africa and other regions during the postclassical period. Finally, though linked to economic efforts, an unusual European family type emerged, from the late postclassical period onward, which had important implications for children.

Western Europe was not particularly important in world history during this period, lagging behind the Asian societies in levels of urban activity and political strength. Western approaches to childhood did, however, combine some unusual qualities with common elements; comparative analysis is complex, with some implications for later developments as well.

As in other regions, levels of child mortality were high in premodern Europe, and obviously families had to find some ways to adjust to the frequency of death. More distinctive were signs of relatively harsh discipline. A psychoanalyst-historian, Erik Erikson, thus has emphasized the frequent beatings Martin Luther – ultimately, the instigator of the Protestant Reformation in the sixteenth century – received at the hands of his coal-miner father. It was Erikson also who commented on the shock North American Indians expressed at European colonists' abundant physical punishments of their children. David Hunt, looking at the upbringing of a future king of France in the seventeenth century, noted how the young man was frequently neglected by his parents, beaten quite deliberately for misbehavior, but also periodically hauled out for the entertainment of guests, as when his father laughingly fondled his genitalia at parties. Swaddling of children was common – not in itself unusual, as we have seen, but the West European practice carried it further, enclosing infants in bands so they could not hurt themselves by crawling or squirming, frequently hanging them on a hook on the wall so that both parents could safely go out in the fields to work, and maintaining the practice for as much as the first whole year, relenting only when the child showed some ability to begin to walk. The practice – designed to require minimal parental attention – accompanied widespread beliefs in the animal-like nature of little children (in contrast to the cute images that dominate more modern approaches, perhaps just as inaccurately, though in an opposite direction). Many people did not like to see children crawl, because this reminded them of the animal phase, preferring not to release them fully until they were able to walk. Children's voraciousness at mother's breast drew comment as well, another sign of animal-like traits that made early childhood distasteful, perhaps until children were mature enough to begin working and helping out. These emphases bore some relationship to the Christian ideas of original sin at birth – with children marked by the stain of Adam and Eve's defiance of God's will – which similarly encouraged a belief in the need for a rigorous, civilizing discipline.

Severity is not, of course, the whole story. Many parents may have steeled themselves against the frequent deaths of infants, but there are also abundant signs of deep grief – as in Martin Luther's own emotional reaction to the death of a child.

Other practices, however, at the least raise some of the same kinds of questions that the specific swaddling practices do. Wetnursing is a case in point. Many European families sent infants out to another woman who had recently had a child, often in the countryside, so that she, rather than the birth mother, could breastfeed. We have seen this practice also in the Russian upper class. Of course sometimes, when a mother physically could not nurse, it was essential. West European practice seems, however, to have been surprisingly widespread, involving many urban women well down the social scale as well as the aristocracy. There is also no question that wetnursing was often counter-indicated from the standpoint of a child's health, because many wetnurses really did not have enough milk to provide for two infants adequately, and sanitary conditions might be bad as well. There is little question that more children died in wetnursing than was average. So why did it occur? Some historians have pointed to wetnursing as a sign of parental lack of interest, perhaps even a sneaking desire for some children to die as a means of *ex post facto* birth control. Others, in contrast, note that parents often visited children who were out to a wetnurse, suggesting concern and affection. They argue that, while some aristocratic women may simply have wished to avoid the messiness of breastfeeding, most urban women who resorted to the practice did so because of work demands, for example in running the business side of the family's artisanal shop. (And a few, of course, had to use wetnurses, or animal milk – donkey milk was preferred – because they simply could not produce an adequate supply themselves.) These more sympathetic historians note that wetnursing continued in the West into the late nineteenth century, again because of work demands and other issues – though admittedly it came under new attack. They argue, then, that wetnursing was not a sign of traditional hostility and that a sharp modern break from it did not occur either.

On another point: poor families in the West often abandoned children – putting them at a church door was a favorite ploy. To some historian critics, this shows lack of love, and indeed many abandoned children did die. To others, the practice reflects sheer poverty and a real hope that someone else, better able than the parents themselves, would care for the child. (And of course the still-more-traditional practice of outright infanticide became rare in the West, as in Islam.)

Another debate involves physical discipline. There were horrific examples of abuse in the traditional West in the postclassical period and on into the seventeenth and eighteenth centuries, as when a German schoolmaster beat a student bloody for not studying. Certainly, physical discipline was widely accepted, even recommended, in family settings as well as schools. Benjamin Franklin, apprenticed to an older brother as a printer, was beaten so often that he finally fled Boston for Philadelphia. But extremes of physical punishment were not accepted, and community control over parental behavior may have been better than it is today, in more anonymous urban settings. The German schoolmaster, for example, was fined for his excess.

Many premodern Western families sent teenagers out to work in another household for several years, often realizing that an outsider family was unlikely to treat a child very warmly. Was this a sign of callousness, or a desire to let other families do the job of disciplining children at a difficult stage of life? (One historian even suggested a twist on this argument: parents actually loved their kids but realized they needed some sense beaten into them after puberty, so they preferred to leave this painful task to others.) Or was the practice simply a reflection of a desire to make sure children received job training, the most important form of education, plus the need for families with more kids than could be put to work at home to spread them out to childless families, as a means of best possible resource allocation? Or, possibly, a bit of all of this? (One problem with the debate between critical historians and more sympathetic revisionists is a frequent neglect of individual variety: surely some parents were harsh, and were perhaps able to use premodern practices to express this harshness, while others were more genuinely affectionate and used the practices for other reasons and/or modified them through the emotional ties they had with their offspring.)

Finally, many historians have pointed to aspects of premodern childhood that may have offered very positive features, sometimes in contrast to characteristic modern constraints. They note how whole villages helped look out for children, providing multiple contacts and safeguards and showing a clear, if not exactly modern, child-centeredness. They stress opportunities for comradeship among children themselves, as they participated in village festivals for example, including the opportunities these festivals might provide to let off steam in a relatively tolerant atmosphere. They note many opportunities for play without intense adult monitoring. Children often played together without much age-grading and without any sense that play should be specifically instructional. They had many traditional games, and they could be creative in finding playthings. Not a few scholars have argued that outlets for children's play-like qualities would actually deteriorate with modernity, among other things because of more schooling and adult supervision – an implicit plus, then, for the traditional centuries.

Historians' debates about the quality of childhood in the premodern West, not surprisingly, mirror ordinary debates. They sometimes generate more heat than light. They often push participants into extreme statements of position, rather than encouraging compromise and complexity. At the same time, they can contribute to the advancement of knowledge, pompous as this may sound, and the debate over traditional Western childhood is a case in point. The debate has died down now, though by no means is everything settled. At risk of some oversimplification, it is possible to sketch how things now stand.

Premodern Western childhood was different from modern childhood in lots of ways. Many of these differences reflected the birth and death rates, and the work roles of children in agricultural societies generally. But there are some specific features, such as frequent wetnursing, that need separate interpretation. Nevertheless, all but the most extreme revisionists admit that a number of changes in ideas, practices, and contexts occurred between pre- modern and modern times – though they also note, quite correctly, that some of the changes occurred later than sometimes imagined, and some of them were less uniformly adopted than general characterizations of the "modern" might imply.

This said, there is also considerable agreement now that premodern Europeans were not as different from modern as some of the critical interpretations have suggested. It is also important – a point for a later chapter – to revisit any notion that modern childhood is not only somewhat different, but clearly better, for this is another claim that must be held up for examination. Rhetoric about children has changed – the idea of kids as little animals began to ease in the eighteenth century – but actual adult attitudes may have altered less. Finally, some of the changes that have occurred may have worsened the experience of childhood, or at least not clearly improved it. Premodern childhood, in other words, was not so bad that change would necessarily mean progress.

Debates about Western childhood have also applied to colonial America, here of course going into a period beyond the postclassical centuries. There is evidence of surprising harshness, as when Protestant ministers thundered against children's original sin and used images of death to try to regulate children. Physical discipline was applied to children not only when in school, but when they dozed off during long church services. But signs of affection and grief were abundant as well, and communities seem to have guarded against abuse. The American experience was itself different, however, from the premodern European in a few respects, which can affect the debate about its quality as well. More abundant land increased the need for child labor and facilitated a higher birth rate in the seventeenth and eighteenth centuries. Death rates were lower, again partly because of better food resources, though they probably rose in the more crowded areas by the later eighteenth century. Because of the need for labor, a lower infant mortality rate, and the open frontier, American families may have been more careful with children than their European counterparts, more eager to keep them positively happy lest they move away. (Stories of children who fled or were abducted became an anxious part of American popular culture.) Correspondingly, American families began to seem unusually open to children's input by at least the later eighteenth century – willing to listen to children and take their opinions into account. Such, at least, was the reaction of many European observers, some of whom liked American family "democracy," others of whom found the children insufferable. Almost surely, by modern standards, even early modern American children were rather firmly kept in line, enjoined to be docile and obedient; but some variance from European traditionalism may have developed earlier, along with considerable overlap.

A revealing way to assess traditional Western approaches to childhood emerges from comparative analysis: was there anything particularly unusual about premodern Western childhood compared with the patterns in other agricultural civilizations? Too often, after all, historians have focused on some standard differences between children in agricultural societies and those in more modern settings, and this has no inherent comparative significance across societies at the same point in time. But there may be some real Western-ness involved as well, which will help us get at premodern childhood from one additional, final angle.

Two Western strands deserve particular attention. One, of course, is Christianity. As Christian nativity art suggests, the religion in many ways encourages sympathetic attention to children. The Bible provides many stories emphasizing the religious importance of childhood, as in Christ's injunction, "suffer the little children to come unto me." There's no question, also, that children could be deeply drawn to Christianity. At one unfortunate extreme, in the year 1212 two people, a teenager called Stephen of Vendôme in France, and Nicholas of Cologne in Germany, preached a children's crusade, in which bands of children were enjoined to recapture the Holy Land that had been lost again to Islamic rulers. Stephen's group reached the port of Marseilles, where it was sold into slavery, while Nicholas' company was turned back. The whole episode may lie at the origins of the Pied Piper story.

For all the attractiveness and attractions of Christianity and childhood, there was the unusual belief in original sin, theologically understandable in light of the emphasis on the need for faith and redemption, not necessarily taken too seriously in the ways many children were treated, but nevertheless available, sometimes inescapable, as the basis for a critical approach to the qualities of childhood. Tainted by original sin at birth, children would continue to sin as part of human nature. This belief could occasion some worried discussions about the fate of the souls of children who died in infancy, and some flexibility developed on this point; it certainly underlay the importance of baptism as a first step in redeeming children's evil nature; but it could also generate beliefs, fierce or well intentioned or both, in the need to impose strict discipline on children lest their impulses lead them further astray. (And this was on top of other superstitions about children who might be born as witches, because their mothers had been frightened during pregnancy or because the children themselves had a fateful birthmark.)

Almost certainly, for many children, Christianity encouraged the use of fear of death and damnation as a regulatory tool, setting up what some historians view as deep-seated characteristic anxieties. Into the nineteenth century, for example, many common readers for children in the United States would stress the fragility of life and the need to prepare for death at any moment. Christianity may have exaggerated, in other words, the impact of one of the inescapable features of premodern childhood everywhere. This tension around sin and death may have intensified in the centuries right after the postclassical period, particularly with the rise of Protestantism in the sixteenth century. For Protestantism brought a greater emphasis on predestination and human sinfulness, creating still further pressures on many children, with fathers supposed to take on the role of moral judge and guardian. Without falling back into ahistorical condemnations of premodern discipline, it is possible that, compared with childhoods in other societies, there were some distinctive disciplinary and even psychological features of Western childhood, some of which may have intensified in the sixteenth and seventeenth centuries.

The second feature of the Western experience that affected childhood, developing from the later postclassical centuries onward, was the special nature of the European-style family. This unusual family type emphasized a relatively late marriage age for people beneath elite status – that is, for the vast majority, marriage at 26 for women and 27 for men was common. Further, a substantial minority, mostly the poorest in terms of economic prospects, did not marry at all. The goal was probably to limit the birth rate in order to protect property holdings from the demands of too many children. The system had several consequences for children besides sheer numbers. It focused attention on nuclear rather than extended families; interaction with grandparents was often limited, because by the time young adults could marry their own parents were often dead. Family work concentrated on the wife and husband, plus able children and perhaps an outside laborer; this probably increased work responsibilities for women, which helps account for practices such as swaddling and the use of wet-nurses. Is this labor pressure, in turn, why Western tradition has tended to limit physical contact between mother and children, compared with societies such as those in Africa, where mothers carried children as they worked, delighting in the closeness of two bodies? Even the timing of children in

Western Europe and colonial America – with a disproportionate number of children born in February and March, apparently deliberately in order to inconvenience women's work the least – reflected labor needs and the results in terms of available attention for offspring.

The system obviously risked more than the usual amount of generational tension at the upper end of youth. When children could not marry until they had property, and when property usually stayed with the father until his death, the chances for harsh relationships were high. In the American colonies, some fathers modified this by turning over some land before death (of course, land was unusually plentiful, compared with Europe), but even here there were many bitter quarrels and some outright violence. In eighteenth-century France, older fathers were the most common victims of murder, at the hands of impatient sons. One peasant expressed nonchalance, if not hostility, even when his father passed away naturally, "My father died today. I went to plough the field."

The European family pattern depended, finally, on considerable sexual control. Most people could not marry until over a decade after puberty. At the same time, both religious codes and the need to protect the family economy against unwanted births discouraged full sexual activity before marriage. Villages monitored youth sexual behavior closely, not permitting individual pairings until there was a clear prospect of marriage; at this point, sexual activity might occur, leading to a number of pre-bridal pregnancies where births, however, occurred well after the wedding. Outright illegitimacy did arise, but rates were relatively low at 2–3 percent of all births. Western youth, in other words, had to accommodate unusual restrictions on sexuality because of late marriage, and it is interesting to speculate about the consequences in terms of individual tensions and the development of alternative outlets. These last included frequent resort to bundling – letting a couple lie together, but clothed – and (to an extent we can only guess at) the use of animals for sexual purposes. There was also some increase in prostitution, particularly in urban areas.

Overall, comparative perspectives suggest some distinctive patterns in the West concerning very young children and also youth, thanks to the combination of religious doctrine and family arrangements. Differences operated within a common range. Wetnursing, for example, was not unique to the West, as we have seen, though the work distractions of mothers may have contributed to higher incidences. The Middle East also featured characteristically strict discipline, though with a bit more debate than in the West, and Islam also encouraged some fearful concern about sin. Interest in obedience was widespread. Distinctive Western emphases in these areas shaded off from standard patterns.

Prolonged youth in the West certainly contrasted, however, with the interest in most agricultural societies in moving more directly from childhood to adulthood, where work could nevertheless still be controlled by extended families. The Western pattern may have had some advantages, though it also encouraged more unrest; much urban protest in Western Europe could be attributed to young men kept back from full economic maturity. The simple fact was that most societies managed youth and sexuality through relatively early marriage ages, particularly for women; Western patterns, with the advent of the European-style family, imposed more individual and community control, and a longer intermediate period between childhood and full adult attainment.

The Western approach toward young children, insofar as it reflected some influence from the idea of original sin, may also have been less indulgent, more guilt-inducing, than its counterparts elsewhere. This might have combined with somewhat less maternal attention, given the labor demands within the nuclear family. Did these differences also affect the wider society? It is certainly interesting, as we will see in Chapter 6, that one of the first targets of reformers in the West focused on the treatment of young children, from swaddling to the very idea of sinfulness. The target did not result from careful comparative analysis, but suggested awareness of some of the drawbacks of the premodern Western approach.

Premodern Western characteristics of childhood did begin to change from the late seventeenth century onward, though many older practices and ideas continued for a long time. Change would gradually modify some of the emphases of traditional Christianity, including the invocation of original sin, and some of the features of the European-style family, including such strict insistence on sexual control. It was a changing Western approach to childhood that would come to have significance not only in the West itself, but, through Western influence, on other parts of the world.

We will pick up on the larger changes in the Western experience in Chapter 6, but one note warrants a place in this discussion. One of the first signs of alteration in the Western approach to children came at the intellectual level. In the late seventeenth century, John Locke argued that children, far from being corrupted by original sin, were actually blank slates, capable of improvement through careful education. In the following century, many Enlightenment thinkers took up this charge, blasting traditional Christianity for its harm to children (among other wrongs) and urging greater attention to schooling. Other intellectuals, such as Jean-Jacques Rousseau, added a more passionate commitment to children's individuality, and to systems of upbringing that would cherish the child, systems of schooling that would nurture the creative spark. It was at this point, for example, that the attack on swaddling began to take shape. What caused this significant revision in outlook – a revision that undeniably prompted some of the more specific changes that would affect children, from more individualistic naming practices to new forms of mass education? Obviously, the rise of science, with its challenge to traditional religion and its apparent demonstration that knowledge could progress beyond Christian dogma, encouraged rethinking. So did growing prosperity for many Europeans, which allowed them to afford new kinds of care for children – ultimately, by the later eighteenth century, including a first set of consumer items deliberately designed for the young. But was there also an implicit realization that aspects of the Western tradition were not only harsh, but counterproductive, in producing tensions between children and parents and in failing to optimize children's talents? Western tradition itself did not directly suggest any basis for leadership in what became a worldwide tendency to reconsider aspects of childhood; but perhaps its very weaknesses encouraged further change.

Even with change in the offing, traditional Western childhood remains important historically, in part because of its involvement in vigorous and ultimately illuminating debate. Earlier practices did not die with the process of change. Wetnursing persisted longer than might otherwise be imagined, given the criticisms that began to be directed at it. Older ideas about discipline persisted as well. Historian Philip Greven has identified continuities amid the evangelical Christian minority in the United States, in the ongoing belief in the need for strict physical discipline and a barely contained anger in parent–child relations. Another interesting expression: as Western society developed new ways to move children around, they tended to repeat the idea of considerable physical separation, putting the kids in buggies or strollers; in contrast, efforts to sell strollers in urban Africa have largely failed because of the continued desire to carry young children close. There is still room to debate what Western childhood is all about, what is distinctive about it, and what complex links to the past remain.

Conclusion

Childhoods in various regions of the world during the postclassical centuries and beyond intermingled the standard characteristics of agricultural societies with particular cultures and local practices, and in broad outline Western Europe was no exception to this generalization. Adherence to one of the major religions produced new kinds of attention to children in many regions, including new types of schooling. In the Middle East, this pushed education to new levels, but there was some expansion almost everywhere. Changing religious ideas could have some impact on discipline, or at least the ways in which discipline was justified, or on reactions to children's death. New levels of contact among major societies – the Americas stood as an exception here – had some impact on childhood, particularly when religious conversions were part of the process, but overall the results seem fairly modest. The growth of trade may have put new pressure on children as workers, though measurements are difficult to come by. The European-style family, probably formed in response to a desire to improve the economics of family formation by assuring access to property, certainly changed the context for childhood, with results that extended into the centuries after the postclassical period. Apprenticeships, particularly in urban crafts, may have become more rigorous, another sign of economic pressures on work, though again it's European evidence that provides the clearest suggestions here. Economic prods did not entirely counter religious factors – religious schooling might expand even when child labor in other respects became more onerous. But the final phases of the agricultural period in world history tossed up an interesting mixture of signals, from religious redefinitions to responses to commercial change. The result created new comparative differences, but it also confirmed the central roles of work and obedience in adult expectations of childhood.

Further reading

On the Americas: Traci Arden and Scott R. Hutson, *The Social Experience of Childhood in Ancient Mesoamerica* (Colorado: University Press of Colorado, 2006); Pedro Sarmiento de Gamboa, *The History of the Incas* (Charleston, SC: BiblioBazaar, 2007); A. Goncu, *Children's Engagement in the World: Sociocultural Perspectives* (Cambridge, UK: Cambridge University Press, 1999); R. Sharer, *The Ancient Maya*, 6/e (Stanford, CA: Stanford University Press, 2005); Michael E. Smith, *The Aztecs* (Oxford, UK: Blackwell Press, 2003).

On Africa: Mario Aguilar, ed., *The Politics of Age and Gerontocracy in Africa* (Trenton, NJ: African World Press, 1998); Benedict Carton, *Blood from your Children: The Colonial Origins of Generational Conflict in South Africa* (Charlottesville, VA: University Press of Virginia, 2000); Jane Guyer, "Household and Community in African Studies," *African Studies Review* 24: 86–137, 1981; John Iliffe, *Africans: The History of a Continent* (Cambridge, UK: Cambridge University Press, 1995). On Japan: S.B. Hanley, *Everyday Things in Pre-modern Japan: The Hidden Legacy of Material Culture* (Berkeley, CA: University of California Press, 1997); Kathleen Uno, *Passages to Modernity: Motherhood, Childhood and Social Reform in Early 20th Century Japan* (Honolulu: University of Hawaii Press, 1999); Mikiso Hane, *Premodern Japan: An Historical Survey* (Boulder, CO: Westview Press, 1992). On Russia: Clementine Creutziger, *Childhood in Russia: Representations and Reality* (Lanham, MD: University Press of America, 1996).

On Europe: Albrecht Classen, *Childhood in the Middle Ages and the Renaissance* (Berlin: Walter de Gruyter & Co., 2005); Andrea Immel, *Childhood and Children's Books in Early Modern Europe* (New York: Routledge, 2006); David Kertzer and Mario Barbagli, eds, *The History of the European Family: Family Life in Early Modern Times* (New Haven, CT: Yale University Press, 2001); Katherine A. Lynch, *Individuals, Families and Communities in Europe, 1200–1800* (Cambridge, UK: Cambridge University Press, 2003).

See also: Don S. Browning, M. Christian Green and John Witte, Jr, eds, *Sex, Marriage and Family in World Religions* (New York: Columbia University Press, 2009); T.W. Rhys Davids, *Buddhism: Its History and Literature* (New York and London: G.P. Putnam's Sons, 2009); Cyril Glasse, *The New Encyclopedia of Islam*, 3rd edn (Lanham, MD: Rowman & Littlefield, 2008); Philippe Ariès, *Centuries of Childhood: A Social History of Family Life* (New York: McGraw-Hill, 1962); Erik Erikson, *Young Man Luther: A Study in Psychoanalysis and History* (New York: Norton, 1958); Mary Hartman, *Households and the Making of History: A Subversive View of the Western Past* (New York: Cambridge University Press, 2004); Stephen Ozment, *Ancestors: The Loving Family in Old Europe* (Cambridge, MA: Harvard University Press, 2001); Linda Pollock, *Forgotten Children: Parent–Child Relations from 1500 to 1900* (Cambridge: Cambridge University Press, 1983); David Hunt, *Parents and Children in History: The Psychology of Family Life in Early Modern France* (New York: Harper and Row, 1972); Lawrence Stone, *The Family, Sex and Marriage in England, 1500–1800* (New York: Harper and Row, 1977); Jean Delumeau, *Sin and Fear: The Emergence of a Western Guilt Culture, Thirteenth–Eighteenth Centuries* (New York: St Martin's, 1990); Philip Greven, *Spare the Child: the Religious Roots of Punishment and the Psychological Impact of Abuse* (New York: Knopf, 1991); John Demos, *Past, Present and Personal: The Family and the Life Course in American History* (New York: Oxford University Press, 1986); Colin Heywood, *A History of Childhoods: Children and Childhood in the West from Medieval to Modern Times* (Cambridge, UK: Polity Press, 2001).

Chapter 6

Forces of change and the modern model of childhood

Developments in the West, eighteenth century to 1914

Historians are cautious about generalization. They frequently prefer to tell stories that hint at wider patterns, rather than laying these patterns out explicitly, at risk of oversimplification. They also tend to be very place-specific, and get nervous about statements that cover too much geographical ground. World historians, while not necessarily quite so cautious as the rest of the breed, are understandably edgy about discussions that pay too much attention to the West, since one of their purposes is to rebalance historical understanding so that the West does not seem to be running the past. A major reason world historians were prone to attack what used to be called "the modernization model" was that it gave pride of place to the West and assumed (in its simplest versions) that the rest of the world would follow Western patterns, or that otherwise there was something deficient that had to be explained.

Too much caution, however, on the modern world history of childhood could seriously mislead; a dash of boldness works better. This chapter begins by sketching a modern model of childhood, lest the woods be lost for the trees. Four major changes separate characteristic modern childhood from childhood in agricultural societies. These patterns do not describe all of childhood, but they do entail several corollaries, regardless of specific place. Furthermore, the changes first occurred in Western Europe and the United States. Other societies have adopted the changes in part through copying the West, but also for independent reasons, beyond mere imitation. It is also true that some societies are still involved in the process of transition, so we're talking about a modern model that remains dynamic, and about the possibility that some societies will reject the model or will modify it substantially. What's claimed here, however, is not a simple version of some modernization of childhood. There were differences between the modern model as it worked out specifically in the West, which is the subject of this chapter, and the way it worked out, or is working out, elsewhere (and these comparisons emerge in the following chapters).

Finally, while the modern model may also seem "good," compared with traditional conditions – which is another way of saying that most of us are so accustomed to the modern model that we have trouble seeing value in alternatives – it will be very clear that the model entailed all sorts of disadvantages. Some of these were emerging in the West by the nineteenth century, some have become clearer since. Because the modern model involved serious change, it also provoked many anxieties, and some of these persist even where the patterns seem firmly established. Some societies are still debating whether to adopt the modern model, even apart from the specifically Western trappings, and this can be seen as quite reasonable. The modern model is not complicated in its essence, but its position in world history must not be oversimplified.

It's important to remember that the focus of this and subsequent chapters enters into several real and complex debates about childhood, initially around the extent to which a modern version of childhood can be legitimately contrasted with a more traditional, agricultural model, and then around the related and complicated issue of the Western role in influencing other societies over the past two centuries. The modern–premodern contrast need not be complete – continuities will undoubtedly accompany change; and it is definitely not the same thing as a good–bad contrast. Western influence, based on its own initial development of new forms of childhood, never completely overshadowed distinctive features in other regions, and frequently Western power and exploitation ironically constrained much capacity to imitate, even on a limited basis. The debates are not simple.

Modern childhood, as it began to emerge first in the West in the eighteenth–nineteenth centuries, involves three fundamentals, which are inter-related. A fourth factor intertwined with the more basic shifts. Change one, the most essential, involves the conversion of childhood from work to schooling. The idea that children should begin to assist the family economy at a fairly young age, and then should be able to cover their own support and perhaps add resources to the family economy by their mid-to-late teens, had been a core element in agricultural societies. In the modern model, this now gave way to the notion that young children should not work at all, in favor of going to school; more gradually, this extended to the notion that even mid-teenagers should not work, again with schooling as the new substitute. This meant, as many parents quickly realized, that children turned from being on balance economic assets, to becoming absolute economic liabilities, which in turn required serious rethinking of the nature and purpose of childhood. All of this pushed well beyond the place schooling had gained in agricultural societies, even in Islam and Judaism.

This, in turn, along with more general urbanization which complicated care for children, encouraged the second element in the modern model: the decision to limit family size to unprecedentedly low levels. Agricultural families had usually sought five to seven children, but this birth rate was simply inappropriate for conditions in which children cost money for food, clothing, and even school expenses, without contributing labor in return.

Accomplishing lower birth rates was not always easy. Many societies went through difficult discussions about what methods were moral and feasible, and discussions still continue even in the United States. Adult adjustment could be difficult as well: if parenting became less important, at least quantitatively, how should family responsibilities be defined? But whatever the anxieties, the process of birth-rate reduction proved central to the modern model of childhood.

The third basic transition in the modern model involved a dramatic reduction of the infant death rate, from traditional levels in which 30–50 percent of all children born had died before age two. The relationship with birth rate changes was variable. In the West, birth rate reduction began first, which encouraged more concern about saving children who were born, which then spurred further birth control needs. In much of the rest of the world, infant death rates dropped first, often as a result of improved sanitation and public health measures, and this triggered an urgent need to cut the birth rate, in part to compensate.

In Western Europe and North America, where the modern changes first took shape, developments stretched over many decades. Schooling began to expand quite early, initially encouraged by the printing press and the rise of Protestant attention to the importance of being able to read the Bible. Learning gains also entered into the growth of manufacturing and technological change, with many manuals devoted to enhancing skills. These developments began to gain ground by the sixteenth century, but the process of change was gradual, and the real commitment to seeing childhood primarily in terms of schooling emerged only in the nineteenth century. Significant birth rate reductions occurred in some social groups by the later eighteenth century. Concern about infant mortality rose during the nineteenth century, but the full conversion awaited the turn-of-the-century decades.

As they accelerated, these changes linked to a fourth factor, the increasing interest of the nation state – itself a modern product, initially defined in the West – in direct encounters with childhood. Few links between states and childhood occurred during the agricultural centuries, with primary responsibility resting on families (usually extended families) with secondary support from religious bodies, particularly from the postclassical period onward. Beginning with the French Revolution, however, states began to enter the picture vigorously, though often amid some real agonizing over boundary lines between parental privileges and state interest. Modern governments wanted some voice over childhood to help improve health, to encourage adequate supplies of troops and workers; to assure political loyalty, mainly through guiding school curricula; and to protect against certain forms of abuse. Government contact with childhood involved the growing commitment to state-run, secular education above all. But child labor laws, public health measures, government-sponsored guidance to parents, and even a willingness to seize children whose parents did not seem to be providing approved types of care all entered in as well. Here was a final source of fundamental alteration in the framework of childhood, and for adults dealing with children, that defines the modern approach.

The basic modern changes brought additional adjustments in their wake, whenever and wherever they occurred. Predictably, the desirable qualities of a child expanded to include specific attention to intelligence: schools and testing programs made it clear to parents that measurable intelligence was a Good Thing.

Greater age-segregation of children followed from the modern model. Most schools allocated children to classes, or to seat sections within classes, by age. Furthermore, with lower birth rates most children grew up with fewer siblings, which reduced crossover relationships and promoted greater interaction with same-age school peers. Age-grading could also affect the ways many adults came to think about children. By the twentieth century, first in the West but then more broadly, a large body of expertise developed about age-sequenced development patterns, including cognitive skills. This expertise built on and enforced (some critics would argue, exaggerated) age-specific patterns inside and outside schools.

Adult–child relationships were affected by the modern model, though various specific formulas could ensue. Schooling reduced parental control over children, obviously in favour of agents of the state. This could cause concern, particularly when schools were seen as representing social class, ethnic or religious values different from those of the family. On the other hand, adult contacts with younger children often increased for the simple reason that, with lower birth rates and with more schooling taking girls out of the home, there were fewer siblings available to oversee preschoolers. Either more parental (usually, maternal) care or some alternative, such as paid help or daycare, became essential. Finally, declining birth and death rates probably increased parental attachments (on average) to individual children. Parents cared deeply for children in agricultural societies, so it's important not to exaggerate. But with fewer children overall, and with each young child far less likely to die, emotional investment in the individual child rose. Certainly, though this is an economic as well as an emotional state-ment, parental inclination to indulge children in low-birth-rate cohorts tends to increase, and evidence of this runs from the West from the late eighteenth century onward to the China of the early twenty-first century.

The modern model of childhood had implications for gender, though these were so radical that they were often long concealed. The objective need for gender distinctions among children declined. With children less assigned to work, with its normal gender links, and with reduced emphasis on mother-hood for girls, at least in terms of numbers of children expected, the need to stress dramatically different orientations for boys and girls was modified. Further, girls and boys could do equally well in school, though this was not realized immediately; indeed, girls might have an edge. Many societies long masked this change, arguing, for example, that girls and boys should study different subjects – no engineering for girls but lots of home economics; or even separate reading books, as in late nineteenth-century France, that would tell girls about their special family and supportive responsibilities. Or when girls and boys were plunged together, as in 1920s American coeducation, other devices, such as separate sports, distinctive clothing, even distinctive colors (it was at this point that American consumer culture introduced pink for girls, blue for boys) could emphasize how different the two sexes were in childhood. But the objective basis for all this weakened, and usually the gap in practice would ultimately narrow as well.

Finally, the modern model on the whole created greater separations between childhood and adulthood than had been true of agricultural society. Children no longer worked alongside their parents when work moved outside the home (with industrialization) and when children were in school. It became harder to see childhood in direct connection to the rest of life. Of course, schools were preparing for life, and many could perceive this; but the connections could be fairly abstract, and in point of fact most of the child's day was now spent apart from the adult's world – the "real world" as Americans revealingly came to call it. This separation could affect adult attitudes toward children, who might now seem privileged, and it could complicate children's efforts to find meaning in their own lives, encouraging new kinds of stress and disorientation.

This was the modern model: school, less death, fewer children in the overall population and in individual families, with a number of further implications and consequences. It's now time to see how this model first emerged in the West, and also very carefully to note some specifically Western baggage that came along with it, but was not essential to the modern model itself.

The first element of the modern model, school rather than work, was ultimately encouraged by the fact that children's work was frequently replaced by machines with industrialization, and that some schooling began to be seen as essential for successful adulthood. But the formula was pre-pared, in the West, by some earlier cultural developments, taking shape in the late seventeenth and eighteenth centuries, that provided a new view of childhood in advance of the more obvious spurs to change. Indeed, the major alterations in childhood provide an intriguing example of cultures changing first, gradually spurring actual behavioral change that would be reinforced by more objective developments, such as mechanization.

Two kinds of rethinking occurred. The Scientific Revolution and Enlight-enment encouraged the growing belief among Western philosophers that children were not corrupted at birth, as Christian and particularly Protestant doctrines of original sin had insisted. Science showed both that old ideas could be discarded and that children could gain access to reason. John Locke argued that children were blank slates at birth, open to learning and essentially good, or at least neutral, unless corrupted by outside influence. These ideas spread widely and encouraged a growing belief that childhood should be devoted to education. Fierce debates raged about this new view, with a strong minority of Protestants, particularly in the United States, still insisting on sinfulness at birth and the attendant need for strict, even punitive discipline. Gradually, however, over more than a century, a more moderate view shaped majority thinking.

The second innovation involved emphasis on the strong emotional ties that should unite a successful family, and particularly mothers with children. The emphasis on familial love was unprecedented. Pictures of respectable families began to feature more expressions of emotion. A corollary was increasingly public displays of grief at the death of children. Another intriguing corollary was a growing openness to the opinions of sons and daughters about marriage arrangements, and a willingness to call things off if an older child claimed he or she could not love the intended spouse; older children were gaining some new voice on the basis of emotional redefinitions.

These intellectual developments linked to other changes in the West during the eighteenth century. Naming practices changed: fewer rural families waited to name children until they had passed age two, and names were no longer reused if a child died. These shifts suggested the growing emotional attachment to children and a new belief in their individuality. In many parts of Europe, swaddling was abandoned in favor of letting infants move their limbs more freely. This increased the burdens of supervision but promoted more healthy development. New criticisms began to be directed at sending children to be wetnursed, though, as we have seen, the actual practice declined only slowly; reformers argued that mothers should take care of their own children and avoid the greater health risks associated with wetnursing. Parents were advised against using anger or fear to discipline children, though of course behavior changed gradually and incompletely. A new interest in purchases for children developed, associated with a desire to educate; books written specifically for children emerged for the first time. By the same token, there was a growing impulse to interfere with unstructured play, in favor of more uplifting recreations. Youth itself won new favor in principle, as adults increasingly tended to claim to be younger than they actually were, if they lied about their age at all. Yet certain rules for youth became more elaborate: increasing emphasis on careful manners, in respectable families, brought new efforts to control table habits and posture. This was a complex mixture of changes, and by no means pure gain for the children involved.

The gradual conversions to the key features of modern childhood meant that key changes, particularly with regard to child labor, were far from complete even by 1914. (Continuity in some patterns was one of the arguments of the revisionists, who disputed Ariès' sharp contrast between Western tradition and modernity.) As industrialization took hold, and cities grew, it was new misery, not basic transitions, that caught the eye of perceptive observers. Many working-class families had to put their children to work in dangerous factories – the experience of working was not novel, but the new setting was troubling. Not a few worker families, including cases involving unwed mothers sometimes impregnated by employers, had to send children to orphanages and foundling homes, where at best they were subjected to hard work and moralizing supervision, at worst abused. Many children lived on the street, not always abandoned but certainly subjected to precarious conditions; not a few fell into minor crime, of the sort described by Charles Dickens in *Oliver Twist*. However, without denying widespread horrors, these conditions were not, in the main, permanent. It was the shift toward schooling that would ultimately reshape childhood across the board.

New attention to expanding and redefining educational systems developed from the late eighteenth century onward. New secondary schools emerged for elite training, while governments began to take a somewhat more hesitant interest in mass primary education; a law encouraging but not requiring schools was passed in France in 1833. Northern American states moved faster, beginning to compel school enrollment in principle in the 1830s, though many children still attended only sporadically. Between the 1860s and 1880s actual attendance requirements became common in the Western world (though American states in the South followed suit only after 1900), and by the 1890s the vast majority of children were literate. More than requirements were involved, though this was one area where governments played a major role in promoting education as beneficial to the economy and modern citizenship alike. Schools, accordingly, emphasized the basic skills of literacy and numeracy along with strong doses of patriotic fervor. By the 1860s, peasant families in France began to acknowledge that some education was good for their sons, as selling agricultural products to wholesalers placed a new premium on literacy and numeracy; a bit later it made sense to send daughters as well, in hopes that they could take advantage of new job opportunities such as school teaching. Along with education came laws limiting child labor, though primarily in the factories; legislation was on the books throughout Western society by 1850, though effective inspections occurred more gradually. For decades, many children would both work and attend school, particularly in rural areas and in the working class; but the trend was clear, and the arguments for the conversion of childhood from labor to schooling were well established.

Gradually, also, growing numbers of middle- and even lower-middle-class parents began to send children to at least a year or two of secondary school. The American high school emerged by the 1840s; European countries introduced new secondary schools, alongside the elite units, later in the century to service growing demand. Youth as well as childhood was being redefined, though at first primarily for the middle classes.

Reduction of the birth rate spread through much of the nineteenth century and beyond. Middle-class and, in the United States, landowning farmers led the way from as early as the 1790s. The working classes followed, mainly after 1870, as did peasants; secular regions, in countries such as France or Canada, changed more rapidly than religious ones. The process required rethinking what both childhood and parenthood involved, and it could be very disconcerting; the unreliability and unrespectability of birth control devices also complicated the process, and many families long relied primarily on sexual abstinence. By the early twentieth century, really large families nevertheless became unusual, particularly in the cities and among non-immigrant groups. It was true that migrants from rural areas, or emigrants from southern and eastern Europe, brought high birth rates still around 1900, but they began to adapt in their new settings, often quite quickly.

The final piece of the modern puzzle, the reduction of the death rate, occurred more abruptly in the West. Heightened grief and a growing tendency to blame parents, particularly mothers, for child death surfaced by the mid-nineteenth century, setting the stage for new practices but initially without much result. Women's magazines, a new genre, blamed mothers for bad practices that caused children to die – such as overwrapping infants, and this reflected a new sense that traditional death rates should be prevented – but in fact they remained stubbornly high. Poor families, with still-high birth rates, indeed could depend on some deaths; an unskilled German worker wrote about how his overburdened wife paced their small apartment, muttering "if only they would die." Increasing use of sanitary measures in childbirth, prenatal checkups, and urban centers designed to help supply milk and infant foods began to achieve dramatic results from 1880 onward; during the ensuing 40 years, on both sides of the Atlantic, infant mortality dropped from 25–30 percent to under 5 percent. (Declining use of wetnurses played into this development as well.) The modern conversion had been essentially completed, though further improvements would continue. With this, in turn, and despite continued regional and class differences, much of the modern model had been installed throughout Western society by the early twentieth century.

These changes were accompanied by several other developments that were not inconsistent, but reflected more strictly Western approaches to modern childhood – approaches that might or might not show up with the modern model in other parts of the world. Several of these accompaniments were interesting, not just in relationship to the basic movement toward the modern model, but also in their contrast with earlier Western traditions, including Christian beliefs and previous tensions about youth and work. Dramatic reconceptualization may have been necessary, at least in principle, precisely because the modern trends strained against some of the distinctive patterns previously dominant in the West.

A striking feature was the idealization of the child, building on eighteenth-century intellectual currents. Children were portrayed, in middle-class literature, as wondrous innocents, full of love and deserving to be loved in turn. Pictures and stories disseminated the image. Motherhood gained new credit as a fundamental source of family love, but siblings were supposed to be joined in loving affection, and even fathers, though now working outside the home, might come in for a bit of joy. While many families doubtless took this new emphasis with a large grain of salt, diaries, and stories such as the American classic *Little Women*, showed how hard some families worked to make it reality. Anger should disappear, in this model, from the bosom of the family, though the new imagery almost welcomed grief. Actual family leisure, in the middle classes and among respectable artisans, built on the same feelings of togetherness. Pianos became vital furniture from the 1830s onward as a focus for family singing; and the idea of family vacations began to gain ground as well. The celebration of children's birthdays, another new habit, expressed family affection and the commitment to children's individuality.

Loving innocence had other corollaries. Parental, and particularly maternal, responsibilities increased, in protecting children from corruption as well as ill-health. Many women worked very hard to maintain a sunny disposition with their offspring. It became harder for children themselves, particularly girls, to express discontent in middle-class families – for discord should not trouble a loving home. By the 1860s, a new eating disorder began to be noted among a minority of girls, particularly middle-class girls. Modern anorexia nervosa, a rejection of food often prepared by doting mothers, might have been an indirect way to react to parental smothering that could not be explicitly faulted; the disease would gain further ground a bit later, when slender body standards became widely accepted as well. While boys had a little more latitude, allowed to engage in some rough play with friends and indeed encouraged not to become effeminate or, as a new word argued, "sissies," they too faced a number of new rules, including the strictures of polite manners and careful body control.

Sexuality was a real problem amid the larger imagery of loving innocence. Middle-class children, particularly males, could not marry very young, because they needed to complete an education and get a start on their career before taking on family responsibility. At the same time, it was vitally important not to burden a family with too many children, and particularly, of course, with children born out of wedlock. A huge new concern about masturbation revealed the rising level of anxiety about sex and childhood, and it generated many very real disciplinary efforts as well. At an extreme, a few children were institutionalized for incorrigible masturbation, which was held to cause all sorts of health disorders and insanities. Children were supposed to be attractive, and girls gained all sorts of training in the art of looking beautiful with an eye to encouraging male interest in courtship, now that marriage should in theory be based on love. New Western standards promoted a complex juggling act in which sex was frowned upon, but a certain amount of sexually laden flirtation was encouraged. Some children, and indeed some adults, found the combination confusing.

Along with the emphasis on loving innocence and the complicated signals about sexual restraint, the West introduced a final basic innovation into its approach to childhood in the nineteenth century: the idea of adolescence. The word came into some use from the 1830s onward, but it really began to gain currency when it was sanctioned by child psychologists such as the American G. Stanley Hall in the later nineteenth century. Adolescence denoted a specific slice of childhood that had never before been identified, having been subsumed in the more general category of "youth." The concept, applied mainly to the middle class at this point, emerged from several of the key changes in the experience of and ideas about childhood. It denoted, first of all, the growing period of dependence for children who were now being sent to secondary schools rather than to work. Adolescence demarcated teenagers' heightened distinction from adults. Adolescence also labeled a period of sexual maturation without respectable outlets for expression. Amid improved nutrition and the greater contacts and temptations of urban life, children in Western society began to experience puberty at an increasingly young age: whereas puberty at 16 was common in eighteenth-century America, the age had dropped at least two years by the 1860s. This very real change obviously complicated the task of sexual control on which middleclass standards depended so heavily, and adolescence helped express this tension. More broadly still, adolescence denoted a period of emotional turmoil for many children, helping parents understand why, despite a loving upbringing, relationships might become more difficult for a few years.

The concept of adolescence fueled a wider social change which, however, had its own double-edged qualities. Because they were so different from adults, and because of the hope to preserve or restore childish innocence, deviant adolescents needed distinctive treatment by police officers and courts of law; they should not, as offenders, be thrown in with adult criminals. Throughout Western society, reformers introduced new codes of juvenile justice by the later nineteenth century, with separate courts and separate penal institutions – the reform schools. At the same time, however, laws governing youth behavior tightened up quite dramatically. Behaviors such as vandalism, that had been tolerated in more traditional times when people had confidence that youth would not unduly challenge community norms, now became illegal in the more anonymous context of growing cities. So, of course, did open sexual activity, and the treatment of female juvenile offenders became particularly severe. Great effort was devoted also to outlawing drinking and, for several decades, cigarette smoking among adolescents.

It became harder for many older children to measure up to social requirements. A variety of new institutions, such as the scouting movement, sprang up to help youth move through its difficult transitions without falling into unwholesome or illegal alternatives. At the same time, often-exaggerated fears about increases in juvenile crime marked the ambiguities with which Western society regarded adolescence in the nineteenth century and beyond.

Some of the tensions in the new approaches to childhood, and the new situations of children themselves, were further shaped by social class and gender factors. Respectable middle-class people might hope to keep their own adolescents in check, but they had no confidence in the immigrants or the working classes. Belief in the inadequacy of many parents grew as the definition of responsible parenthood became more rigorous. Class differences help explain the reliance on policing and a number of other efforts at intervention against working-class parents, including moralistic supervision of particularly vulnerable groups such as unwed mothers. Working-class youth did develop recreational interests – for example, in the new amusement parks – that the middle class frowned upon, and premarital sexual activity might be tolerated in working-class culture as well, so long as pregnancy was followed by marriage. Early in the nineteenth century, in fact, an increase in the rate of illegitimate births among teenagers and young adults helped spur new levels of middle-class vigilance. Clashes over respectability in children expressed the combination of middle-class standards and deep social divisions in nineteenth-century Western society.

Gender presented another divide. Girls and boys were held to be very different, and they were destined for different roles – wife and mother versus productive worker or businessman. While the new imagery emphasized the loving innocence of all children (unless corrupted by debased parents), girls were particularly innocent, held to be by nature anger-free and far less burdened than adolescent boys with sexual desire. These standards imposed severe constraints on girls, though many measured up successfully; failure, particularly in the sexual arena, was severely sanctioned. Respectable boys faced their own complexity. They were supposed to be gentle in the household but capable of forceful action outside. They should honor sexual restraints in courtship (though there were some breakdowns here, even in the middle class), but they should also realize that men were by nature sexual aggressors. Some late-adolescent schoolboys could reduce this particular tension by sexual liaisons with lower-class girls or prostitutes, enjoying a sexual double standard compared with middle-class girls. Highly gendered childhood was another legacy of the particular Western take on modern childhood more generally. While its hold would decline in the twentieth century, it continued to influence the West itself, and also Western judgments about childhood in other societies.

Nineteenth-century Western society accompanied the creation of the modern model of childhood with a series of embellishments that simultaneously placed almost impossible hopes in childhood and generated a number of new restrictions and constraints. The most obvious strictures were directed against children of the less respectable classes, where a combination of new laws and moralistic laments were designed to keep the lid on, while explaining why childish innocence could not readily be preserved. But the standards applied to middle-class children themselves were demanding as well. At the end of the nineteenth century, the Viennese psychologist Sigmund Freud basically argued that the new standards distorted children's natural impulses and created frustrated, even mentally ill, adults. More generally, the concept of adolescence was meant to explain a problem period without throwing out the idealization of childhood. Not all of these features were essential to the demographic transition and the embrace of schooling, though they seemed vital at the time. Some would drop off in the twentieth century, as the modern model itself matured. Many would be ignored or modified by other societies seeking their own transitions to modern childhood – though the weight of Western authority and insistence made it difficult to distinguish what was non-essential.

Further reading

Recent surveys include: Marianne N. Bloch, Devorah Kennedy, Theodora Lightfoot and Dar Weyenberg, eds, *The Child in the World, The World in the Child* (New York: Palgrave Macmillan, 2006); Hugh Cunningham, *Children and Childhood in Western Society Since 1500*, 2nd edn (New York: Longman, 2005); Anthony Krupp, *Reason's Children: Children in Early Modern Philosophy* (Lewisburg, PA: Bucknell University Press, 2009); Alan Prout, series ed., *The Future of Childhood: Toward the Interdisciplinary Study of Children* (Abingdon, UK: RoutledgeFalmer Press, 2005).

Earlier books that dealt with basic change include: John Gillis, *Youth and History: Tradition and Change in European Age Relations, 1770–Present* (New York: Academic Press, 1974); Philip Greven, *Protestant Temperament: Patterns of Childrearing, Religious Experience and the Self in Early America* (New York: Knopf, 1977); Rachel Fuchs, *Abandoned Children; Foundlings and Child Welfare in Nineteenth-Century France* (Albany: State University of New York Press, 1984); Stephen Humphries, *Hooligans or Rebels? An Oral History of Working-Class Childhood and Youth* (Oxford: Oxford University Press, 1981). See also Colin Heywood, *Childhood in Nineteenth-Century France: Work, Health and Education among the "Classes Populaires"* (Cambridge: Cambridge University Press, 1988) and *A History of Childhood: Children and Childhood in the West from Medieval to Modern Times* (Cambridge, UK: Polity Press, 2001); Lee Shai Weissbach, *Child Labor Reform in Nineteenth-Century France* (Baton Rouge: Louisiana State University Press, 1989); J. Robert Wegs, *Growing Up Working Class: Continuity and Change among Viennese Youth, 1890–1938*

(University Park, PA: Pennsylvania State University Press, 1989); Nancy Janovicek and Joy Parr, eds, *Histories of Canadian Children and Youth* (New York: Oxford University Press, 2003); Peter N. Stearns, *American Cool: Creating a Twentieth-century Emotional Style* (New York: New York University Press, 1998); Mary Jo Maynes, *Schooling in Western Europe, A Social History* (Albany: State University of New York Press, 1985).

See also Paula Fass, *Children of a New World: Society, Culture and Globalization* (New York: New York University Press, 2006); and with Mary Ann Mason, eds, *Childhood in America* (New York: New York University Press, 2000).

On demographic change: Ansley Coales and Susan Watkins, eds, *The Decline of Fertility in Europe* (Princeton, NJ: Princeton University Press, 1986); Michael Haines, *Fertility and Occupation: Population Patterns in Industrialization* (New York: Academic Press, 1989); Wally Seccombe, *Weathering the Storm: Working-class Families from the Industrial Revolution to the Fertility Decline* (London: Verso, 1993). Steven Mintz, *Huck's Raft: A History of American Childhood* is an important recent study (Cambridge, MA: Harvard University Press, 2004).

Chapter 7

Alongside the modern model

The pressures of colonialism

Even as the modern model of childhood began to be formulated in Western society, in the eighteenth and nineteenth centuries a quite different set of changes affected children in many other parts of the world. These changes were not always as striking as those involved in the modern redefinitions of childhood, but they did move, quite dramatically, in opposite directions from the modern model in many ways, involving more rather than less work, frequently high birth rates, and certainly elevated levels of death and disease.

It is vital to remember that, even as changes took shape in the West, most of the rest of the world remained locked in basically agricultural patterns, sometimes with relatively little change involved. Indeed, this is true to some extent even in the present day, with some parts of rural India, for example, only slightly affected by developments like campaigns against child labor or schooling requirements. The gap between the areas of even gradual shifts toward the modern model, and agricultural patterns, was even more striking in the eighteenth and nineteenth centuries.

This is not, however, the whole story. Beginning with new forms of colonialism from 1500 onward, global economic and political changes were creating new pressures on childhood even in areas that remained basically agricultural. Directly or indirectly, Western-sponsored pressures heightened the exploitation of many children, even as reforms were under discussion in the West itself.

Three related developments, from the sixteenth century onward, central to world history, had substantial impact on many children. The first involved the massive expansion of slave trading, from Africa to the Americas, and of slavery itself. The second featured growing European colonialism, particularly in the Americas. And the third, most generally, centered on the expansion of production for an increasingly commercial world economy.

All three of these developments impinged on children, rarely benignly. Some results simply highlighted or extended common features of agricultural childhoods for the lower classes – hard work for children, to take the most obvious example, was not new, but it sometimes became even harder. And there were also some novel results, leading to new challenges for childhood and new indignities for children themselves. The resultant patterns extended well into the nineteenth century and in some cases beyond.

This chapter uses examples of change from several locations, but with particular focus on Atlantic slavery and on the development of new forms of childhood in Latin America, where European, African, and Native American influences mixed for children as they did for the civilization more generally.

Some world historians have recently argued that, globally, the pressure to work harder increased from the sixteenth to the nineteenth century, a pattern that had been hinted at even earlier in the postclassical centuries. Growing populations in many places required more labor to sustain their numbers. Expanding export markets attracted merchants and growers with a greater interest in extracting more labor as well. The results showed in more work in old age, an increased production intensity among adults – and greater pressure on child labor. The argument is plausible, though hard to prove in the absence of reliable statistics. What is clear is that particular systems, such as Atlantic slavery, changed the work equation for children and more besides. And many of the effects would continue to 1900, and in some places even beyond.

In 1756, Olaudah Equiano, age 11, was seized into slavery from his village in Nigeria. Youngest in his family, he had been indulged by his mother and trained in various sports and military skills. His community was aware of the possibility of kidnapping, and usually had someone watch children as they played together. But two men and a woman got through anyway, while Equiano's parents were working in the fields, and seized him and his sister. Both children were filled with fear and grief – but soon the gang separated the two, so, as Equiano put it, "we were soon deprived of even the small comfort of weeping together." The boy, joined with various other captives whose languages he rarely understood, was finally put on a slave ship, where, among other things, he thought that the white sailors were going to eat him. Refusing food, he was whipped into willingness and ultimately put to work on a plantation in Barbados. There he saw again the tragedy of children being separated, in this case by sale – "and it was very moving on this occasion, to see and hear their cries at parting." "Why are parents to lose their children, brothers their sisters. ... Surely this is a new refinement in cruelty which ... adds fresh horrors even to the wretchedness of slavery."

Slavery was not new in world history, of course, and it had always involved potential trauma for children. Adolescents were in high demand as slaves, for their work and breeding potential. The new slave trade and American slave institutions were unquestionably worse than most traditional slave systems, however; Islamic societies, for example, barred slave mothers from being separated from young children, and protected slave women who had children by free men. And for the most part, in Islamic slavery, tasks for children were lighter than would be the case in the new Atlantic economy.

American slavery also thrust children transported from Africa, like Equiano, into a far stranger and more remote culture than had normally been the case, though later generations of slave children would not face this degree of uprooting.

The actual experience of American slavery had two components: first, some standard features of lower-class childhood, though somewhat intensified; and second, some decidedly unfamiliar difficulties. Most African parents already insisted on obedience from their children, and their childrearing maintained many African customs including, for many decades, the habit of naming children for other relatives. A white observer noted, "The rarest thing to hear are disrespectful words from a child to his parent." Elderly slaves often provided childcare while parents worked, again a not unfamiliar arrangement. And there was the work itself: slave children were supposed to start working quite young – "as soon as us could toddle," as one slave put it in a reminiscence. Little children gathered firewood; children by age 10 worked the fields. Some, particularly males, learned some craft skills. But there was also a certain amount of time for play and community revelry.

The harsher features of slavery involved the possibility of being separated from the family by sale – either of the child itself, or of one of the parents. Slave-owners looked at children explicitly in terms of dollar value – "Her oldest boy is worth $1,250 cash, and I can get it." Fear of separation was even more common than the fact itself, though once the Atlantic slave trade was abolished, in 1808, sales of young slaves from the coastal states to the deep South and the West increased considerably. There was also the demeaning position children encountered in front of whites. They might play, as youngsters, with white children, but soon the latter would learn to lord it over them, requiring that they obey "young masters and mistresses." Whites often commented on the ragged and dirty appearance of slave children, the results of poverty and work. Harsh punishments were frequent for children who stepped out of line. A master talked about selling an "unruly" girl, a "very dangerous character." Whippings were common. Slave parents worked hard to instill deference in children. Boys were taught to "bend their body forward with head down, and rest the body on the left foot, and scrape the right foot backward on the ground, while uttering the words 'how do Massie and Missie'." Even white owners who viewed blacks with some sympathy, seeing them all as children, exasperating but lovable regardless of age, displayed a patronizing quality that children could not help but pick up. And finally, there were the common denials: most slave-owners long opposed even minimal education for slave children. This stood out at a time when other sectors of society were increasingly emphasizing schooling, and in which many slaves (like Equiano) originally came from families in Africa, where certain kinds of education had been assumed. Cruelty, visible inferiority, and relative deprivation combined to create a distinctive childhood in the Americas, experienced by large numbers of people. By 1859, 56 percent of all slaves in the United States were aged under 20, and their childhoods would carry over into their experiences, and to those of later African-American children, long after Emancipation.

A variety of new migrations occurred from the seventeenth through the nineteenth centuries, and while the experience of migration was certainly not new, the modern patterns had various implications for children. Some adolescents migrated on their own, though more commonly there was family support on either the sending or receiving end, or both. Even when they traveled with families, children often found themselves in the position of mediating between their parents and their new home. Often, to take an obvious and familiar immigrant example, they learned a new language far better than their parents ever managed. Service as intermediaries gave children new opportunities, but it also caused tensions with parental standards, and no small amount of identity confusion in children themselves.

Large numbers of children were also pushed to migrate in conditions that were less than free. During the eighteenth and nineteenth centuries, many charity organizations in Europe sent children to the colonies, because there was insufficient support at home. Indentured service was another device often applied to youth, requiring several years of work in the new land prior to independent adulthood. The indenture experience involved many Asians in the later nineteenth century, transported to places such as Hawaii or the West Indies as the search for available labor spread to new areas. Adults were involved as well, but children's participation was vital, based on the standard assumptions, in agricultural society, that child labor was normal. And while indentures involving children in principle were negotiated – though often by parents or an orphanage, rather than by children themselves – some children were effectively sold into migrant labor.

Other types of migration could have an impact. European men, traveling abroad, not infrequently fathered children with local women, whom they then usually abandoned when they went home. In Canada, the Hudson's Bay Company offered a small payment for children left behind. (The disavowal of native illegitimate children was common in Protestant countries, particularly Britain; the situation in Catholic countries such as France and Spain was more complex.) The disproportionate numbers of men in migration (including forced migration) increased the incidence of mother-led families in Europe and Africa; or alternatively, if mothers migrated along with fathers, children might be left behind with female relatives.

The impact of migration – on migrants themselves, and on societies that received them – could combine with the larger results of European colonialism, as the Latin American experience abundantly demonstrated. As the Spanish and Portuguese colonized Latin America from the late fifteenth century onward, they affected childhood in several ways. Intense labor needs prompted an obvious emphasis on children as sources of work – again, a standard feature of agricultural societies, but given urgent attention.

Larger attitudes toward native peoples could include a sense that reforms of childhood were needed to bring these colonial subjects up to civilized levels (as determined by the conquerors). Sexual unions between Europeans and locals, not infrequently involuntary, generated a culture in which large numbers of children were at least technically illegitimate, requiring in turn a set of social mechanisms that would allow them to be utilized and cared for. The results, however, might well encounter additional official disapproval from those in the colonial elite.

The work needs were obvious, and included the use of children in slavery on the sugar plantations of Brazil or the West Indies. Many Native American children were compelled, with their parents, to work on Latin American plantations, particularly the *encomiendas*, where forced labor was particularly extensive. Work had been part of childhood in pre-Conquest America, but the element of compulsion and the service for European owners rather than the local community added new components.

Because Incas and Aztecs had long operated in an agricultural economy, their approaches to childhood did not, in fact, always differ greatly from those of the Europeans. As we have seen, they too, for example, stressed not only work but obedience. There are indications of some harsh disciplinary practices before European arrival, particularly among the Incas and Aztecs. The Aztecs featured a variety of punishments for children from age eight or so onward, including slaps and, at an extreme, exposure to the smoke from burning chili peppers (which created an effect rather like pepper spray, from which a few children might actually die). They, too, highlighted gender distinctions. Despite overlap, however – for Europeans also emphasized physical discipline – Europeans often scorned native ways. They frequently found Indian children badly behaved, and they often interfered with an Indian belief that children had obligations to the entire community, more than to individual families. European leaders, headed by the missionaries, worked hard to stop traditional practices such as the use of children in religious sacrifice. They also interfered with local practices by imposing missionary-based education on a minority of children. European colonists did not have a dramatic new approach to childrearing, but they did want to impose religious change where possible, and they highlighted specific differences – whether apparent permissiveness or specific methods of punishment – on the assumption that their own practices were superior.

Most strikingly, the colonial experience in Latin America created unusually high rates of illegitimacy, and this in turn became a durable characteristic of childhood in this society. High rates of illegitimacy developed in the colonial period, for several reasons. Most obviously, many European men had sexual contact with local women, and rarely did they officially acknowledge any offspring that resulted. But sexual activities within the lower classes themselves – a *mestizo*, or mixed race man, for example, with an Indian or African partner – also often occurred without the formality of marriage. Again, illegitimate children and mother-based families were the frequent result. The percentage of all births that were illegitimate was considerable. In a São Paulo (Brazil) parish in the 1740s, 23 percent of all children were illegitimate, mainly as a result of sexual activity between different racial groups. Percentages in the nineteenth century had risen even higher, to 30 or even 50 percent in some cases.

The results, for children themselves, varied widely. Some fathers maintained loving contacts with children even though they did not acknowledge them officially. A planter specified in his will that an illegitimate son should receive "a canopy from the bed in which I sleep and ... four shirts of mine and four white pants" – the point being gifts that would express real and personal affection. Other fathers ignored the children entirely. Mothers raising children on their own often received a great deal of help from other families, some of whom took the children in directly. Reliance on wetnurses was common (except, interestingly, among the upper classes, classes where, in contrast to Europe, mothers were expected to care for children themselves). Tremendous numbers of children in Latin America "circulated" – that is, they went to families that were childless or needed extra labor, where their own work service could make a crucial difference. Labor was the key component. It was sometimes accompanied by extremely harsh discipline, and there were cases of immense cruelty. But other adults treated their child workers kindly, even incorporating them into essentially familial relations and providing for them in their wills. Ironically, Latin American laws did not allow for legal adoption (this situation changed only later in the twentieth century), but *de facto* this often occurred. In one city in Chile, 17 percent of all children at one point around 1880 were living in houses run by adults who were not their parents. Large orphanages supplemented this system of child circulation, often taking in infants for wetnursing and then allocating them for labor to other families once they reached age five or six. For a time after the abolition of slavery, Brazilian planters used orphan labor in what was little more than a replacement slave system.

The elites and middle classes of Latin America profoundly disapproved of these features of lower-class childhood (even though upper-class men frequently sired children with maids or other lower-class women). For these people, European standards of childrearing were fully applicable, and this meant conventional two-parent families. Statements thus referred to illegitimacy as "infamous," leaving an "indecent and shameful mark." Two-parent families were essential to have children who are "more educated, deferential, and apply themselves to work." Outrage mounted from the later nineteenth century onward, as European standards were taken as vital signs of civilization itself. Thus a Chilean politician in 1928 praised Europe for its family life, in contrast to the lower classes in his own country: "where illegitimacy reigns, populations are closer to a primitive state ... and backwardness prevails." Particular concerns applied to health, with assumptions that lower-class children "transmit infections that devastate the population."

Clearly, Latin American upper classes and governments were moving toward a modern model, at least for their own families and in their own minds, by the later nineteenth century. Schooling advanced. Laws made special provision for juvenile offenders. Programs attempted to combat high rates of infant mortality and also infanticide. But the traditions and conditions that produced a different kind of childhood, devoted to labor amid a fluctuating, though often quite effective, family structures, did not really recede. The colonial heritage of Latin America produced a bifurcated set of childhoods, each functional in different ways, one moving toward European-defined modernity, the other based essentially on agricultural standards but with some special twists introduced by colonialism. The pattern continues to inform many Latin American countries even today.

Not all versions of colonialism replicated the Latin American experience. Always, however, colonial attitudes toward natives as children, and native children as particularly problematic, had some impact. Always, European sexual relationships created new categories of children – though not necessarily the same level of illegitimacy. Always, there was attention to maintaining child labor and even assuring that children would be available for work for the colonial masters themselves, as household servants and as producers in the fields. Always, some tension developed, by 1900, between efforts to introduce new institutions for children such as schools – whether by Europeans or by local reformers – and the actual conditions of the majority.

Developments resulting from slavery, colonialism, and new economic relationships encouraged new forms of child labor and new attitudes toward certain kinds of children. The developments occurred simultaneously with the emergence of the modern model. Here was a crucial source of divisions within particular societies such as Latin America, but also in the world at large. Both patterns were important, but their irreconcilability was most important of all. World society is still dealing with the results, early in the twenty-first century.

Colonialism and slavery were not the only forces shaping childhood outside the West during the early modern period and the nineteenth century. Chinese childhood, though hardly unvaried or unchanging, continued to reflect many of the patterns established in the classical and postclassical periods, which obviously contrasted in many ways with the modern model. Most striking was the continued emphasis on obedience and hard work. Indeed, work obligations may have increased in the period 1600–1900, as China became more urban, with greater emphasis on training for productive labor. Here was a link to patterns in other parts of the world. While many children carved out some space for themselves, and while parents varied in severity, many families restricted children considerably, even attempting to forbid play in the interests of jobs or of rigorous schooling. Harsh physical discipline was common. Model children were still described as having essentially adult qualities. One was praised as "having a solemnity almost like that of an adult," while another, ultimately a successful intellectual, was described as having been "born with a serious and solemn outlook, never taking part in play." Hints of change developed late in the nineteenth century. The government certainly began to consider new forms of schooling, sending some youth and young adults abroad, and missionaries imported change as well, including new stirrings against foot binding. Some adults began to take a possibly novel delight in bringing new and imaginative ideas to children, as in the case of an uncle who liked to encourage creative thinking in his nieces when he visited. But, as in Latin America, the basic imperatives of childhood in agricultural societies still predominated, modified mainly by increasing labor demands.

Further reading

See William A. Corsaro, *The Sociology of Childhood* (Thousand Oaks, CA: Sage, 2005); Ernest Bartell and Alejandro O'Donnell, eds, *The Child in Latin America* (Notre Dame, IN: Notre Dame University Press, 2001) (contemporary in focus but with historical references); Tobias Hecht, ed., *Minor Omissions: Children in Latin American History and Society* (Madison: University of Wisconsin Press, 2002); Dirk Hoerder, *Cultures in Contact: World Migrations in the Second Millennium* (Durham, NC: Duke University Press, 2002); Wilma King, *Stolen Childhood: Slave Youth in Nineteenth-century America* (Bloomington: Indiana University Press, 1991); Ping-chen Hsiung, *A Tender Voyage: Children and Childhood in Late Imperial China* (Stanford, CA: Stanford University Press, 2005).

Chapter 8

Modern childhood in Asia

Japan adapts the new model

In 1984, the Japanese government ordered an inquiry into the declining use of chopsticks among schoolchildren. Preference for knives and forks was growing rapidly among children who wanted to eat more quickly, and also to become still more attuned to international patterns. The government hoped to encourage tradition as part of the sense of what childhood, both modern and Japanese, should entail. Not a major historical moment, obviously, but an interesting comment on change and counterpressure in one of the most dynamic societies in modern world history.

Japan's rapid adjustment to unprecedented Western pressure from the 1860s onward was a striking development on the international scene. American and British fleets sailed into Edo Bay in 1853 and 1854, demanding that Japan end its isolation and open to Western trade. Over a decade of struggle followed, amid further Western interference, as Japanese leaders debated how to respond, at times falling into near-civil war. But in 1868, the decision was made: massive reform was the answer. All this is familiar as well as important; what must be added now is the extent to which a major redefinition of childhood formed a basic part of the process.

Japanese reformers quickly grasped the essentials of the modern model, as they visited Western Europe and the United States, with schooling at the forefront. They were prepared for this to some extent, for Japan had expanded Confucian and Buddhist schooling rapidly earlier in the nineteenth century and, after the West, had the world's highest literacy rate. Upwards of 30,000 private schools had been set up between 1800 and 1868, bringing exposure to primary education for large numbers of commoners. But conversion to mass education, and of course the new commitment of the government to this extension, constituted a major shift, nevertheless, and it brought a surprising number of additional changes in its wake. The Japanese case suggests how many ramifications could attach to the modern model, at least when the model was borrowed directly, often eagerly, from the West.

At the same time, Japanese childhood did not become Western. Leaders were at pains to construct a genuine modern model that would nevertheless retain distinctive Japanese values in childhood, either in traditional ways or through new inventions, such as a particular version of nationalism. Here, too, the Japanese case, distinctive in its own right, is an extremely instructive caution against a simplistic application of modernization thinking.

Finally, as early as the 1920s, and certainly after World War II, Japan proved capable of influencing childhood in other parts of the world, particularly through consumer exports. Its speed in taking up new opportunities to sell to children is a fascinating part of its own adjustment story, and would ultimately become a significant element in the globalization of childhood. Again, Japanese-sponsored change complicates any portrayal of the modern world history of childhood in strictly Western terms. Patterns took shape clearly from the 1860s through to postwar American occupation in the later 1940s.

Childhood had been changing in Japan even before full consideration of the modern model. Schooling spread to a large minority of children, though disproportionately to boys, in the early nineteenth century. Private Confucian and Buddhist schools won growing popularity, building on, but altering, the influences from China of several centuries before. These developments undoubtedly helped prepare Japan for a fuller conversion to an education-based childhood after the Reform Era began in 1868. In other respects, however, the conditions of agricultural society largely prevailed. Most children worked from a fairly early age. A full concept of childhood as a distinct stage of life was not developed, as evidenced, for example, by the mixing of children and adults in punishments for crime. Dominant Confucian principles emphasized hierarchy and discipline.

Discussion of school reform heated up in the 1860s. Government-sponsored missions abroad brought back reports on the merits of Western education; many of the emissaries would themselves shape the later Ministry of Education. Particular attention was devoted to the need to introduce more science, and to break the Confucian habit of looking toward tradition rather than innovation for sources of knowledge. Considerable caution attached to these discussions, for almost no-one advocated complete Westernization: as one leader put it in 1868, "foreign learning must be made to subserve the interests of Japan."

The reform movement obviously inserted the national government strongly into the redefinition of childhood, an innovation for Japan, where (as in many traditional societies) childhood had been seen as a largely private matter. Now the nation itself had a stake in children's achievements, just as it would develop greater involvement in promoting children's health, providing advice to parents, and other matters. This paralleled the process emerging in the West, though the government initiatives were more sudden. It would take a few decades, however, for the government to agree on standards within schools that could ensure students would gain a modern education, but also a distinctively Japanese set of values compatible with emerging commitments to nationalism.

As the Ministry of Education was formed (in 1871), and then an ambitious new Education Code was introduced the following year, several major changes gained emphasis. First was the new attention to science, modern foreign languages (particularly English), and other new subjects. Even in families where schooling was already established, this meant that children began learning many things their parents did not know, and ignoring some cherished subjects as well – an interesting development in a society where age hierarchy had long been esteemed. A host of foreign books and advisors were welcomed into the system, particularly during the 1870s. Second, education at all levels was opened to qualified citizens regardless of social rank – "learning is no longer to be considered as belonging to the upper classes." And third, and most important for Japanese childhood generally, universal primary schooling was mandated, with a goal of opening 54,000 primary schools under government control. Here, surprisingly early in the reform process, and with dramatic scope, came the introduction of the essence of modern childhood, an insistence that schooling become the core obligation of childhood. Reform leaders explicitly argued that "if the ordinary people are poor and illiterate, the wealth and power of the entire country cannot be summoned." Clearly, larger social goals, not explicit attention to childhood, dominated this change, but such had been the case in the West to some extent earlier, and it did not modify the massive impact of schooling on childhood across the social spectrum.

It was vitally important that these measures involved girls as well as boys, again a striking innovation in a gender-conscious society, and a major change in childhood in its own right. Attention to girls' education followed from the desire to imitate the West, where at least basic education for females was gaining ground rapidly. It also resulted from a belief that, in a modern society, mothers must be educated in order to raise their children properly. In other words, even if the basic interests still involved boys' training, the need for literate mothers seemed inescapable.

Not surprisingly, actual change proved slower and more hesitant than the early proclamations implied. Only half the required primary schools had opened by 1900, in a society that was still very poor. More interesting still, though hardly surprising amid what was nevertheless an ambitious pace of change, considerable popular resistance emerged. Many peasants believed that schools were nothing more than a channel for military recruitment, and they rebelled, in a few cases quite literally, against this extension of government control over childhood. It would take some time for Japanese peasants to realize, like their counterparts in the West, that there were practical advantages in letting children acquire basic literacy and numeracy skills, including opportunities for upward mobility – as in becoming a teacher. There was also pushback against too much openness for girls, and by the late 1870s greater emphasis on domestic skills such as sewing helped reaffirm the importance of gender in childhood, even amid new levels of schooling.

By 1900, despite various constraints, essentially all Japanese children were attending primary schools (sometimes crowded ones) and were becoming literate, a massive reorientation in childhood. Japan was also promoting an unusually long school year, of 200 classroom days, a clear indication of the seriousness of this redefinition away from child labor, and remarkable in a society with limited resources. Change extended far less widely into adolescence at this point, however; and a number of children even of primary school age were still sent to work at least part time, forming 15 percent of the factory labor force. Anomalies increased after age 12. To be sure, secondary and university education expanded, with even a few opportunities for women, but the emphasis lay on identifying talented children who could be trained toward the kind of technical expertise that an industrializing society required – in fields (for boys) such as engineering, which ballooned rapidly. For most teenagers, work continued to describe life for several more decades. Indeed, reliance on young workers, particularly women, became central to Japan's industrialization process. Needing cheap exports to pay for expensive imported equipment and fuels, and lacking significant raw materials for export, Japan rapidly expanded production in silk textiles, taking over world leadership from China. Sweatshops, using manual methods, eagerly recruited young girls from the countryside, often essentially buying them from family members. Resultant conditions, with long hours, no freedom to leave the work site, and low pay, represented change, but not in the direction of a fundamental redefinition of later childhood. By the 1930s, however, the number of children in secondary school was rising rapidly.

For the longer run, the most significant adjustment in the Japanese process of change toward the modern model of childhood involved a successful attempt to infuse schooling with principles that differed from those the Japanese saw in the West, and particularly to emphasize collective loyalties and obedience for children, as opposed to the more individualistic approaches in Europe and the United States. (Western authorities themselves tried to limit individualism by stressing national loyalty, but they placed more emphasis on individual achievement and less on group affiliation in the classroom.) Balancing changes in childhood became a crucial issue for Japanese identity. Conservative counterattack against too much Western influence crystallized in a pronouncement by the Emperor in 1879. An ensuing Memorandum for teachers insisted that "loyalty to the Imperial House, love of country, filial piety toward parents, respect for superiors, faith in friends … constitute the great path of human morality." Secondary schools, similarly, were urged to regain "the virtues of loyalty, filial piety, honor and duty, which had been cultivated for several centuries." Attention to science and new knowledge was fine in the technical fields, but it should be balanced by this more traditional moralism, including the emphasis on community among children that had developed far earlier in Japanese villages. For girls, this approach heightened the emphasis on gender-specific education, toward becoming a "good wife, wise mother," preached even for upper-class girls in the higher schools – even as opportunities beyond primary training continued to expand. In the sciences themselves, at least in the early grades, Japan continued to stress rote learning, parroting the teacher while embracing schooling more generally in an elaborate maze of rules and codes of conduct. Here, too, Japan continued to generate a culture among children that, while no less modern than that of the West, was genuinely distinctive. Also important was the encouragement to students to form close bonds with each other, promoting group cohesion; by the later twentieth century, this quality would continue to distinguish Japanese education in the early grades, taking precedence even over obedience to adults. This same group emphasis encouraged Japanese teachers to rely considerably on shaming as a disciplinary tactic, even as its use declined in the West, and particularly the United States, because of concerns about children's self-esteem. By the early twenty-first century, Japanese students who faltered in math were still publicly identified to their classmates – a practice that was actually illegal by this point in the United States on grounds of protection of privacy. Whatever its other drawbacks, the Japanese approach remained more successful in encouraging academic performance.

For its qualities, both old and new, education became more important in Japanese society than it was in the West, in terms of defining access to later careers. Like Western Europe, and in contrast to the United States, the Japanese system placed great stock in qualifying examinations, which would ultimately open the path to university for the minority of successful students. Parents who aspired for their children's success accordingly added to their own responsibilities to childhood the need to work hard to promote academic achievement, including providing opportunities for entertainment and letting off steam amid the seriousness and intensity of preparation for exams.

Education brought additional changes in its wake, many of which rather unexpectedly moved Japan closer to the Western version of modern childhood. Two of the changes were predictable enough. Birth rates began to drop rapidly during the nineteenth century, which followed logically from decreased family reliance on the labor of younger children, and from increasing costs, including getting children ready for school; this pattern began to emerge amid the expansion of schools even before 1868, and accelerated thereafter. Birth rates remained higher than in the West through the 1930s, though dropping; after the 1950s, Japan changed even more rapidly, moving from 2.7 children per woman in 1950 to a mere 1.4 in 1995, well under the levels needed to sustain the population. Government-sponsored public health measures, one of the other early interests in copying from the West, rapidly cut into traditional child mortality rates during this period as well. Infant mortality had dropped to 16 percent by 1920, 10 percent by 1939; the level the West had achieved by 1920, 5 percent, was reached by 1950. And the process continued, with 0.04 percent infant mortality, one of the world's lowest rates, by 1995. These fairly rapid changes in children's demography, as earlier in the West, made the individual child a more precious commodity within the family.

Other adjustments followed. Japan had not offered a particularly clear definition of childhood as a separate phase of human life, or of society, prior to the later nineteenth century. It had an extensive premodern school network, but this was conceived as a system, not a definition of discrete childhood. Other than the private schools themselves, there were no separate institutions, particularly public institutions, for children – youthful offenders were mixed with adults, for example, in the prison population. Even as the school reforms took hold, government leaders rarely mentioned children themselves – national goals were paramount. But the implications of childhood devoted to schooling, plus further contact with the West, began to generate a more explicit view of childhood itself.

As early as 1874, one reformer, Mitsukuri Shuhei, commented on the need to protect young children as part of the preparation for successful education, sounding remarkably like earlier Western thinkers in the process:

> From infancy until they are six or seven, children's minds are clean and without the slightest blemish while their characters are as pure and unadulterated as a perfect pearl. Since what then touches their eyes or ears, whether good or bad, makes a deep impression that will not be wiped out until death, this age provides the best opportunity for disciplining their natures and training them in deportment. They will become learned and virtuous if the training methods are appropriate, stupid and bigoted if the methods are bad.

Similar ideas encouraged reformers to argue that parents had a special responsibility to care for and enlighten their innocent offspring – but that most parents, at least given Japanese traditionalism, did not know how to do this properly. Teachers and child experts were essential not just to educate, but to promote proper care for children more generally. As in the West, and partly because of the Western example, childrearing manuals and other advice literature began to proliferate. The new ideas gained force as Japan was urbanizing rapidly, taking many parents away from the extended family structures that had once helped care for children in the villages; and often both husband and wife had to work outside the home, compounding the childcare problem. Worries about children roaming free in the cities, and sampling urban life independently, clearly promoted the new ideas about devising special care for the young. Childhood became an increasingly common topic of discussion in the popular press as well as in expert literature. A host of new periodicals, such as *The Family Magazine*, attempted to communicate the new ideas about children, urging careful attention but also a modern belief that, rather than seeing them as problems, Japan should convert to the idea of "the child as treasure."

Many reformers focused on the poor, who so often lacked the means to pay proper attention to the children they loved. This sentiment helped generate the first daycare centers in Japan, sometimes under Christian missionary sponsorship. By 1912, there were 15 centers nationally, mainly in the biggest cities; by 1926, the number had grown to 273. The centers offered not only physical care, but also advice to poor families about promoting children's health and providing psychological support. Center employees often took whole families on excursions to places such as city parks, hoping to convince them of "the limitless joy expressed when the whole family is together."

Another set of developments that sprang from explicit concern for children, and from the Western example, involved special juvenile courts and reform houses for offenders, again pulling children away from undifferentiated contact with adults even amid deviance. The government mandated a reformatory in each district in legislation of 1900. Other legislation in 1911 banned factory employment for children aged under 12, a crucial measure that occurred much earlier in Japan's industrialization process than had been true in most Western countries. Additional protective efforts included the outlawing of smoking by children, which lasted for several decades. Government and private agencies pushed the creation of orphanages, nursery schools, clinics for children, and vocational counseling for youth; by 1920, programs for children were consuming 60 percent of the budget of the Home Ministry. For the middle class, the same basic impulse encouraged a growing range of toys produced especially for children, designed "to liberate the child to freely explore its own interests and curiosity," while a playground movement created new public spaces for children. One playground created by child psychologists in 1917 included a zoo, a wading pool, a plant garden, seesaws and slides, and a sumo wrestling ring.

By the 1920s, through a combination of new ideas about children and global economic opportunity, Japan began to become a major toy exporter. The Japanese had imported toys from Europe during the early stages of reform, but with Western manufacturers distracted by World War I, the chance to participate in the world market became obvious. Japanese toy exports tripled during the war, and then tripled again by 1920. By this point, European competition resumed, which put new pressure on Japanese industry to innovate; and reformers were urging greater imagination, to help compensate for a presumed national tendency merely to copy and learn by rote. One firm that led the way in this direction was Nintendo, initially founded in 1889. A highlight of the Japanese approach, differentiating it from Western European toymakers, though resembling the more innovative efforts in the United States, involved a self-conscious willingness to deal with children as children, not miniature adults. European toys, such as model soldiers, were well made, popular and influential, but they were oriented to preparation for adult activities, including war. Japan, from the 1920s onward, approached child consumers more directly and appealed to their fantasy life. A popular comic book, *The Adventures of Sei-chan*, thus led in 1924 to spinoff products including playing cards and hats. Dolls carried on comic book themes as well. Toys based on commercial fantasy narratives were separated from the expectations of adults. And this theme continued once Japanese toy manufacture revived after World War II, leading the nation to a dominant position in the global export market and in defining children's tastes. Japan easily retained a position, along with the United States, as the leader in the imaginative (some would say, exploitative) design of toys and products for children, even as actual manufacturing shifted to centers of cheaper labor such as China.

In childhood, as many other topics, Japan's dramatic process of modern change requires some reasonably subtle analysis. Change was fundamental as Japanese of all classes moved within a very few decades (much more rapidly than had earlier been the case in the West) to a childhood of schooling and good health, amid a declining birth rate. We have seen that by the 1950s, with more explicit government encouragement, the Japanese birth rate had dropped to Western levels, though with greater reliance on abortion than in the West. Equally important was the fact that, as in the West, the installation of modern childhood encouraged a wider array of reconceptualizations of childhood, leading to a variety of new institutions and practices. Assimilating many characteristics from the West, Japan began to be able to contribute influences beyond its borders as well. At the same time, change did not create a fully Western type of childhood. The qualities sought and promoted in children retained distinctive values.

It is also important to note that, partly as a result of differentiated imitation, partly because of domestic impulses, Japan generated some aspects of childhood that were closer to those of the United States, and some that were closer to Western Europe. The educational and testing systems, with emphasis on intense academic standards before university and on careful tracking, were quite similar to those in France and Germany, from which they were borrowed. But the desire to promote educational advancement among all children in the primary grades and, as we have seen, the child-centeredness of commercial toy manufacture, more closely resembled aspects of the United States. The complex combination, of course, furthers the impression of Japanese distinctiveness.

This complexity also means that there was, and is, active debate about childhood in Japan, both among social groups and within leadership ranks, and a continuous stream of change. While rote learning and group loyalties differed somewhat from emphases in the West, there were, and are, plenty of Japanese reformers encouraging more individualism and creativity.

American occupation of Japan from 1945 to 1952 inevitably brought additional outside influences that colored Japanese childhood. Nationalism, and particularly emperor-worship, were downplayed in the schools, while greater individualism was encouraged. As social distinctions declined further, both secondary schools and universities expanded rapidly. It was at this point, in 1947, that nine years of schooling (through the lower secondary grades) were required by law. But debate continued as well, as conservatives in the 1960s rallied against the more individualistic ideas of citizenship Americans had promoted, talking about a renewal of "the cultivation of ethical consciousness." Yet another burst of reform, in the 1980s, attacked undue emphasis on rote learning, urging a new attention to thinking ability and innovation as essential to Japan's success in the global economy and the information age; the Ministry used phrases such as "from uniformity and homogeneity to more diversity and the expansion of freedom of choice" and a need "to identify and develop the personality, abilities, and aptitudes of individuals." At the same time, Japan was producing children who did exceptionally well in international academic competitions, and not surprisingly there were some nationalists who argued that it was the rest of the world that now had catching up to do. And the special moral education theme did not go away, with references to "proper national awareness" and the "unique culture and traditions of Japan;" as one conservative put it, "you have to teach tradition to the children whether they like it or not." Here, as in other respects, Japan participated in setting standards for modern childhood, sharing key issues with many other societies, but operating as well with some distinctive vocabulary and several special themes.

Further reading

Recent surveys include: Paula S. Fass, *Children of a New World: Society, Culture and Globalization* (New York: New York University Press, 2007); Kathy E. Ferguson and Monique Mironesco, *Gender and Globalization in Asia and the Pacific* (Honolulu: University of Hawaii Press, 2008); M. Gutman and N.D. Coninck-Smith, *Designing Modern Childhood: History, Space and the Material Culture of Children* (Piscataway, NJ: Rutgers University Press, 2008); Jyotsna Pattnaik, *Childhood in South Asia: A Critical Look at Issues, Policies and Programs* (Charlotte, NC: Information Age Publishing, 2005).

Also see: Brian Platt, "Japanese Childhood, Modern Childhood," *Journal of Social History* 38: 965–85 (2005); Gary Cross and Gregory Smits, "Japan, the U.S., and the Globalization of Children's Consumer Culture," *Journal of Social History* 38: 873–90 (2005); Kathleen Uno, *Passages to Modernity: Childhood and Social Reform in Early Twentieth Century Japan* (Honolulu: University of Hawaii Press, 1999); Mark Lincicome, *Principles, Praxis and the Politics of Educational Reform in Meiji Japan* (Honolulu: University of

Hawaii Press, 1995); Joseph Tobin, ed., *Re-Made in Japan: Everyday Life and Consumer Taste in a Changing Society* (New Haven, CT: Yale University Press, 1992); Michael Stephens, *Japan and Education* (New York: Macmillan, 1991); Donald Roden, *Schooldays in Imperial Japan: A Study of the Culture of a Student Elite* (Berkeley: University of California Press, 1980); Helen Hopper, *Fukuzawa Yukichi: From Samurai to Capitalist* (New York: Longman, 2004), on a leading educational reformer; Peter N. Stearns, *Schools and Students in Industrial Society: Japan and the West 1870–1940* (Boston: Bedford, 1998); John Traphagan and John Knight, eds, *Demographic Change and the Family in Japan's Aging Society* (Albany: State University of New York Press, 2003).

Chapter 9

Childhood and communist revolutions

The process of spreading versions of the modern model of childhood continued in the twentieth century in many parts of the world, though legacies of colonialism, economic dependence, and even the prior experience of slavery complicated global change. The West and Japan continued to adjust to still-novel patterns. Latin American cities worked toward a more schooled childhood, but social divisions complicated the process. The most striking new force in childhood change in the first half of the twentieth century, however, came from the new burst of political and social revolutions that became such a vital part of the century's landscape.

Major revolutions marked twentieth-century world history at many points, and most of the really important ones – Russia, China, Cuba, and Vietnam – occurred under communist inspiration. All the twentieth-century revolutions attacked Western influence, with communist leaders deliberately intending to introduce arrangements vastly different from those of the bourgeois West, dominated by capitalism. On the whole, however, the revolutions advanced the major elements of the modern model of childhood, and indeed they provided one of the major vehicles for the spread of this model during the twentieth century. The challenge in dealing with the cases of Russia and China (and their huge populations) is to tease out the standard modern features, some special traditions that survived change, but also the deliberate attempt to forge a distinctive communist childhood.

Some halting reforms of childhood had begun to spread in Russia and China before their revolutions, which helps explain why the revolutionaries, even amid their zeal for systematic change, found the modern pattern logical, particularly when it came to schooling. The leaders also believed that education could be shaped to offer particular advantages for a communist future, that it did not have to be guided by specifically Western models. Communist regimes also introduced other innovations in their approach to children – for example, in a heightened emphasis on youth groups – that added to the force of change. It is also important to note that simply introducing the modern model in a context such as Chinese society, with its longstanding traditions concerning childhood, often involved factors very different from those present in the West. Distinctive kinds of disruption and opportunity might arise, heightened by the heady fervor of a revolutionary experience.

The communist approach to childhood certainly involved an even more explicit recognition of the role of the state than had developed in the West and Japan. Substantial government control of childhood, not only through schools, but through youth groups and other mechanisms, aimed at socializing children to be better workers and (sometimes) soldiers, and certainly to be loyal citizens – goals shared with other modern states; but it also sought to mold children to be different from their parents, to develop values and characters more appropriate to communist goals. In principle, at least, children had to be remade. In fact, of course, communist manipulations did not always work; even efforts to control children's reading might misfire. And the big changes in reality focused more on transitions to schooling and low birth and death rates than on the special communist flavor. The state's role, however, did take a significant further step.

We're dealing, then, with another set of cases of fundamental transformation, overlapping with the experience of the West and Japan in many ways, but distinguished by separate traditions and by the power of revolutionary aspirations. The revolutions themselves were heavily staffed by youth and young adults, willing to risk violence to tear down established structures in societies where the percentage of young people in the population remained very high. This fact, along with an ideology that sought to create new kinds of people according to communist values, and along with the obvious power of the modern model itself, assured dramatic change. Familiar modern patterns blended with the special circumstances of a new revolutionary age.

The Russian Communist Party had not formed special youth groups prior to the 1917 revolution, in large part because the whole party had to operate clandestinely. Nor had tsarist Russia developed a particular interest in childhood – there was virtually no Russian research on childhood before the twentieth century – beyond the gradual expansion of education. In a heavily agricultural country, the basic conditions of agricultural society, including frequently harsh discipline for children, largely prevailed.

New attention to children, however, surfaced almost immediately after the 1917 rising, even as the communist revolutionaries struggled to seize and then maintain power. A first congress of youth organizations, for example, occurred in 1918. A year earlier, a new law forbade work before age 14 (though it was not well enforced). A Decree on the Eradication of Illiteracy followed in 1919, and while some of this was designed for propaganda – a key problem in dealing with Russian communism was its desire to trumpet its beneficence to children to score points with its own people and internationally, not always with strict regard to truth – the regime early on began to establish new schools, including a network of nursery schools and kindergartens. Efforts to improve children's health and also to abolish the use of physical punishments on children began early as well – the latter a really interesting effort explicitly to reverse common patterns of prerevolutionary Russian schools and society. The overall commitment to children was remarkable, given the many problems confronted in the early years of revolution and the real poverty of Russian society.

Why – propaganda goals aside – this extensive interest? Schooling had already been expanding in tsarist Russia, so it probably seemed logical to build on the effort – though in dramatic new ways. The new regime also faced several years of real crisis among children: the results of World War I, including malnutrition, and of the revolutionary years and civil war, including widespread famines, greatly increased the death rate among children. The mortality rate for young children, about 30 percent before 1914, soared to 50 percent or more by 1921 (some estimates as high as 90 percent of newborns). New attention to children was partly prompted by truly menacing problems.

It was also true that the new regime, though defiant of much of the rest of the world, wanted international approval, and committing to more of the modern model for childhood was appealing for this reason. Above all, however, communism as an ideology was deeply imbued with the belief that children were born good, innocent, and improvable; problems with childhood resulted from imperfect social arrangements, poverty, and inequality among classes. The new Russia must be built, as a result, on the strengths of greatly enhanced efforts to protect and educate children. This belief, born of the same basic Enlightenment ideology that had informed the early phases of the modern model in the West, strongly shaped revolutionary aspirations and policies. It pushed both toward the modern model, and to a concerted effort also to produce a different kind of child from the emphases current in the West, viewed as fatally corrupted by capitalism.

The communist belief in the innocent child, but also in the faults both of capitalist childhoods and of prerevolutionary conditions in Russia itself, had several interesting corollaries. One was, simply, that revolutionary experts believed they knew far more than parents did about what children needed. This was a belief among experts in the West as well, but it had even greater vigor in Russia: to improve childhood, parents needed to be guided and their hold over children limited. Revolutionaries even believed that well trained communist children should assume the task of educating their backward parents in key respects. The state had to gain an active hand in childrearing – this meant schools, of course, as in the modern model more generally, but in additional activities as well. "The child is the object of state upbringing," one party leader claimed, and while families remained extremely important, the state role loomed large as well. The beliefs in childish innocence and a communist mission for children also helped explain the fervent propaganda: improving children was so fundamental to the revolutionary ideal that it was almost impossible publicly to admit basic problems (except insofar as they could be blamed on prerevolutionary remnants such as religion). Issues such as juvenile delinquency, as a result, were largely swept under the rug.

The restructuring of childhood under communism had four components: the modern model itself, with its usual facets, one of which, however, was hotly debated. Second, the specifically communist apparatus added to the modern model. Third, continuities from earlier Russian conditions that persisted despite considerable objections from the leadership. And finally, some changes, particularly toward a more consumerist childhood, that began to emerge from the 1950s onward despite equally considerable official objections.

As we have seen, the regime quickly resolved on extensive schooling, at least in principle, and improvements in children's health, including the effort to reduce mortality rates. Progress in schooling was truly remarkable, even as the revolutionary leadership continued to struggle with limited resources; the commitment ran deep. Primary schools spread quickly, in a society where literacy rates had reached only 28 percent in 1914. Expansion of secondary schools and universities quickly followed. Between 1929 and 1939, there was a doubling of students in grade schools but an eightfold increase in attendance at middle schools and an elevenfold increase in secondary schools. University slots quintupled by 1939, and more than doubled again by 1951, to 1.3 million students. The government also invested in extensive research on pedagogy, seeking new teaching methods that would be compatible with communist goals and would bring out the best in students' learning capacity; there was a real, if possibly naïve, hope that in a socialist state learning would be enjoyable and spontaneous. Prizes were established for good students. Families, realizing the importance of education for their children's prospects, increasingly worked to support school success, particularly in the growing cities. This was a real conversion: childhood now meant schooling, above all.

Much of this development was a fairly standard illustration of the modern model, but there were some distinctive twists. The regime wanted schools to combat vestiges of the old regime and prepare for a better society to come, so much effort was invested in attacking religion ("superstition") and in instilling the principles of Marxism, along with a strong emphasis on science. Enthusiasm for Marxism sometimes involved memorization exercises for very young students, who probably understood little of what they were told to drill into their heads; by the 1950s, more careful age-grading saved Marxism for the later primary grades and beyond. Most interesting was the ambitious attempt to expand kindergartens and nursery schools, in order to begin the preparation of children early and to reduce family influence. The program also responded to the large number of mothers who worked in the Soviet Union, and the resultant need for childcare provision. Kindergartens did spread rapidly, though resource constraints sometimes reduced the effort;

by 1929 about 10 percent of the relevant age group had formal kindergarten slots, though other institutions added to the program somewhat. Rural families accepted kindergartens slowly if at all, preferring more conventional family supervision, so this aspect of the process of change was more halting in the countryside.

The push to reduce child mortality was impressive, though events – including the German invasion in World War II – could generate setbacks. A 1918 decree insisted on new goals, claiming that too many children had died "as a result of the ignorance and irresponsibility of the oppressed populace and the stagnation and indifference of the class [tsarist] state." The government rapidly expanded clinics and prenatal services, and tried to expand the corps of pediatricians as well. Increasingly, clinics actively reached out to parents, particularly mothers, sending reminders and even venturing personal visits if children were not brought in for checkups, a far more interventionist approach than in the West. The state also issued a series of advice manuals, again on the assumption that parents were not fully reliable – as one authority put it early on, "family upbringing is in need of additional guidance." Or again, as another expert claimed, discussing basic housing and feeding standards for children: "even this, most parents do not do well." Hygiene was strongly emphasized, in schools and elsewhere, again a pattern very similar to that in the West and Japan. By 1960, infant mortality rates had dropped 900 percent from 1918, to 3.8 percent of all children born, and by 1989 the figure was 2.5 percent. These rates remained a bit higher than in the West, reflecting lower overall standards of living and some undeniably substandard medical facilities; but the change was dramatic, nevertheless, and clearly brought the Soviet Union into the modern model of childhood in this important respect.

With children increasingly going to school instead of working (at least for the family economy), with a falling death rate, and with other issues such as endemic housing shortages and problems with childcare, it was hardly surprising that the people of the Soviet Union began participating in the third area of modern change, the reduction of the birth rate. Attacks on religion also, if unintentionally, reduced some of the traditional barriers to birth control, and it was interesting that the more religious minorities in the Soviet Union, notably Muslims, retained higher birth rates than average. Government policy, however, vacillated. During the 1920s there was open discussion of birth rate reduction and experimentation with various methods. But Stalin returned the nation officially to a pronatalist policy, seeking a larger population for economic and military purposes. The state outlawed abortion in 1926. Birth rates continued to drop, however, in part because of widespread illegal abortion; here, Russian families and Russian women drove behavior in quiet defiance of government goals. The state, recognizing the ill effects of illegal abortions, reversed its policy here in 1951; by the 1980s the majority of Russian women were experiencing at least one abortion.

With some interesting internal variations, the Soviet Union became a low-birth-rate society. Increased parental attention to individual children was one common result, including parental support for success in school, linking this society to modern patterns in Japan and the West.

Communist additions to modern childhood were at least as interesting as the substantial conversion to modern childhood itself. Marxist indoctrination and the propaganda claims about Soviet children were fairly obvious, though not unimportant. The Soviet Union eagerly supported international human rights movements for children, partly at least as a means of suggesting its own special virtue. Citing the tremendous hardships for children in World War II, for example, Soviet spokespeople used the theme as a means of opposing what they argued were Western efforts to promote militarism: "We must direct the attention of all who love children to the effects of the arms race."

More substantive developments, for Soviet children themselves, involved the extensive youth-group apparatus established as a supplement to schooling and as a means of furthering Communist Party influence over children, while limiting independent parental controls. Youth groups were an important development in modern world history generally, beginning with programs such as the Boy Scouts in Western Europe and the United States; they aimed to help discipline young people and make them socially useful. Fascist governments employed youth groups such as the "Hitler Youth" for indoctrination and paramilitary training. But the Soviet system took the widespread impulse much further.

Almost all children by age nine were organized in the Young Pioneer organizations, which sponsored a variety of activities – dance lessons, sports training, summer camps – and collective work efforts. Many who graduated from Young Pioneers at age 14 then went on to participation in the *Komsomols* (communist youth groups), where the party controls were more overt, and the explicit political indoctrination more intense.

Youth groups, schools, and official advice all pointed to the seriousness of childhood and its collective focus. Children were still meant to do quite of bit of work; schools organized various production activities, appropriate to the age level, and the youth groups certainly called on children's service in harvesting grain, helping take care of veterans, making toys, and a wide variety of other activities. The goals were to aid the state – not the family economy – while not interfering with the primary educational mission, and to teach children both relevant skills and the nobility of work itself. While youth groups provided leisure activities also, and in schools children managed, when called upon for "social labor," to put more emphasis on the social than the labor, the state itself was not very interested in play, but rather in readying children for adulthood. In this it reflected a mixture of communist beliefs and some strong remnants of agricultural tradition, both providing interesting variants on the modern model. In 1984, an education code urged honesty, courage, and so on as character goals for children, but also "exactingness toward one another," a duty to the collective good – not a combination that would be found in Western manuals by this point. Youth organizations were highly moralistic, another sign of the seriousness of childhood and children's social responsibilities. One *Komsomol* chided a girl who threatened to wander off to find her divorced father, "But Galena is a *Komsomol*, she should have the courage and honesty to tell her comrades what kind of life she is going to lead." Intensive involvement of talented children in dance academies or sports training institutions provided another example of the effort to use childhood for social purposes and to inculcate adult-like seriousness.

The Soviet system also toyed with some changes in gender divisions, based on its formal belief in male–female equality in a communist society. Various lessons attacked traditional downgrading of women. But school uniforms emphasized gender division, with very feminine outfits for secondary school girls. The state itself soon began placing emphasis on women's family duties, including motherhood. And children themselves picked up gender cues, noting as one boy did when asked to treat girls a bit better, "Lenin was a boy." The spread of education undoubtedly reduced gender divisions in childhood, but there was no full revolution.

The communist approach to childhood was by no means entirely successful. Partly because of wars and dislocations, many children suffered from abuse and poverty; there were many strays and orphans. Divorce rates also rose, and so did the number of children in female-headed households. Juvenile delinquency and, by the 1980s, drug-taking were undoubted problems, though their dimensions were hidden by official secrecy. The communist system also failed in disrupting family control of childhood and traditional pleasures as fully as intended. Many Russian children continued to play traditional games and listen to traditional stories, including very superstitious ones. Their parents took them to puppet shows and circuses, both widely popular. Many adults recalled happy excursions to the woods or the countryside with families. Official campaigns themselves revealed the persistence of family celebrations regarding children. A major effort against Christmas trees, for example – "we must battle against the old way of life" – showed the pervasiveness of older habits.

Finally, new kinds of rebellion, particularly by adolescents, emerged by the 1950s, directed not against the modern model so much as against some of the communist additions, headed by undue seriousness and preachiness and the increasingly inflexible bureaucracy of the *Komsomol* movement. As early as 1955, a *Komsomol* intoned, "we have begun to wage an uncompromising struggle against these idlers who imitate trashy foreign 'fashion'." Consumer-minded youth were "completely divorced from the varied, full and beautiful life of labor and romanticism lived by our Soviet youth." Growing interest in Western music, clothing styles including blue jeans, and other early hints of a global youth culture, though battled against by the government, gained increasing interest from young people as the communist system slightly loosened its grip from the death of Stalin until the collapse of the system in 1991.

The Russian revolution included a revolution in childhood, though not, of course, a complete overturning of all traditions. The purposes and activities of children shifted dramatically. As the Soviet system did finally end, there seemed no doubt that the modern model would retain its force. The real questions involved the sudden disappearance of the communist organizations and doctrines that had impinged so heavily on Soviet childhood. Even though many children had not fully accepted the system, it was not clear what kinds of alternatives would become available.

Chinese communists, as they assumed full control over the mainland by 1949, were even more fiercely determined than their earlier Soviet counterparts to construct a society radically different from modern Western models. They also had to contend with the powerful Confucian tradition and its implications for childhood. Not surprisingly in this context, the regime periodically introduced some dramatic experiments, concerning schooling, for example, and the role of youth in the wider society. There was also an even stronger impulse than in the Soviet Union to encourage large families as a source of economic and military strength, part of the sense of embattlement against the rest of the world, and a symptom also of more traditional thinking about the usefulness of large numbers of children. In the long run, however, the new regime did work toward the main features of the modern model, ultimately including a particularly dramatic birth control policy. Youth groups and a strong emphasis on social service resembled features developed by the Soviets.

Two assumptions, similar to those of the Soviets, guided policy toward children: first, an optimistic belief that children were innocent and improvable with the right kind of guidance; and second, a deep conviction that past policies toward children, including Confucian traditions and extensive parental controls, were deeply flawed, responsible for crucial problems in China's past. Family influence, as a result, had to be curtailed in the interests of appropriate training.

School reform was not a new topic in China. Chinese reformers and Western missionaries had worked hard, from about 1900 onward, to create more modern schools, freed from Confucian assumptions about the need to instill conformity in children, and more open to scientific subjects and to intellectual inquiry generally. Communist experts, borrowing in part from Russian research, emphasized the need to identify individual characteristics and to encourage creativity. How much this actually affected schooling is open to question. Chinese teachers, according to outside studies, continued to assume that children should measure up to established norms for each age; the emphasis was on the standards rather than on individual development.

In the early grades, getting children to recite in unison, partly as a means of controlling individual impulses, was a common ploy, suggesting more than a hint of Confucianism. Furthermore, the new emphasis on Marxist indoctrination added another layer of memorized conformity for many children. Children were taught about communist heroes, beginning with Chairman Mao, and the need to devote their lives to the struggle for communism – though as one interviewee noted, recalling his school days, "to tell the truth we didn't quite yet know what communism was."

There was no question, however, about the rapid spread of schooling itself. During the 1950s, the number of children in primary schools tripled, to 90 million – an immense investment in a still-poor nation. The increase at the secondary school level was even greater, in percentage terms. This process of expansion continues to the present day. The regime in 2003 made a commitment to educate 15 percent of the relevant age group in universities – this is a lower percentage than in Japan or the West, but given the size of the population, a tremendous assignment, leading to a massive building boom in new campuses. For children themselves, and for their parents, schooling increasingly replaced work as a focus.

As in the Soviet Union, a huge effort also went into the development of nursery schools and kindergartens, to provide childcare for parents, both of whom increasingly worked outside the home, and as an opportunity for indoctrination. A variety of youth groups served the same goals. The communists had established Little Red Soldiers during the revolutionary struggle itself, using children for sentry duty and other tasks. This group continued for grade (primary) schoolers, and was supplemented by Young Pioneers and the Communist Youth League. Tremendous pressure was applied to shame children into joining. Young Pioneers, for example, got to wear a distinctive scarf, and if a child lacked a scarf by the sixth grade, he or she could be ostracized by peers.

Work duties were combined with schooling and the youth groups, again both for serious production on behalf of the state-run economy and for training in proper values. Middle schoolers could spend as much as a month in school workshops, making items such as electric circuits for cars and trucks; and they also were often sent for labor stints in the countryside. A fascinating use of some children involved street patrols to prevent adults from spitting in public: this coincided with a strong hygiene emphasis in the schools, but more significantly it stood Confucianism on its head by making children the monitors of wayward elders. During the 1966–67 Cultural Revolution, Mao Zedong almost turned against education itself, worrying that too many students were picking up bourgeois values. Millions of secondary school and university students were sent to the countryside to do agricultural labor. This impulse was transitory, and emphasis on educational achievement resumed in the 1970s, but it was an interesting moment. The Cultural Revolution also saw a use of communist youth gangs to intimidate adults – tradition-minded teachers, for example – in another deliberate inversion of Confucian hierarchies. Here, youth themselves sometimes found outlets for rebellion against the discipline and competitiveness of the school system itself.

In addition to schooling, the new regime worked hard on improving children's health. Neighborhood clinics were established in the cities, while "barefoot doctors," combining modern and traditional medicine, provided care in the countryside, including immunizations against the major childhood diseases. Child mortality dropped rapidly from the 1950s onward; at an 18 percent annual average between 1955 and 1960, infant mortality had dropped to 3.7 percent by 2003.

Chairman Mao raised some questions about the final element of childhood's modern model, arguing in the 1950s that a high birth rate was an asset to China, supplying needed labor, and attacking Western population experts, who were urging nations such as China to cut back. By the 1960s, however, the turn to population control began. State policy was heavily involved, but so was parental reaction to the decline of children's work for the family economy and the pressures of parental jobs outside the home. By the mid-1960s, clinics and the barefoot doctors were distributing birth control devices, including pills and IUDs, and were performing abortions. Led by the cities, birth rates began to drop rapidly – in some neighborhoods, 50 percent reductions were registered in two-year intervals in the middle of the decade. In the 1980s, the post-Maoist regime tightened policies even further, banning marriage before age 25 and penalizing couples who had more than one child. Here was a tremendous assertion of state power, and an equally tremendous departure from China's customs concerning children.

In practice, revolutionary innovation combined with selective traditions – and not all the innovations actually followed communist scripts. Parents and children alike were told that the family must be downplayed, that children must be "concerned with the people's benefit and the state's interests." Specific measures attacked parental control: a 1950 Marriage Law, for example, allowed young people to choose their own spouse, without parental consent. But the hand of family remained strong. While up to 30 percent of Chinese children were in kindergartens by the 1970s, particularly in the cities, far more were being cared for by grandparents. Tradition also shaped reactions to new population policies: with only one child allowed per family, many rural people undoubtedly returned to a practice of female infanticide (so that their "one child" would be a boy); and the ratio of girls to boys in orphanages was 9:1. A considerable excess of males developed in consequence. The one-child policy also encouraged new levels of emotional investment and material indulgence of children, creating tighter parent–child bonds in some respects – a familiar development in the modern history of childhood, but not exactly the communist goal. By 2000, school authorities were reporting tremendous pressure from "4–2–1 groups" to make sure beloved only children were treated well. The four were the grandparents, grouping with the two parents, all banking on the success of the one child, and introducing a significant new ingredient in the conduct of schools themselves.

With the adoption of market economic policies by the communist regime in 1978, and with rapid economic growth ensuing, urban Chinese childhood in fact began to overlap with childhoods in many other societies in additional ways. Some of the experiments with collective work faded in favor of outright emphasis on school success and advancement toward university. (Demand for university slots in fact exceeded supply.) New consumer interests developed, on the part of children and parents alike. Imported baby goods became fashionable in the 1980s, for example, including toys, diapers and, for older girls, cosmetics. Many urban Chinese children began to participate in a global youth culture.

The communist contribution to changing the nature of childhood in the twentieth century was of great significance. Wherever communism seized control, changes in concepts of childhood and in government initiatives toward children followed quickly. The communist example could have influence as well in other parts of the world, pushing toward elements of the modern model. The particular emphases brought by communism itself were intriguing and vital to many children for over half a century, as they devoted themselves to youth groups and political awareness. With communism receding after the mid-1980s – even in China, with its swing toward a market economy – the durability of these emphases came into some question, and with it the range of options for a modern childhood that would not be defined by Western standards.

Further reading

On the Soviet Union and more recent developments in Russia: Marina Balina and Evgeny Dobrenko, *Petrified Utopia: Happiness Soviet Style* (London, UK: Anthem Press, 2009); Catriona Kelly, *Children's World: Growing Up in Russia, 1890–1991* (New Haven, CT: Yale University Press, 2007); Christina Kiaer and Eric Naiman, *Everyday Life in Early Soviet Russia: Taking the Revolution Inside* (Bloomington: Indiana University Press, 2006); Clementine Creuziger, *Childhood in Russia: Representation and Reality* (Lanham, MD: University Press of America, 1996); Lisa Kirschenbaum, *Small Comrades: Revolutionizing Childhood in Soviet Russia, 1917–1932* (New York: Routledge, 2001); Landon Pearson, *Children of Glasnost: Growing up Soviet* (Seattle: University of Washington Press, 1990); Jim Riordan, ed., *Soviet Youth Culture* (Bloomington: Indiana University Press, 1989); N. Vishneva-Sarafanova, *The Privileged Generation: Children in the Soviet Union* (Moscow: Progress Publishers, 1984); Kitty Weaver, *Bushels of Rubles: Soviet Youth in Transition* (Westport, CT: Praeger, 1992).

On China: Brian Power, *The Ford of Heaven: A Cosmopolitan Childhood in Tientsin, China* (Oxford: Signal Books, 2005); E. Stuart Kirby, ed., *Youth in China* (Hong Kong: Dragonfly Books, 1966); Anita Chan, *Children of Mao: Personality Development and Political Activism in the Red Guard Generation* (Seattle: University of Washington Press, 1985); Jon Saari, *Legacies of Childhood: Growing up Chinese in a Time of Crisis, 1890–1920* (Cambridge, MA: Harvard University Press, 1990); Ni Nan, *Hometowns and Childhood* (San Francisco: Long River Press, 2006); Sing Lau, ed., *Growing Up the Chinese Way* (Hong Kong: Chinese University Press, 1996); Thomas Bernstein, *Up to the Mountains and Down to the Villages: The Transfer of Youth from Urban to Rural China* (New Haven, CT: Yale University Press, 1977); Luo Xu, *Searching for Life's Meaning: Changes and Tensions in the Worldviews of Chinese Youth in the 1980s* (Ann Arbor: University of Michigan Press, 2002); Beverley Hooper, *Youth in China* (Harmondsworth, UK: Penguin Books, 1985); Ann-ping Chin, *Children of China: Voices from Recent Years* (Ithaca, NY: Cornell University Press, 1988).

Chapter 10

Childhood in the affluent societies, twentieth and twenty-first centuries

Childhood experienced major changes in the advanced industrial societies during the twentieth century. Two patterns predominated, and of course they interacted. First, societies in the United States, Japan, and Western Europe continued more fully to implement what we have described as the characteristics of modern childhood. That is, they added commitments to schooling, and further reduced at least the more traditional forms of child labor; they completed the dramatic reduction of child death rates that had begun in the late nineteenth century; and, with a few zigzags, they made a fuller conversion to low birth rates (Japan joined this particular parade mainly after World War II, with government encouragement, at first relying heavily on abortion before turning to other forms of birth control). There were real changes involved in the fuller implementation, even though the principles had been established earlier.

But second, the advanced industrial societies also innovated further in the treatment of children, reconsidering traditional methods of discipline and adding growing interest – and anxiety – in treating children as consumers. The United States introduced changes in these areas as early as the 1920s. In Western Europe, the more dramatic shifts – generally speaking in the same directions – occurred from the late 1950s onward.

The role of government in organizing childhood expanded further as well, beyond previous staples such as requiring/providing education and regulating labor. Two somewhat clashing approaches were involved, both aimed in principle at making childhood better and protecting children even further. Many governments passed new protective measures in the decades after World War II. American states required children to wear helmets when bicycling, and safety stipulations for riding in automobiles escalated steadily. The Italian government sought to regulate the age at which children could ride elevators alone. Many governments, by the early twenty-first century, sought to intervene against childhood obesity. Efforts to control the commercial fare directed at children formed another large category, toward limiting access to undue violence or pornography in the media. Continuing earlier "child-saving" efforts, many governments discussed situations in which the state should take children from presumably inadequate parents, not only in cases of abusive violence, but where there seemed to be excessive alcohol or drug use or even, again by the twenty-first century, lack of control over excessive eating. Not all the regulations were thoroughly enforced, and children and adults alike found ways around some of them. But the belief in government oversight of childhood extended fairly consistently. At the same time, however, post-World War II rhetoric also talked about children's rights as a category of human rights more generally. Much of this discussion focused on developing countries, where attempts to defend children against excessive work to assure them opportunities for schooling seemed particularly urgent. The human rights efforts might also apply to freedom from abuse even in the West, or, more tentatively, to freedoms of expression against overzealous censorship programs in schools.

In dealing with social change more generally, in places such as the United States and Western Europe, some scholars used terms like "postindustrial" or "postmodern," suggesting dramatic shifts away from the industrial patterns of the nineteenth and early twentieth centuries. Eye-catching labels like this may have captured some important changes, such as the shift toward more white-collar jobs and the relative decline of factory work, but for childhood their usefulness is questionable. Most of the world, after all, was still just moving into the industrial age. Even for the industrial pioneers, many of the developments in defining modern childhood increased; new efforts – for example, the widening safety regulations – sought to limit child death still further. Even some of the clearer innovations, such as the expansion of children's consumerism, in part reflected parental responses to the lower birth rates, seeking to demonstrate to the one to three children per average family how much they were cherished. The new elements were important, but they operated within ongoing adjustments to the earlier, more basic changes. Of course, the claim can and should be debated, but there seems to be no reason to use terms suggesting that the modern model was being unseated by some brand new postmodern variant.

For the West, specifically, some observers, finally, have found in recent history an "end to childhood," as children are exposed to more and more adult-level consumer items, and the idealization of childhood innocence fades a bit. Changes in the lives of women, taking shape from the 1950s onward, toward more work outside the home even when children were young, also cut into the childrearing patterns so romanticized during previous decades. It's important to remember, however, that childhood innocence was itself a fairly new idea, not a traditional notion; and it had surfaced mainly in the West, in part in reaction to older ideas such as original sin. The disappearance of childhood innocence, in other words, was not a clearly global development. Even in the West, however, some notions of innocence, and certainly of protectiveness, still lingered, at least for children before adolescence. And in point of fact, studies by the early twenty-first century showed that working mothers spent more time actually with their children (as opposed to being in the same vicinity) than their housewife counterparts had done in the 1950s.

Without question, changing conditions did prompt some significant rethinking. In the process of change beyond the trinity of schooling, low birth rates, and low mortality, Western societies modified some of the emphases that had characterized their approach to childhood during the nineteenth century, apart from the basic modern model. Manners became more flexible; by the 1940s, parental injunctions about posture were being abandoned. Other issues, including a more informal style suitable for consumerism, were becoming more important. Sexual concerns remained, particularly in the United States, but both culture and practice shifted toward greater permissiveness. The intense concern about respectability, as against the lower classes or immigrants, yielded amid these changes also, without disappearing entirely. Images of cute and loving children actually intensified – they proved very effective in advertisements for relevant products, or as movie fare – but they became more complicated; and attention to adolescence, an innovation in the nineteenth century, became a recurrent, anxiety-drenched obsession with many adults.

Differences persisted within the advanced industrial category. Western Europe and Japan, for example, placed much more emphasis on competitive examinations, to track students into different levels of secondary education, as well as, later on, to determine university eligibility, than did the United States. This meant, in turn, that many children were subjected to greater school pressures during their early years than was generally true in the United States. At the later end of childhood, American universities normally charged tuition fees, often substantial fees, whereas Japan and Western Europe supported most schools with tax revenues, offering essentially free rides for most students who qualified for entry: here was a huge difference for youth, but also for definitions of family responsibility. Children's consumerism went farther, faster in the United States and (by the late twentieth century) Japan than in Western Europe, though there were certainly similar trends. Diets varied. Between 1950 and 2004, European children, as they grew, gained rapidly in height – the Dutch became the tallest people, on average, in the world. But American children registered fewer gains, possibly because of new sources of immigration and greater social inequality, but probably also because of a diet richer in junk foods that deterred height gains.

Dramatic differences opened in childcare after the 1950s, despite common concerns such as encouraging children's performance in school. In Western Europe and the United States, more and more mothers began to take jobs outside the home. This raised obvious issues about caring for children, though everywhere women expressed initial discomfort at their new roles, claiming, even as they went to work, that mothers really should stay home.

In Western Europe, daycare centers became increasingly common, and most parents became comfortable with this recourse. In the United States, anxieties about care were greater, as many mothers preferred to rely on relatives or patchwork solutions rather than commit their children to institutional care. Finally, in Japan, fewer mothers worked, preserving a much more direct role in tending young children and indulging them as a reward for diligence in school. In all three regions, of course, differences were leavened by a common pattern of falling birth rates (aside from a brief baby boom), which confined the problem to some extent.

It is important also to remember the differential impact of events. Children in West European countries such as Germany and France suffered greatly during World War I, because of constraints on food and living standards as well as the absence and often the loss of fathers; the experience would be repeated even more widely in World War II. Children in the United States, though affected, experienced much less disruption. Bombing scarred children, literally and psychologically, in Western Europe and Japan during World War II. American children experienced a brief period of anxiety as the nuclear arms race developed during the 1950s, as part of the growing Cold War. And some analysts have argued that deeper fears of devastation lurked amid adolescents even after Americans largely seemed to cast off apocalyptic concerns in favor of growing consumerism by the late 1950s. But certainly American children never faced the literal confrontation with modern war that affected at least two generations of their counterparts in Western Europe, and one major generation in Japan.

Social and gender differences also continued to matter, in addition to geography. Working-class kids were fully drawn into schooling by the 1920s, as attendance laws began to be fully enforced. But they remained less likely to complete high school or go to college than their middle-class counterparts, which meant that their adolescence was different as well. For a minority of children, particularly in societies such as the United States, where the welfare state did not fully develop, deep poverty and malnutrition persisted; by the 1980s in the United States, the number of children below the poverty line began to expand rapidly, particularly in households headed by single mothers – the twin result of reduced government attention and disrupted family life. Racial minorities – expanding in Europe as a result of new immigration after World War II, as well as the United States – also provided distinctive contexts for childhood, reacting to prejudice and less abundant job opportunities, and frequently forming separate gangs and musical styles. While gender arguably declined in importance, it still affected the types of education chosen, dress and other consumer options, and household duties. Certain kinds of gender distinctions occasionally expanded, as in the United States during the 1920s, when pink and blue were chosen to identify gender in young children, and when largely separate extracurricular activities were emphasized to highlight masculinity or femininity.

Still, with all the caveats, there were a large number of common trends for the children of affluence. Beginning with the completion of the installation of modern childhood, the trends described a number of serious alterations in the ways childhood was defined and experienced, across national boundaries. They also prepared a number of deliberately shared activities, also across these boundaries, including clothing styles, many toys and recreations, and popular music. What resulted, obviously, was a combination of deliberate imitation – including use of the same childrearing manuals, such as the widely translated Dr Spock from the United States – and shared conditions of affluence and the need to prepare more and more children for adult work roles that depended on substantial education.

It was no accident, to take a particularly striking symbol, that Disney theme parks won success in all three areas, as a symbol of family devotion to child-oriented leisure and consumption. The parks began in the United States in the 1950s. A Japanese version near Tokyo won quick success. Europe was a bit tougher, because there was resistance to children's commercial culture and to Americanization in general, including US eating and snacking habits; but with a few adjustments, Euro Disney succeeded as well, becoming France's most visited tourist spot, muscling out less child-centered attractions such as Notre Dame or the Louvre.

Completing the modern model of childhood involved some additional refinements and a host of additional results. It is important to remember how recently, even in places such as the United Kingdom and the United States, some seemingly obvious features of modern childhood were installed.

Residual work was an obvious target, with particular attention to lingering working-class reliance on child labor as a family support, along with the continued willingness of some businesses to seize on this source of cheap workers. Basic child labor laws had been passed during the nineteenth century in the industrial countries, but there was still a lot to be done. The decades around 1900 saw the peak of child labor in the United States, for example, in terms of sheer numbers. In 1890, about a million children between the ages of 10 and 15 worked (12 percent of the total); and in 1910, the summit, almost two million (18 percent) were formally employed, and this did not include ongoing farm labor. Middle-class opinion had already concurred that work and children should not mix, so the figures, widely publicized, predictably spurred a spate of new reform initiatives. The National Child Labor Reform Committee originated in 1904, and for over two decades the press recurrently publicized stories of abuse. The twin focus was on damage to children's health in sweatshops or in factories involving chemicals, and on the impediments to proper schooling. Moral dangers also loomed large, with child workers open to sexual exploitation or the lure of criminal activities on the streets. Many former child workers themselves testified about the abuse they had endured. According to the reformers, children should enjoy the right to be protected from work, even on the farms, and this right trumped the powers of parents to organize this aspect of childhood.

There was debate, of course. Business and agricultural interests often defended child labor. They cited benefits to families, to training, and to the protection of children themselves from the vice of idleness. But gradually, through a combination of changes in industry, laws including school enforcement, and decisions by parents themselves, child labor did begin to decline. Technology also contributed: urban message boys, for example, were increasingly replaced by telephones, while household appliances reduced the need for teenage maids. By 1920, the percentage of children in the 10–15 age category who were formally employed was down to 8 percent, and by 1940 it had dropped to a mere 1 percent.

There were a few interesting exceptions. Newspaper owners, for example, argued that delivery boys were still essential – which was ironic, given newspapers' loud role in the larger crusade. They pitched their message in terms of training children for work and for business skills, and many parents, including middle-class parents, agreed for several more decades, until these jobs, too, were phased out by adult delivery services. And the use of children by migrant farm workers, almost entirely minority or foreign, escaped full regulation. Several hundred thousand children still worked in American agriculture by 2001, and only 55 percent of migrant working children completed a full high school program. In the main, however, in the United States and Western Europe by the 1930s, and in Japan by the 1950s, children and formal work simply did not mix. For a time, work-free childhood was defined in terms of 15 and under, but gradually required schooling moved up to age 16 – Western Europe implemented this extension in the 1950s – while the school day and year expanded, reducing work opportunities for the majority of children at least until the end of high school.

These changes, in turn, completed the economic redefinition of childhood. Children were liabilities, not assets. Families that had not realized it before, could not avoid this conclusion by the second quarter of the twentieth century, and it provided a further spur to the declining birth rate. Revealingly, the great Depression of the 1930s, which might have encouraged greater reliance on child labor, given falling wages and massive adult unemployment, had the opposite effect: birth rates dropped to an all-time low as families realized they could no longer afford more than one or two versions of the modern child. Other changes related to this further transition. Between the 1930s and 1950s, most industrial societies developed new pension funds – in the United States, this was the Social Security system, which began contributing to retirement in the 1940s. This had the effect of reducing older people's dependence on their children as sources of economic support; again in the United States, whereas the elderly in the 1930s listed children as their main hope if and when they could no longer continue to work, by the 1940s this had shifted to reliance on the government. Here was a further motivation both to reduce the birth rate and to complete the redefinition of childhood – and even young adulthood – away from work.

A few anomalies and hesitations remained. By the 1960s, France and some other European countries began experimenting with a work–school combination for certain children from age 15 onward. The argument was that for about a quarter of all children who did least well on academic tests, on-the-job training in manual labor – hopefully, skilled manual labor – while still blended with some schooling, provided the best assurance for an economically viable adulthood. In essence, programs of this sort revived the idea of apprenticeship, though for the benefit of the individual, not the family of origin. The modern model of childhood might be modified, in other words, for a minority, though only in mid-adolescence, when it seemed possible to make firm judgments about capacity for further schooling. By age 16, of course, when it became legally permissible to leave school altogether, a minority of children, or their parents, made this decision themselves, though this number steadily dwindled as attendance at least through high school became the increasingly accepted norm, and as it became clear that adult opportunities improved greatly with the possession of a high school degree or better.

By the 1980s, a growing number of older American children began working by age 17, in part-time jobs after school and during the summer. In principle, their work commitments were secondary to school focus, though in fact conflict often resulted, with jobs and other activities distracting from school and homework, and leaving adolescents fatigued or disengaged. Even less than the experimental school–work programs was this a revival of older definitions of work-based childhood. The children who worked after school were mainly working for themselves – for consumer goods such as a car, or to help with college expenses (particularly challenging in the United States) – not for their family, though of course there were exceptions. In the main, also, they were not doing jobs that prepared them in any direct way for adult activities, performing mostly low-level service tasks. Still, the change was an interesting reminder that modern childhood was not always easy to define, particularly by mid-adolescence.

The most interesting residual discussion about childhood and work, however, focused on children's jobs around the home. During the 1920s, many American commentators assumed that household tasks would continue to make children useful to their family, despite lack of earnings, and would help instill a work ethic. In fact, however, chores declined steadily. Machines replaced child labor here, too – for example, gas furnaces removed the task of shoveling coal into furnaces, dishwashers reduced that task, smaller families lessened the need to watch younger children. But more was involved: parents, particularly when mothers started work, often found it easier to do chores themselves rather than teach and monitor the kids; and the pressures of school performance also made parents leery of asking too much.

New kinds of advice to parents warned against exploitation – as one put it, "take great care not to overburden the child with responsibilities." And children themselves became more resistant, particularly after the age of 10 or 12. Girls still did more than boys; children did pitch in a bit in single-parent households (but work was at its lowest when a step-parent was present). And work did decline rapidly: in 1976, 41 percent of all American high school seniors said they did something around the house every day, whereas by 1999 this figure had dropped to 24 percent. In many families, fathers replaced children as the mother's principal household assistant. Here, too, in unexpected ways, work and childhood separated even further.

None of these changes constituted a huge problem, but there was some confusion. Many parents, despite accepting school as children's prime responsibility, still felt slightly aggrieved that kids did so little work, and wondered what the commitment to family was. From the children's stand-point, further removal from work also meant further removal from adult-hood. For those who identified readily with schooling, this might pass unnoticed. But some children clearly themselves wondered what their purpose was, and this, in turn, could contribute to problems with identity and meaning that so often entered into commentary about contemporary children in affluent societies.

The most obvious counterpart to declining work was heightened schooling. We have seen that schooling now became a universal experience, and it extended later into adolescence and even what used to pass for young adulthood. In the 1950s, a noticeable minority of children in the industrial countries still quit high school before graduation – particularly boys, who found it easier to get jobs than did adolescent girls, and whose culture, at least in some cases, was more resistant to schooling in any event. But by 1960, the number of children not completing high school had dropped pre-cipitously; school now equated not just with childhood but with adolescence. Everywhere in the industrial world, finally, attendance at post-secondary schools exploded as well. The United States led the way, with well over half of the relevant age groups attending at least some college by the 1970s. By the 1990s, similar trends were affecting Western Europe, Canada, and Japan, where higher education had longer preserved an elite status. Of relevant age groups, 40–50 percent attended either university or advanced technical school. As with high schools previously, women outnumbered men, in a ratio of 55:45 or more. For both sexes, the spread of college expectations and experiences in some measurable ways pushed youth and some degree of economic dependence (on family, or state, or both) well into their twenties, delaying full adulthood accordingly. The modern equation, childhood = schooling, was open to additional innovations.

Furthermore, the intensity of schooling also changed, at various levels, partly because of the expansion of schooling itself. It was only in the twentieth century, for example, that grades and report cards became standard practice in American schools; previously, loose pass-or-fail procedures had prevailed. New tests were introduced and old ones expanded. The College Board tests were introduced early in the twentieth century as a means of sorting high school students for the elite colleges. Their range and impact broadened steadily, until by the early twenty-first century they had become something of a rite of passage for most middle-class children, some of whom took them several times, on top of cram courses, in an effort to boost scores. Tests loomed even larger in Europe and Japan. Tests and teachers' reports helped sort children into various secondary tracks around age 11 – and kids who didn't make it into the college preparatory track would find it difficult to win reassignment. Another set of tests awaited completion of secondary school, as a basis for college entrance and assignment. The names varied – A- and O-levels in Britain, the *baccalauréat* or *bac* in France – but the pressure was immense. Small wonder that completion of the tests often triggered massive youth celebrations, with street demonstrations, even riots in Paris; or drunken revels, complete with special costumes, in post-Soviet Russia.

Here, too, change involved the experience of both childhood and adult perceptions and anxieties. Encouraging school performance became a vital aspect of parenting. This could mean choosing appropriately enhancing summer activities, or the maternal coddling of children's letting off steam in the Japanese home. Subjecting young children to intelligence tests, to find out their potential and determine possible remediation, was another new way of rating one's own offspring. With the spread of procedures for artificial insemination of infertile partners, school success began to shape criteria for selecting donors (along with height, good looks and, though genetically irrelevant, religious background). Sperm or egg donors were preferred who had a high IQ and a degree from a top college. All societies doubtless had valued some perception of intelligence in children, but now it became a virtual obsession with some adults, and for children's self-perception as well.

Given these changes, it was not surprising that some hesitations surfaced. British working-class parents usually talked about hoping for school success, envisaging their children as doctors and lawyers, but in fact they did little to help their kids, and often showed scant interest in school results or activities; class differences, in other words, affected the school–child equation. In the United States, where suspicion of intellectualism had a long history, even the middle class could worry about the impact of too much schooling on children's wellbeing. Through the first half of the twentieth century, many parents' groups successfully pressed governments to limit or even ban homework, on grounds that it imposed undue strain. Later in the century, movements to provide more self-esteem for children, along with extensive inflation of average grades, addressed similar concerns. Traditional shaming methods, such as posting grades publicly, were actually outlawed. Many schools went to considerable lengths to provide different kinds of children with a sense of reward. High schools, for example, began identifying multiple valedictorians – 16, in one California case – in order to reduce hurt feelings; awards for attendance and citizenship boosted another category of students; bumper stickers noting that "I have an honor student at Crestview Elementary" constituted a further outcropping of the self-esteem movement. While the United States served as the epicenter of the self-esteem movements, systems in Britain and elsewhere began to adopt some similar language and policies. The adjustment of children, and their parents, to the focus on schooling was a work in process.

Widespread adoption of lower birth rates simply became a fact of life in the industrial societies. Everywhere, in the modern model, poorer families tended to have larger families than the middle class, a reversal of premodern patterns, reflecting differences in knowledge about birth control and, probably, some lingering beliefs that children could be economically useful at the lower end of the social scale. At times, governments also encouraged larger families. France, for example, adopted a policy in favor of a higher birth rate in the 1930s and again after World War II, being concerned about low population levels that, among other things, could affect military strength. Part of the French welfare state involved payments to parents with more than two children; some other European governments offered similar, though smaller, programs. The result may have slowed the birth rate reduction trend, but it did not halt it – governments, in the industrial societies at least, could not really regulate parents' decisions about family size.

The most interesting anomaly in the low birth rate pattern involved the baby boom from the late 1940s to the early 1960s, headed by the United States, but with more modest echoes in Western Europe. For over a decade, middle-class families began to seek three to four children, often closely spaced, while working-class families eased up on their own birth rate reduction. Some of this zeal for more children reflected pent-up demand from the Depression, when families had not been able to meet their own desired goals; some involved reactions to World War II. Growing postwar prosperity enabled many families to think about having more children, fueling a boom in suburbanization that, in turn, supported a larger family ideal. Media presentations encouraged an emphasis on stable families and intensive mothering, and many women did pour new energy not only into caring for their own brood, but into serving on school committees and other agencies designed to assist children. In turn, the baby boom caused school crowding and other tensions that played a role in the outburst of student protest in the United States and Western Europe during the 1960s.

The baby boom itself, however, played out within 15 years. The costs of extra children competed with other consumer goals. Many women clearly tired of that degree of parental obligation and of the isolation of suburban motherhood. The leading salvo in the revival of American feminism, Betty Friedan's *Feminine Mystique* (1963), directly attacked the 1950s family model as a distortion of women's lives. The influx of mothers into the labor force directly competed with the birth rate, and work won out. Birth rates resumed their downward trend. By 2000, several European countries, headed by Spain and Greece, had birth rates so low that, without immigration, population levels would actually begin to decline. Despite the interesting interruption, the modern model seemed confirmed.

Low birth rates had their own consequences, of course, extending the impacts that had already emerged in the nineteenth-century demographic transition. Many parents lavished extra attention on the children they did have, at least in terms of gifts and careful arrangements to foster school success. In these respects, low birth rates encouraged some of the more obvious apparatus of the affluent childhood. Smaller family size meant that children themselves had fewer siblings for interaction; this could promote greater contact with adults (parents or other caretakers) in early childhood, and it certainly encouraged heightened reliance on friends of the same age, mostly encountered in schools. Many parents reported increased concern about sibling rivalry, as the average two children per family warred for parental attention, though the anxiety may have outstripped actual problems. More obviously, siblings declined in importance in children's lives simply because there were fewer of them.

Most generally, low birth rates furthered a redefinition of age structures in ways that could affect society's approach to childhood. With the baby boom as a brief exception, children declined rapidly as a percentage of the overall population in the industrial world, and at the same time, thanks to greater life expectancy, the percentage of older people rose. Quite understandably, new levels of attention began to be devoted to the elderly, through social security and medical programs. And while this did not necessarily detract from policy attention to children, it might yet have that effect. During the last three decades of the twentieth century, for example, the percentage of elderly below the poverty line fell in the United States, thanks above all to pension programs, while the percentage of children in this category rose. In a related pattern, older people began to take advantage of the political process, with high rates of voter participation; in contrast, younger citizens became increasingly unlikely to vote, presumably because the leading political issues did not seem to affect them. But this voting disparity contributed further to the policy gap between adults and young people.

Ironically, then, falling birth rates could increase parental attention to individual children while constraining resources and policy attention available to children society-wide. Here was a clear challenge for industrial societies in the twenty-first century.

Finally, completing the implementation of the modern model, all the industrial societies continued to experience rapid reductions in children's death rates, particularly in infancy. Only active involvement in war or other disasters might briefly challenge this pattern. Here, further, was one area where social commitment remained strong: children should not die, and industrial societies poured massive resources into keeping children alive.

Growing affluence and new government programs expanded efforts in children's health well beyond efforts to eliminate child mortality. Specific programs varied, and the United States stayed somewhat apart, but most governments in advanced industrial societies developed comprehensive healthcare coverage which expanded the medical services available to children. Massive investments also went into children with special needs, providing not only medical attention, but school support for children with various disabilities.

Not surprisingly, even with a trend that almost everyone could embrace, there were anomalies and problems. While death rates fell for all groups, social inequality showed clearly. Infant death rates for African-Americans were often three times the level for those of whites, because of poverty, less access to medical care, and more risky teenage pregnancies. (African-Americans also suffered disproportionately from high rates of death by violence in the teenage years.) On the other hand, some observers worried that some children were being kept alive at excessive cost, or with clear prospect of adult ill-health. The widespread commitment to keeping children alive unquestionably made it harder to accept deaths that did occur. In the United States, few marriages could survive the death of a child, in contrast to the nineteenth century, when grief was supposed to help hold a family together; the sense that someone must be at fault for a child's death became hard to bear. Grief counseling for children close to death – for example, in case of the death of a schoolmate – became widespread. The whole issue of the relationship between children and death came in for new attention. During the 1920s, many American experts argued that children should be kept away from grief and funerals, and while this attitude eased a bit by the 1970s, concern persisted. One nursery school went so far as to ban references to "dyeing" Easter eggs (it was all right to refer to "coloring") lest children be traumatized by the word. And many experts argued that contemporary children no longer understood death, because they were so unlikely to have direct experience. The psychological implications for childhood were intriguing.

There were, of course, some new problems. Modern equipment posed new accident hazards for children. Household appliances could be dangerous, and cars were a menace. Not surprisingly, huge campaigns developed from the 1920s onward to keep children safe; many involved placing growing responsibility on parents, though new safety devices such as seat belts and "childproof" bottle caps ultimately came into play as well. The United States went particularly far in imposing safety restrictions on children, with one revealing exception: American dependence on the automobile encouraged relatively easy driving tests, and at a relatively young age, compared with Europe or Japan. Driving and adolescence became intimate partners in the

United States, with accident rates to match as the greatest cause of adolescent deaths; in contrast, most European countries banned driving before age 18. Death and childhood were farther removed, in the industrial societies of the early twenty-first century, than ever before in human history, but issues remained.

Three new or heightened trends added to the changes in childhood in advanced industrial societies through the twentieth century. The first involved new forms of family instability, particularly the rapidly rising divorce rate. By the late twentieth century, 50 percent of all American marriages, and 35 percent of all British, ended in divorce, capping a fairly steady increase for several decades. Instability itself, of course, was not new. Earlier families had faced the death of one or both parents, or dire poverty that could force parents to institutionalize children. These pressures actually lessened in the twentieth century overall; in particular, there were fewer outright orphans. But deliberate family breakup undoubtedly affected many children adversely, as they found themselves caught in parental conflict and sometimes harmed economically. Legal trends favored custody by mothers through most of the century, though there was some rebalancing after the 1970s. Bitter custody battles could add to the burden on children. Few parents divorced because of their children, and for a time experts argued that divorce was preferable to conflict, a view that was revised by the 1990s. Clearly, however, many parents were deciding that their personal happiness was more important than keeping a family together for the sake of children, and this was a significant change in its own right.

Divorce and growing sexual permissiveness often heightened the phenomenon of bad fathering, though this, too, was not new. Large numbers of fathers of illegitimate children, and not a few divorced fathers, refused to meet financial obligations to their children, sometimes abandoning them altogether. Various governments introduced new measures to attempt to enforce child support, but the gulf between some fathers and their children was not healed. This was not the whole story of twentieth-century fatherhood, for many fathers began to devote new levels of attention to children; some divorced fathers, feeling guilty, lavished children with gifts when they saw them, as another sign of new commitment. And the whole pattern of family instability varied by region as well as social class; France, secular but in the Catholic tradition, had lower divorce rates than Britain; Japan, with high rates early in the century, saw families become more cohesive.

The second new trend involved massive reconsideration of child discipline. As early as the twentieth century, American childrearing experts urged parents to reconsider older patterns. Children were psychologically vulnerable, in the new view, and needed to be treated carefully. Not only should they not be frightened as part of discipline, they should not even be made to feel guilty, because this would damage their self-esteem and lead to later problems. The rise of psychological research, and of psychology as a profession, generated dramatic new levels of advice to parents, many of whom began to believe that their own instincts might be faulty, and that reliance on a childrearing manual or a parents' magazine was indispensable. Here again, an American trend soon spilled over to other parts of the world. Thoroughly modern parents prided themselves on reasoning with their children, or keeping them out of situations that might promote bad behavior. At an extreme, many parents now resorted not to physical discipline, not even to guilt-laden harangues, but to the punishment called "grounding": cutting children off from their peers and from consumer enjoyments for a time, hopefully without indications of guilt-inducing anger. For their part, many children learned that a warning to their parents that they were causing guilt was a valid means of correcting parental behaviors.

Not all parents bought into the most up-to-date expertise, of course. Physical discipline was, however, rather widely reconsidered. Ireland offers an interesting case study. Corporal punishment was recommended by courts of law, tolerated in families, and actively used in schools through the first half of the century, without much debate. In one classroom, students were even hit with a strap across the hand for bad grades. By the 1930s, some voices were being raised against extreme abuse, and a few teachers were called to account. More criticism developed by the late 1940s. A group of parents in Dublin formed a children's protection group to publicize school abuses. New laws limited physical punishments in the 1950s and 1960s, though there continued to be voices in favor of the necessity of spankings. Finally, in 1982, physical punishment in the schools was banned outright; suspension or expulsion became the most extreme school penalties. The government ruling insisted that teachers should treat their students "with kindness combined with firmness and should aim at governing them through their affections and reason and not by harshness and severity." Even sarcasm or "remarks likely to undermine a pupil's self-confidence" were disallowed.

The trend was fairly general. Childrearing experts almost uniformly urged against spankings from the 1920s onward. Britain and a number of American states (though not all) outlawed corporal punishment in schools by the 1980s. Scandinavian countries even banned spankings in the home. More diffusely, in the United States and elsewhere, definitions of child abuse became more rigorous, and acts that earlier might have passed unnoticed – severe bruising, for example – were now criminalized. Violence against children still occurred, but it almost surely declined, and the stance of society at large had changed decisively.

Perhaps most obviously of all, the twentieth century, building on earlier trends, enthroned the child as consumer. Parents and others began buying children lots more toys, from infancy onward. Early in the century, a few experts warned against surrounding babies with stuffed animals, but most adults agreed that having things to love was useful for children. By the 1920s, American parents were being told to use consumer items as bribes: a child who feared the dark might be lured into a room with a piece of candy, drawn farther in each night until the consumer pleasure had overcome the phobia. Holidays and birthdays became consumer celebrations – experts in the 1920s even urged gifts for siblings on a birthday, to prevent any rivalry. By the 1950s, parents began to take on tacit responsibility to make sure their children were not bored. Boredom, a modern notion in any event, had previously been treated as a character issue: children, particularly girls, should be taught not to bore others. Now, however, boredom shifted to a state for which someone else was responsible, beginning with parents. "I'm bored," correspondingly, became a legitimate childish complaint.

Children as consumers set up some obvious new issues concerning sources of authority and control. With many children boasting spending money – the practice of giving allowances began in the United States in the 1890s, and spread; and of course some older children earned money on their own – they often had direct access to goods. Furthermore, new media, radio and then television and finally the Internet, reached children directly, bombarding them with both images and advertisements. Many parents worried about this direct commercial interaction with children, and governments sometimes stepped in to regulate, as in encouraging the rating of films according to acceptability for children; or, as in Sweden, banning TV adverts aimed at children. Recurrently, modern societies were assailed with warnings about the dire effects of comic books, radio, movies, video games – the common argument being that children might be led into violence or inappropriate sexuality. Without question, the range of experiences to which children and adolescents were exposed through the media widened steadily. Without question, children's consumerism was laced with violence and sexuality. How great an impact all this had was, however, open to some debate. And many parents found themselves divided: concerned about the fare their children encountered, they also had their own obligation to entertain, and often some real guilt that they could not, or did not, pay more attention to their children. So consumerism gained ground steadily, even in the poorest sectors of the industrial societies. Having and wanting things became a central part of a child's life. Indeed, many aspects of consumerism set up a special world for children, with distinctive music, clothing, and other attributes treasured in part because adults disapproved.

The bargain struck for contemporary childhood both resembled and differed from the bargain developed in agricultural societies. In the latter, children were supposed to work, but were given some special roles in festivals as partial recompense. In the current version of modern childhood, children are supposed to tolerate schooling, ideally even to excel, but are given unprecedented consumer abundance and latitude in return.

Advancing children's consumerism had some corollaries. Grandparenting changed. In Western society, most older people began maintaining their own homes from the 1920s onward, rather than sharing housing with adult children. In that sense, their interaction with grandchildren might decline. Some families continued to depend on grandparents for childcare, particularly when single mothers had to work. But the dominant image of grandparents shifted to that of consumer-indulgers, bringing goodies for their grand-progeny along with lots of open affection, and expecting thoroughly enjoyable, if often brief, interactions in return. The role was important, but it was also novel.

For adolescents, consumerism was associated not just with sexual imagery, but with changing sexuality, throughout the industrial world. In the United States, the practice of dating began around 1920. Different from more traditional courtship, dating involved a boy and girl seeking some kind of commercial entertainment outside the home and outside any systematic chaperonage – dining out, going to a film – as the central feature of their encounter. Some level of sexual interaction might follow, whether merely "necking," or "petting" or "going all the way." In principle, girls were supposed to regulate the level of sexual activity, given the continued assumption that they had more sexual restraint and, certainly, more to lose by excess. Dating did not usually lead to intercourse, but sexual activity undoubtedly increased. By the 1950s in the United States (earlier than was recognized at the time or since), rates of premarital pregnancy began to increase, even though most respectable girls were urged to conceal their activities. The 1960s brought more accessible birth control devices, notably the pill, which furthered the trend of growing sexual activity among people in their mid-to-late teens. Without question, the age of first sexual encounter went down, particularly for girls, though there were both individual and social class differences. By the 1960s also, marriage ages began to rise, particularly in the middle class, as women as well as men sought to complete education and gain a professional start; this increased the sense of a period of youth – mid-to-late teens to later twenties – as a time of some sexual experimentation, sometimes encouraged also by drink or drugs. The commercial media faithfully represented, and somewhat exaggerated, this impression of youth indulgence.

Countercurrents developed. Some feminists worried that young women, now less free to reject sexual advances, were being exploited, and a certain number of young people deliberately bucked the trend, for religious or personal reasons, embracing celibacy until marriage. A major movement developed in the United States during the 1990s to encourage young people to "just say no" to sex as well as other vices, and considerable federal funding went to celibacy education programs. Birth control devices were not officially encouraged, because they might facilitate sex, though access was not too difficult. Teenage pregnancy did drop a bit, but whether sexual activity changed much was open to question. Campaigns against sexual harassment of students and against date rape reflected real problems for American youth, but also societal nervousness about the new youth sexual culture.

Responses to the new sexual patterns in Europe and Japan were different, as birth control devices were made more readily available and teenage pregnancy dropped noticeably.

Changes in consumerism and discipline had one final effect, this one more visible in the United States, but increasingly affecting Europe as well. By the 1980s, building on earlier trends, childhood obesity became a major problem. Children who were indulged by their parents, or who indulged themselves, with ubiquitous sodas and snacks; children whose eating habits were not carefully monitored because parents feared to discipline or thought that food might compensate for their absence at work; children whose entertainments were increasingly sedentary thanks to television and computers, and who were often driven by car to other activities – many of these children got fat. A 1994 study found 25 percent of all American children to be obese, up over 50 percent from the 1970s; and by 2004 this figure had risen to over 30 percent. By the same point, 13 percent of French children were obese, an increase of over 50 percent since the early 1990s.

In 1907, a Swedish authority, Ellen Key, proclaimed the twentieth century as the "century of the child." The motto won wide currency in the United States. With gains in health and schooling clearly visible, with new expertise available, with discussions of gentler discipline and more consumer abundance beginning to advance, her prediction was plausible and was widely hailed. In some ways, it has worked out: children in industrial societies are better educated, less likely to work in harsh conditions, much less likely to die, less likely even to be spanked than had been true in the nineteenth century. But, by 2005, few authorities would be comfortable with Key's optimism. The picture is more complex.

First, gains have sometimes brought further problems in their wake. No-one could anticipate childhood obesity in 1900; a century later, it was inescapable. Death is down, but tragic accidents continue to erase many teenage lives. There are more amorphous downsides as well, including new problems of stress and identity: all available statistics show that depression and suicide among children, particularly teenagers, have risen markedly.

Second, even aside from clearcut problems, adult anxieties about children have in some ways increased, particularly in the United States. While consumerism brings some new chances for children and parents to play together, a real source of family joy, it is hard to be fully comfortable with children's consumerism overall. The growing gap between teenagers and parents, based in part on very different consumer tastes and values, is palpable, and it is hard on adults. Children are less likely to die, but because death is now so unacceptable, adult worries about health and safety have hardly abated. New responsibilities for the emotional and psychological wellbeing of children, including the need to avoid anger (or to feel guilty if avoidance fails), add to the mix. The rise of inescapable expertise is double-edged as well: while parents find valuable advice and comfort in childrearing manuals, they are also being told that their own impulses are likely to be wrong, and this hardly increases delight. Growing psychological expertise brought many adults to question their own childhood and the way they were raised: blaming parents for one's problems became more acceptable than ever before, another interesting development. A stark fact: between the 1950s and the 1970s, the number of American parents who said they enjoyed parenting declined markedly; and, according to polls, the happiest married people were childless.

Third, despite widespread rhetoric about the joys of parenting and the cuteness of the child, industrial societies have clearly become ambivalent about childhood. Adults clearly often prefer work, or their separate consumer pleasures, to dealing too extensively with kids – though they may also feel guilty in the process. The sheer decline in the number of children inevitably shifts attention, and while it results from new economic calculations about children's work and costs, it encourages a reorientation of interests as well. In the 1970s, Germans began to identify a phenomenon they called *Kinderfeindlichkeit*, or hostility to children – manifested particularly by couples who avoided parenting altogether. While the United States seemed a bit friendlier, the number of communities for older adults that banned children, except as occasional visitors, was an interesting innovation as well. The relationship between childhood and advanced industrial societies was still being worked out; it brought many advantages, but the paths were less clearcut than they had seemed 100 years before.

Further reading

Donna Bee-Gates, *I Want It Now: Navigating Childhood in a Material World* (New York: Palgrave Macmillan, 2007); Peter N. Stearns, *Anxious Parents: A History of Modern American Childrearing* (New York: New York University Press, 2003); Neil Postman, *The Disappearance of Childhood* (New York: First Vintage Books, 1994); Gary Cross, *Kids' Stuff: Toys and the Changing World of American Childhood* (Cambridge, MA: Harvard University Press, 1997) and *The Cute and the Cool: Wondrous Innocence and Modern American Children's Culture* (New York: Oxford University Press, 2004); Martin Guggenheim, *What's Wrong With Children's Rights?* (Cambridge, MA: Harvard University Press, 2005); Joan Jacobs Brumberg, *The Body Project: An Intimate History of American Girls* (New York: Random House, 1998); Mary Ann Mason, *The Custody Wars: Why Children Are Losing The Legal Battles And What We Can Do About It* (New York: Basic, 1999); Stephanie Coontz, *The Way We Never Were: American Families and the Nostalgia Trap* (New York: Basic Books, 2000); Howard Kushner, *Self-Destruction in the Promised Land: A Psychometric Biology of American Suicide* (New Brunswick, NJ: Rutgers University Press, 1989). On Japan, see Merry White, *The Material Child: Coming of Age in*

Japan and America (Berkeley: University of California Press, 1994); Muriel Jolivet, *Japan, A Childless Society?* (New York: Routledge, 1997); Roger Goodman, *Japan's "International Youth": The Emergence of a New Class of School Children* (Oxford: Oxford University Press, 1990). On Germany and Europe: R.H. Samuel and R. H. Thomas, *Education and Society in Modern Germany*, repr. edn (New York: Routledge, 2003); Fritz Ringer, *Education and Society in Modern Europe* (Bloomington: Indiana University Press, 1979). A pioneering comparative collection is Joseph Hawes and N. Ray Hiner, *Children in Historical and Comparative Perspective: An International Handbook and Research Guide* (New York: Greenwood, 1991). See also Colin Heywood, *A History of Childhood: Children and Childhood in the West from Medieval to Modern Times* (Cambridge: Cambridge University Press, 2001).

Chapter 11

The dislocations of the twentieth and twenty-first centuries

Children face war and violence

The past 100 years have seen a host of horrors inflicted on children in various parts of the world. Putting the same point another way: many of the very worst aspects of recent history have been visited on children. One need only think of the huge number of children caught up in the Holocaust during World War II, forced into camps, witnessing the degradation and deaths of parents, often themselves killed in the gas chambers. One and a half million children died in the Holocaust, of the estimated 1.6 million Jewish children alive on the European continent (outside Russia) in 1939. They were killed as Jews, of course, in the Nazis' anti-Semitic frenzy, and not as children, but no beliefs in the special position of children offered them any protection. The many bloody wars of the twentieth century, the displacements of populations, including hundreds of thousands of children, that continue into the twenty-first century, are an integral part of the recent history of childhood. Contemporary war has blurred the boundaries between civilian and military, and this involves children in many ways. New levels of open hatred, as between ethnic groups, prompt direct attacks on children in ways less common in the nineteenth century.

Children have been victims of collective barbarity in past times. Remember the fate of many of those who went on the children's crusade: being sold into slavery. Attacks on children, as a mean of intimidating adults or destroying the future of groups that might never seem trustworthy in the eyes of a conqueror, were hardly twentieth-century inventions. The past century, however, stands among the bloodiest, because of the frequency and scale of warfare and internal strife, and the new levels of weaponry involved. For many children, the "century of the child" proved to be a bad time to be one.

The process began early, for example with the forced migrations, amid great bloodshed, of Greek and Turkish populations after World War I. It continues today in civil strife in many parts of Africa and elsewhere.

The subject is an inescapable part of the recent experience of many children, and it moves us a great distance from the lives of most children in more settled societies and the implications of increasing adherence to the modern model of childhood. Without detailing all the episodes, this chapter offers some examples of physical and psychological hardship. It describes some of the most common results of displacement, in exploited labor, sexual servitude, and the emergence of new kinds of child soldiers.

A bit of subtlety is called for. This chapter deals with truly significant as well as shocking aspects of the conditions of many children in the contemporary decades. There is no attempt to provide a complete list of atrocious situations, but a sampling is shocking in itself. The result shows the inadequacy of many international protective efforts and well intentioned proclamations. While the conditions are not characteristic of children around the world, they demonstrate that the spread of schooling and consumerism cannot be taken as fully characteristic either. The great variety in children's experiences, however, imposes several further complications. First, some similar horrors lurk in societies that are not obviously torn by war and ethnic hatred, but simply suffer from dire poverty; there too, sales of children's sexuality, labor, and even body parts respond to desperate situations. Several observers have noted that African-American children in violence-torn housing projects in Chicago have experiences not entirely different from children in outright war zones. Second, while there should be no sugar-coating the fate of children in war-torn regions or refugee camps, not all the stories lack some redemption; once in a while, a combination of outside intervention and family ingenuity produces unexpected improvements, including some access to modern schooling. And third, it remains important to remember that children in more stable societies, though sheltered from maimings and massive post-traumatic stress, face drawbacks of their own, some of them seemingly inherent in the modern model and in pervasive consumerism.

There is a division in contemporary global history between societies under siege, with children spared almost no imaginable atrocity, and societies working to install or expand the more widely recognized modern conditions of childhood. Children in the former societies deserve far more effective attention than they have often received, for despite some powerful commentary, the damage to children seems to proceed unabated. The horrors should not, however, distract us entirely from the issues, milder but nevertheless genuine, that children face in other settings.

While the contrasts between children in war or civil strife and the consumer-rich children of the Western or Japanese middle classes are vivid and real, some observers have nevertheless suggested an unexpected link: even children in many affluent sectors are increasingly exposed to violence, in media and video games, for example, even though their "real" lives are less touched. Are the distinctions between childhood and violence breaking down, though in different ways, on a global basis?

No single process in the twentieth and twenty-first centuries killed as many children as the Holocaust did, but the pattern of violence seemed to accelerate with World War II and the ensuing decades. Distinctions between military personnel and civilians declined, and children were often caught up in the process. Many children, of course, were caught directly in wartime sieges and bombings from 1939 onward, a massive explosion of violence deliberately directed at civilians. Some children were sent out of wartime London, and there was even an effort to evacuate some children from Leningrad (St Petersburg) before it was surrounded and besieged by German forces. Even evacuated children faced severe problems, in unfamiliar surroundings away from family, and suffering massive guilt that they had been sheltered while others were dying. Far worse conditions afflicted children who stayed amid bombings and artillery shellings that could reduce blocks of housing to rubble. Death and injury, loss of family members, inadequate food supplies, and massive psychological stress touched many. The problem was not European alone: children in Chinese cities under Japanese attack, and then children in the Japanese cities targeted by American bombers, had similar experiences.

After World War II, attacks relevant to children eased briefly. The most obvious exception was the violence and dislocation surrounding the formation of the state of Israel and the periodic wars and Palestinian uprisings that continue to this day. Violence on an even wider scale resumed with Vietnam and its aftermath. One of the most powerful photographs in the Vietnam War features a girl, her back aflame from American napalm, running naked down a street (she survived, amazingly). Subsequent civil war in Cambodia brought further massive bloodshed.

Children were heavily involved in the violence in Central America during the 1970s, and more recently in the drug-related strife in Colombia. Civil wars in Myanmar (Burma), including raids on Thailand, constituted another center. The collapse of the Soviet Union brought violence and displacement in several new nations in Central Asia and the Caucasus. Warfare in the former Yugoslavia, compounded by deliberate attacks on certain groups in the name of ethnic cleansing, involved many children. Two rounds of American and allied attacks on Iraq – particularly the Gulf War of 1990 and then the new invasion of 2003 – and an intervening period in which foods and medical supplies were limited by embargoes, involved many children. Hundreds of thousands were killed or wounded, or affected by lack of food and medical supplies. Endemic warfare in Afghanistan, from the Soviet invasion of 1979 through the oppressive Taliban regime to the American-led combat in the early twenty-first century, helped produce a situation in which children's life expectancy rates plunged to among the lowest in the world. Tragically also, on an even larger scale, the several trouble spots in Africa, convulsed by civil strife and government counterattack, involved children from Sudan and Uganda to Congo and the dreadful genocide in Rwanda, and other places in the center and west.

It has been estimated – and estimates are all that can be offered – that 150 million children have been killed in war and civil war since the 1970s, around the world, and another 150 million crippled or maimed. It was as if every North American child born in the same period had been killed or injured. Further, estimates calculate that 80 percent of all people killed in late twentieth and early twenty-first century conflicts have been women and children, in struggles that have relatively rarely involved extensive engagements between conventional armies of adult males.

Sometimes, children have been deliberately targeted. In the 1930s and early 1940s, Japanese troops seized young girls in Korea, using violence to force them to become sex slaves; in one military brothel, 400 girls serviced 5000 Japanese troops on a daily basis. Forty years later, Cambodian Khmer Rouge forces, bent on ethnic cleansing, might club children to death in front of their parents, or hammer a three-month-old against a tree. Death pits could contain hundreds of children's bodies. African combatants have killed their share of children in recent decades – a third of all those dead in the Congolese bloodshed in the 1990s were under five, but still more frequent have been maimings – an arm sliced off with a machete – and frequent rapes of young girls, deliberately designed to hurt and degrade. From yet another site of battle: 58 percent of the Palestinians injured in clashes with Israelis have been under 17.

The aftermath of war could be dangerous as well. Many twentieth-century struggles have involved land mines, easy for children to explode after the battles ended. A Cambodian boy loses a leg to a land mine on his way to get water from a well; it will be a year before he qualifies for a crude replacement, because the list of eligibles is so long.

Much of the world knew that these episodes contradicted approved international standards. One of the most common impulses of people under attack, including Iraqis protesting American invasion, was to highlight pictures of dead or injured children, knowing what resonance this would have when projected to world opinion. But the sense of horror did nothing to break the pattern.

Throughout the century, but again particularly from World War II onward, children were often forced to flee the scenes of war. Millions of children, in various places, have lived in refugee camps during the past 60 years, amid varying conditions but always facing considerable stress. As many as 4 percent of all people on Earth have had to flee their homes at least once in the past century, including over 20 million children. A 17-year-old in Azerbaijan explained his flight simply: "We left our village when the bombs began falling. ... The bombs were like earthquakes that didn't stop. You spend many years building up a home, and then, in one moment, it is destroyed."

The worst camps are those still perched on the edge of violence. A camp in Thailand is shelled by rebel forces. Two boys lose their mother in the attack, seeing her die before them; one will also die because of wounds to vital organs; the other has had his stomach replaced by a plastic bag.

Outright violence aside, most refugee camps have been woefully short on food and medical supplies. Many children in the camps suffer medical problems, including sexually transmitted diseases contracted from earlier rapine. Malnutrition is rampant, outright starvation all too common. In one Cambodian camp, children could qualify for extra food only if they were in the lowest 25 percent of their weight category – in other words, suffering already from serious malnutrition – and they lost their rights if their weight rose above that level. Many camps on many continents have featured children dying from hunger, incapable of caring for themselves.

Many children in camps or related institutions have lost their parents, sometimes forced to watch them die at the hands of rebel forces. In Cambodia in 1970 – a country where, traditionally, parentless children were cared for by other relatives or fellow villagers – there were three orphanages, with 1600 children. Then war tore tradition apart: by 1974 there were 3000 orphanages, with 250,000 inmates, often living in appalling conditions because needs had so far outstripped resources. Because of deaths of parents, or simply losing track of them during the long flight from violence, as many as 65 percent of the inhabitants of some refugee camps are children. This was the figure, for example, for a camp in Afghanistan filled by people fleeing the Taliban regime. In Rwanda in 1994, 100,000 children were separated from their parents, though aid officials later helped reunite some families.

Always, in the camps, there was immense stress among the displaced children. Often they were living in a region where they did not know the language and where they had no sense of control over their lives. In a refugee camp in the nation of Georgia, 83 percent of the displaced children were diagnosed as suffering some degree of psychosomatic stress.

Prolonged life in a camp splintered families, even when they had arrived intact. Parents, particularly fathers, possessed no resources, and so had no traditional bargaining power with their children. Not surprisingly, large numbers of children tried to fend for themselves, ignoring parental pleas. Some girls sold their bodies. Boys and girls both often turned to stealing. Respect for parents dwindled, and alignment with other children replaced conventional loyalties.

In other cases, parents themselves pushed their children into prostitution or thievery, as a means of providing some support for the family. Many parents approved of their daughters selling sex for food, if they saved some scraps for other family members. Not infrequently, troops sent in to assure order were eager customers for child sex, a problem encountered in several United Nations expeditions. Children's lives, in sum, could be disrupted in almost every imaginable way, even if they survived war itself.

Some happier endings were possible. United Nations agencies and private relief groups tried to do more than relieve suffering, though the task was frequently too great. Often the aid workers organized youth groups as a means of providing some order and purpose, and sometimes the skills gained could be applied to life outside the camps. Youth councils played a significant role in recovery in Kosovo, in the former Yugoslavia. The youth groups were sometimes able to help younger children. Many agencies tried to establish schools, though supplies were an obvious problem. Again in Kosovo, the Save the Children Fund managed to set up outdoor schools for over 40,000 children.

By the 1990s, some criminals against children were put on trial before international tribunals. A man in Rwanda was convicted for encouraging and tolerating violence and the rape of children; several war criminals were also identified in the former Yugoslavia, again in part because of actions against children. There were, in other words, international standards, and occasionally they displayed some teeth.

Occasionally, also, children (often with some family members) made their way out of camps to a better life. After months, even years, many Vietnamese and Cambodian refugees were admitted to the United States, and some built positive lives despite the hardships they had endured. Jewish children who survived the Holocaust and subsequent camps for displaced persons, and managed to get to Israel, were also often able to rise above their pasts. In both these cases, opportunities for later schooling played a significant role in recovery.

Sometimes, finally, if a bit more modestly, children might be saved by their enemies. Some Rwandan Tutsi tribespeople, under attack by the Hutu tribe, simply sent their children to their Hutu neighbors, who did in fact take care of them. The parents cited a local proverb, "He who wants to punish an assassin trusts him with his own child."

War and flight contributed also to the spread of child soldiers, directly involved in war, often against their will, but often also desensitized to the violence that surrounded them. It was estimated that, in any given year in the later twentieth and early twenty-first centuries, some 300,000 children were bearing arms, particularly in parts of Southeast Asia and Africa, but also in Latin American battlegrounds such as Colombia.

A bit of historical perspective is vital on this widely lamented phenomenon. Children have often served in military forces. A 13-year-old boy, fighting for the French revolution and killed by royalist forces, was praised as a martyr to the cause, with no sense that his military participation was unusual or inappropriate. A good portion of the soldiers in the American Revolution – on the patriot side, but also among German mercenaries serving Britain – were boys of 14 or 15, and some children were involved as young as eight. Some, undoubtedly, were pushed into battle against their will, but many fought willingly. In the conditions of agricultural society, war might seem a desirable alternative for many youth, a chance for excitement and escape from the family economy.

So what was new about the child soldiers? Different international standards, for one thing. It no longer seemed proper, according to dominant world opinion, for children to be involved in military service; the United Nations emphatically agreed.

But it was also true that contemporary child soldiers were dealing with far more lethal weaponry than their earlier counterparts. More of them, almost certainly, were forced into battle than had been true in past conflicts. More of them suffered dire consequences, as in sexually transmitted diseases that could kill. The furor over child soldiers reflects a complex mixture of new (if ineffective) global standards and a real deterioration in many children's lives.

Most child soldiers are in their early teens, but some are under ten. Most are boys, but girls are often recruited for supporting roles, including forced or willing sex, and some combat. In the Moro Islamic Liberation Front in the Philippines, for example, girls are used to prepare food and provide medical care, but each leader also is assigned a girl for sexual pleasure.

Force is often central to service. The UNITA rebel group in Angola forcibly recruited child refugees from Rwanda, seizing them in the Congo. Many child soldiers ended up facing violence not only from their captors, but also from opposition forces, who often tortured them for information and as retaliation. The Tamil rebel group in Sri Lanka seized children from orphanages for its all-child "Baby Brigade;" the same children were often treated brutally if they fell into the hands of the government. Some child soldiers were deliberately exposed to extreme violence, even forced to attack their own families, to initiate them into a life of bloodshed.

There were other reasons for service, of course. Families sometimes approved, as did wider communities. Many Palestinian children were drawn into formal or informal fighting because of what they perceived as Israeli attacks on their society.

And the child soldiers could be inspired fighters. An adult soldier from Myanmar commented on the children he fought: "There were a lot of boys rushing into the field, screaming like banshees. ... We shot at them but they just kept coming." By the same token, many child soldiers, once initiated into war, could become quite brutal, delighted in their gun-induced power, frequently killing, maiming and raping for no apparent reason other than to demonstrate their dominance. Children who did serve often found it hard to go home, even if they had been forced to fight: home seemed tame, parents had often disappeared, communities were understandably hostile.

War, flight, and soldiering were not the only afflictions for masses of contemporary children. At the end of the twentieth century, another new scourge appeared in the form of AIDS. Disease had continued to play a role in the lives of many children in the twentieth century, but the big story had been its progressive retreat, as immunizations and public health measures improved this aspect of children's lives. AIDS, in some regions, provided the first counterthrust. By 2000, the disease had directly killed 4 million children and had orphaned another 13 million. Africa, particularly southern and eastern Africa, suffered the most. By 2001, teenagers were contracting the disease at a faster rate than other age groups in Africa, as a result of ignorance or defiance. Many men insisted on sex without the protection of a condom, and many young women, eager to please or dependent on male favor for their own upkeep, felt they had to oblige. War, with its frequent sexual attacks, facilitated the spread of the disease in some regions as well. But the child deaths occurred almost entirely from transmission from the mother at birth. As high rates of the disease spread to other relatively poor regions, there were understandable fears that one of the great gains of modern childhood might be rolled back by the new scourge.

Work conditions worsened for many children at various points and in various places during the past century, another trend running counter to the modern model, and affecting a substantial minority of those children in the labor force. Deterioration is often associated with migration, particularly from countryside to city, a process which – even when not tied to war – can both reflect and cause new problems for children.

The emphasis here is on change. It's abundantly clear that, since the arrival of agriculture, most children have worked, so the mere fact of work, often hard work, is not new. And part of the perception of deterioration results from new global standards based on the modern model of childhood: to many journalists and scholars, children simply should not be working beyond some assistance around the house or in a family business; they should be going to school. This modern evaluation is important in its own right, but it sometimes complicates a judgment about the novelty of the economic exploitation of children. For even in traditional societies, some children might be exposed to very poor working conditions, including outright slavery; beatings at work, atrocious housing on the work site, very low pay for child labor – these are hardly brand-new inventions of the modern world.

Here's the basic picture: though more and more children are not in the labor force, an increasing percentage of those who are find themselves in exploitative situations, in jobs that often endanger them and certainly offer no real preparation or training for adult work life. Though they are often trying to work to help the family, and are often placed in their situation by impoverished parents, they are largely cut off from the kind of guidance and protection the traditional family economy used to provide. Again, the result is not in fact entirely novel, for children had suffered at work in the past as well; but it has become increasingly common among laboring children in the contemporary world.

A related comment involves social and geographical place. The vast majority of work-exploited children are in the world's poorer regions, not in the world as a whole. Even in their locations, they typically come from the lowest social groups. Working children in Peru, for example, are Amerindians or *mestizos*, not white. Children laboring in India's rug shops are drawn from the traditional lowest castes, not from the population more generally.

Exploited labor increasingly reflects and confirms inferior social place, both in the global community and in one's own society.

The root cause of heightened economic exploitation of child labor has been the increasing dislocation of many children from traditional family economies in the countryside. Population growth and competition from other sources of supply prevent many families from using child workers in customary ways. The carpet industry in India is a case in point. Children have long assisted in carpet production in Indian villages. Increasingly, however, carpet production has moved to urban factories. Children are widely employed in these factories because of their extremely low wages – well below the presumed national minimum wage. Many child rug workers are migrants from the villages. Some have been kidnapped outright; many are beaten, particularly on their face and hands, as part of work discipline, and a few are branded. Their work can run up to 15 hours a day.

Children in many cities in Africa and Central America, again including many migrants from the countryside, work as domestics. They carry packages and do other street errands. They help bag groceries. They beg. They perform street entertainment, like the child fire-eaters in Mexico – here and elsewhere, child entertainers are often at the bottom of the heap. Many of them sleep on the street as well. They are subject to various diseases, related to both work and housing; some get involved with drugs; they are also exposed to considerable police violence.

In Togo, a former French colony on the West African coast, the nature of apprenticeship has changed, again reflecting new problems in the traditional economy. The lack of adequate jobs in the countryside forces families to seek more urban programs for their children, so the number of apprentices grows rapidly – up to 23,000 by 1981 in the country's cities, in fields such as clothing and construction. Growth means a new upper hand for employers, who charge more to families for the positions, and who increasingly use children as sources of cheap, unskilled labor, ignoring training goals. So apprentices end up doing housework for their employers; they are required to keep watch in the shop overnight. Some small businesses have as many as 80 apprentices, some aged under 15, almost all of whom have dropped out of school. This number precludes any pretense of training: the goal is a low-paid labor force, often beaten to stay in line. Here is another contemporary example of brutal childhoods with no clear springboard for adulthood. The argument for exploitation is strong.

Many children during the past 100 years have been victimized by several interconnected factors. Moving to cities, many children lost the protection of extended families and close-knit communities. More of them, particularly women, might find themselves engaging in casual sex or outright prostitution. This, of course, put them, and any children they might have, at greater risk of disease. Orphaned children often had fewer economic choices available, which again could drive them toward dangerous or degrading work. When war or dislocation was tossed into the mix, the situation could become truly hopeless.

The numbers of children caught up in one or more of the modern world's disasters are impossible to calculate, in part because many of them died before reaching adulthood, victims of violence or disease. Rates have been estimated for each kind of problem, from war to AIDS. Cumulatively, only a minority of the world's children have been trapped in the worst horrors. For them, clearly, the modern model of childhood, whatever its problems and promises, has been largely unavailable, often indeed contradicted by rising mortality rates or more intense labor. Contemporary conditions have divided childhoods into two very different kinds of experience, with, admittedly, some intermediate conditions between the two extremes. A few children – the lucky ones schooled or rescued in the refugee camps, for example – have managed to move from one type of childhood to the other; but some, victims of unexpected conflicts such as those in the former Soviet Union or Yugoslavia, have been plunged just as abruptly from expectations of schooling into a life on the run.

One final factor demands consideration. In the last decades of the twentieth century, new levels of contact among almost all of the world's societies, often summed up as globalization, added important new elements to childhood. We turn to the consequences in the next chapter. Unfortunately, while globalization adds some interesting ingredients to the modern model of childhood, it can also intensify economic deterioration for many children as well, and it has not, at least to date, healed the inroads of war and disease. Divided childhoods persist.

Further reading

Recent surveys include: Elizabeth Goodenough and Andrea Immel, *Under Fire: Childhood in the Shadow of War* (Detroit, MI: Wayne State University Press, 2008); David M. Rosen, *Armies of the Young: Child Soldiers in War And Terrorism* (Piscataway, NJ: Rutgers University Press, 2005); P.W. Singer, *Children at War* (Berkeley: University of California Press, 2006); Lauren St John, *Rainbow's End: A Memoir of Childhood, War and an African Farm* (New York: Scribner, 2008). See also: James Garbino, Kathy Kostelny and Nancy Dubrow, *No Place to be a Child: Growing Up in a War Zone* (Lexington, MA: Lexington Books, 1991); James Marten, ed., *Children and War: A Historical Anthology* (New York: New York University Press, 2002); Graca Machel, *The Impact of War on Children* (New York: UNICEF, 2001); Marc Vincent and Birgette Sorenson, eds, *Caught Between Borders: Response Strategies for the Internally Displaced* (London: Pluto Press, 2001); Bernard Schlemmer, ed., *The Exploited Child* (London: Zed Books, 2000); Rachel Brett and Irma Specht, *Young Soldiers: Why They Choose To Fight* (Boulder, CO: Lynne Rienner, 2004). See also the Human Rights Watch website: www.hrw.org/en/search (enter search term 'abuses of children').

Chapter 12

Globalization and childhoods

Two developments in the later twentieth century ushered in a new era of globalization – an era of intensifying contacts and interactions among societies literally around the world. The most obvious development, and with direct impact on children and youth, was technological: satellite TV broadcasts facilitated global communications, including networks such as MTV, crucial in dispensing at least a version of international youth culture; and in 1990 the introduction of the Internet created an unprecedented means of contact, which many young people seized upon in societies otherwise as different as the United States and Iran. The second development was political: the decision of first China, then Russia to open to new kinds of international contacts. The Cold War ended; multinational companies expanded their outreach amid growing inducements to create market-based economies.

Globalization was not an entirely new process, and historians debate the chronology. Important influences from inter-regional contacts had affected childhood in earlier periods. More intense connections in the later nineteenth century, including Western imperialism, reshaped childhood in many areas and many ways. For Japan, for example, decisions about relationships to the external world brought global forces to bear on childhood from 1868 onward. There is no question, however, that globalization accelerated in the twentieth century, and particularly in the final decades, with a new variety of impacts on childhood.

Contemporary globalization was not a simple process. It was not entirely new, even in its impact on youth and childhood. The global spread of key sports such as soccer and baseball, as part of the spectator life and athletic aspirations of young people from Latin America to Asia, had begun in the late nineteenth century. Another complexity: globalization provoked new kinds of resistance, some of them winning allegiance among groups of young people. Some Muslims, for example, feared the impact of globalization on their traditions, seeing it as a new means of Western dominance. Many Latin Americans feared the impact of American consumer culture on their offspring. On another front, groups of young people in the West and the Pacific Rim openly worried about globalization's impact on labor conditions and the environment. It was not certain that globalization would triumph over the various oppositions. In the West and Pacific Rim, polls showed that young people were more favorable to globalization, overall, than older adults were, priding themselves in their tolerance and openness to new ideas; but in Latin America, Africa, and other parts of Asia, young people and adults agreed on a certain wariness. Third complexity: globalization's emphasis on increasing international contacts did not point in a single direction, and this was of great importance to childhood. Economic globalization, for example, worsened the work situation of some children; but political globalization – that is, the growing outreach of international government and nongovernment organizations – moved toward increased advocacy of children's rights.

Globalization did not assume command of childhood; major regional patterns persisted, and the earlier trends embodied in the modern model of childhood, already well under way, largely persisted. Key aspects of globalization actually provided new support for this model, as we will see. Nevertheless, globalization deserves separate consideration as a new force in the history of childhood, creating additional kinds of change and resistance in the later twentieth and early twenty-first centuries. Four facets of globalization had particular impacts: new patterns of migration; the efforts of international political groups to provide international standards for the treatment of children; economic globalization, or the growing involvement of almost all regions of the world in a common process of production, along with the retreat of state-sponsored economies; and cultural globalization, or the spread of global consumerism.

Migration, of course, was not new, and it had always had consequences for children. Immigrant children in the United States around 1900, for example, had often played a special role as intermediaries between parents, whose English was often uncertain, and the new society in which they worked and, often, went to school. It was a challenging but sometimes invigorating experience, though frequently confusing to parents. At the same time, prejudices often surfaced that found targets among immigrant children; job opportunities might be limited thanks to ethnic bias, and gang activities embodied tensions among many urban youth in immigrant neighborhoods.

Two aspects of migration in the later twentieth century, loosely associated with globalization, added to this mix, along with familiar elements. First, migration occurred over unusually long distances and involved people of very different cultures. Pakistanis and West Indians poured into Britain; Turks and North Africans created large Muslim minorities in France, Germany and the Netherlands; Filipinos and Palestinians flocked to the oil-rich Persian Gulf states; Latinos and Asians created new diversity in the United States. In this situation, children's role as buffers between parents and the new society became if anything more important, but also more demanding. Opportunities for generational clashes within the immigrant community could increase, around issues such as dating or female dress.

Opportunities for expression of prejudice could expand as well. Many immigrant youth in Britain faced growing hostility, punctuated by outright violence and race riots; gang activity could form in response, as in the rise of Latino youth gangs on both coasts in the United States by the early twenty-first century, or the emergence of (Asian) Indian gangs on Canada's west coast. Several riots by Muslim youth in France broke out in the early twenty-first century, reflecting high levels of joblessness and discriminatory treatment by police. Different kinds of youth music, such as the reggae styles brought from the West Indies, but also the sometimes racist punk rock, expressed creativity but also obvious tension in this intermixture of groups of young people in urban settings.

The second innovation, for some immigrant youth, involved the growing possibility of return visits to the home country, thanks to relatively cheap air travel or other facilities; Indians and Pakistanis often went home for vacations, preserving ties to extended families, and often providing occassion for marriage arrangements for young people themselves. The opportunity for many youth to become "bicultural" in this situation, conversant with two cultures and comfortable in switching back and forth, increased. This could involve young people who did not migrate, but whose contacts with cousins who did provided familiarity with the habits of other societies. Here was an obvious spur to globalization, though not to a single cultural model.

Efforts of international organizations to assist children and reshape childhood had begun in the aftermath of World War I – a sign of political globalization and the growing force of humanitarian world opinion. A variety of groups distributed food and other aid to children displaced in the war, including children in former enemy nations. While this applied mainly to Europe, the principle of special international charity for children gained ground steadily. After World War II, this would blossom into further efforts for refugees and for children in poor countries. Private organizations such as the Save the Children Fund, and political bodies deriving from the United Nations, both solicited philanthropy and distributed funds and products. The needs of poor children regularly outpaced donations, but the aid was significant, as were the new principles involved.

In the 1920s, also, the new International Labor Office, affiliated with the League of Nations, began to pass resolutions against child labor up to age 15. The goal was to extend the criteria now common in industrial societies to the world at large. This effort also broadened out under the United Nations after World War II. A host of conferences and resolutions attacked excessive work, while urging the right of every child to an education. The United Nations drafted formal statements on children's rights (the Convention on Rights of the Child was issued in 1989), and most nations signed on, at least in principle: the main goals were promotion of health, avoidance of abuse, access to education, plus more standard rights such as freedom of religion and expression – a familiar roster, but now conceived in terms of a global approach. A key focus by the 1990s was an effort to ban executions of children and youth for crimes, and virtually all societies in the world accepted this agreement, with the United States one of the only holdouts (until 2005). The World Health Organization worked hard to promote children's survival and wellbeing, and a number of improvements occurred under its auspices – from inoculations that largely defeated some traditional killers, like polio, to educational programs designed to improve maternal care of infants. In the late 1970s, world opinion, as well as international organizations, became actively involved in attacking the Nestlé company for distributing infant milk formulas to regions where unsanitary water and parental ignorance led to higher death rates than occurred with breastfeeding; after initially resisting the international campaign, the giant company dramatically revised its approach in the 1980s. Other United Nations programs worked actively to promote some form of population control, in the interests of economic stability and children's wellbeing alike: a major conference in 1996 agreed on this goal, despite tensions with religious authorities in the Islamic world and in the Catholic Church; greater education for women was particularly recommended as a means of reducing population pressure. Finally, a variety of United Nations and private agencies worked to spread the most up-to-date principles of education and childrearing, often distributing materials urging parents to pay attention to their children as individuals.

The commitment of large numbers of well intentioned people, primarily from the more affluent countries, to a global vision of children's rights, health, and economic protection was an important part of globalization more generally. The idea of children's rights was novel in any society, but the notion of international agreement was at least as dramatic. It could have important effects, even aside from the resounding proclamations. In 2003, for example, the United Arab Emirates banned the use of children as jockeys in camel races: they had long been favored because of their light weight, strapped to the great beasts despite obvious terror. Here was an established pattern that had to be rethought by a nation eager for growing international contacts and a successful world role. The United States was affected as well. A Supreme Court ruling in 2005 held that minors could not be subjected to capital punishment, an area where the United States had, for several decades, differed from almost every other country in the world; international legal standards were cited as a key basis for the decision. More generally, along with imitation of the modern model of childhood by individual governments, the global movement on behalf of children helps explain the steady (if quite varied) decline of the birth rate and, even more, the decline of infant and child mortality; the same applies to the steady reduction of child labor in the final decades of the twentieth century, and the consistent increase in the percentage of children receiving at least some education.

There were, however, important limitations on the range of global action for children. In the first place, open disagreement flared on certain issues.

A campaign in 1973 to win global agreement on a ban on child labor under age 16 failed, because not enough countries would sign on. Several poor countries believed that their economies depended to an extent on cheap child labor, and that many poor families had the same need; countries such as the United States refused to sign as well, both because of reliance on child labor among migrant agricultural workers, and because of a general resistance to international infringement on national freedom of action. A replacement agreement in 1989 was important, but more modest: extreme abuse of child labor was now outlawed in principle, with particular focus on sexual exploitation, sale of children to pay family debts, and use of children in military forces. Most countries did sign this document. There were also disagreements about birth control, with the United States, from the 1980s onward, withholding funds from international agencies that distributed birth control devices or in any way countenanced abortion. Catholic and some Islamic opposition added to disputes on this issue.

In addition to disagreements, many international political measures fell short because the problems were too severe, or because individual regions simply ignored the principles involved – sometimes even when they had signed the international convention in order to seem up-to-date and civilized. Many countries signed documents on children's rights to schooling, but because of lack of resources and family dependence on child labor, many children were left with no educational access at all. Other international standards provoked outright disagreement locally. Conflicts over birth control might pit wives against husbands, doctors against priests; and while the birth rate did drop overall, with major reductions in Latin America and in China, high rates persisted in Africa and in many Islamic regions. A huge gap opened, as discussed in Chapter 11, between ringing international rights statements and the actual treatment of children in cases of war and civil conflict: rights workers strove to mitigate the effects of war, with occasional success, but clearly they could not keep pace with the magnitude of the problem. Global influences on children were undeniable, but there was hardly a single, effective global voice.

Trends in child labor showed some of the limits of global standards efforts, and the modern model itself, while ultimately providing evidence of impact as well. The issue bridged between global politics and global economies. By the later twentieth century, rates of child labor were falling almost everywhere, with schooling on the rise, which did not negate the fact that a large minority of children still worked in some places, often amid extensive exploitation. But the case of South and Southeast Asia was particularly challenging because the region not only failed fully to comply with international efforts to curb the use of child workers, but actually experienced rising rates in the 1990s, bucking the global trend outright. Clearly some comparative regional analysis was essential, for even by 2008 United Nations' reports showed that up to 44 million children aged 5–14 were at work in the region, and while some decline was reported by this point, it was noticeably slower than in other areas. Explanations varied, in comparison with other regions where poverty was as, or even more, extensive. For India, the persistence of large rural populations was surely a factor, compared with societies such as Latin America, where poor families are more urbanized. A related point was the lack of a fully available school system, and some government hesitancy in pushing school requirements. Literacy rate gains lagged in consequence, which might also explain the tenacity of commitments to child labor. Within South Asia as a whole, localities in particular economic distress, or disrupted by civil war, as was the case until recently in Sri Lanka, saw more child labor simply as a function of families trying to make ends meet. A persistent claim was the strength of the long-standing view that children are simply supposed to work, and that they are ready to work at a young age.

Yet regional distinctiveness, and the incomplete hold of global standards, was not the end of the story. By 2008, after some lag, the South Asia region did seem to be pulling into the global trend of replacing work with schooling, particularly once some modest improvements in prosperity began to register. India had 17–20 million children working in 1999, but the figure had dropped to 12.6 million by 2008, a dramatic reduction. Global influence and the sheer impact of a more modern economy had a real, if gradual, effect.

Economic globalization added greatly to the complexity. Not only levels of trade, but also basic systems of production, shifted with this central development. Multinational companies, based in the United States, Western Europe, or the Pacific Rim, began setting up production facilities wherever they could find favorable labor costs, environmental regulations, and useful resources and transportation systems. Complex products such as automobiles were assembled from parts made in Asia, the Americas, and Europe. For simpler items such as textiles, giant sales companies such as Gap or Nike usually hired subcontractors who ran the actual factories in places such as Indonesia, Vietnam, or Lesotho.

Labor conditions in the multinationals were not always good – they were seeking low-wage areas, and they often skimped on safety equipment, while requiring long hours. They employed relatively little child labor, however – only about 5 percent of the children working by the early twenty-first century were in any sense directly working in the global economy. Economic globalization's impacts were more indirect, but they were huge. There were two major pressures. In the first place, global production often displaced more traditional manufacturing, in which children and young people had been employed. Along with continued population growth in places such as Africa and the Middle East, this led to massive rates of youth unemployment – figures of 30 percent or more in the cities were not uncommon. This became a key source, in turn, of various forms of unrest among young people, including participation in extremist religious and political movements.

The second result of economic globalization involved a steady retrenchment of social programs by governments in societies such as Brazil or India. The reigning philosophy argued for freer market economies, rather than government spending, and agencies such as the International Monetary Fund and the World Bank, as conditions for development loans, often pressed for smaller welfare programs as well. Eager to advance economic growth, and hoping that growth would yield ultimate benefits to the poorer classes, governments pressed ahead, with very few exceptions. Family assistance dropped as a result.

Patterns were complex. Despite the pressures of globalization, the percentages of children working continued to drop steadily, as we have seen, from 6 percent of the total workforce in 1950 to 3 percent in 1990 – or from 28 percent of children under the age of 14 in 1950 to 15 percent in 1990. The declines accelerated during the 1980s and thereafter. By 2004, 88 percent of all children of the relevant ages, around the world, were attending primary school. Globalization was not, in sum, reversing the movement toward the more modern model. Nor were some of the horror stories straightforward. An Indian social scientist commented on newspaper reports lamenting the long hours and close confinement of child workers in fishery industries along the coast; the children had been recruited from other areas, often disputing with their parents, who wanted them closer to home. Yet the children themselves found work entirely normal, and rejoiced that they had escaped far poorer conditions in their villages of origin. They were pleased, as well, that they could send a bit of money to their families. Exploitation? Definitely, by many standards. But the key problem was grinding poverty. Globalization contributed to harsh child labor mainly insofar as it failed to resolve, and in some cases surely worsened, the economic constraints faced by so many families in the developing world.

Global competition and the reduction of social programs had a very clear result: an increase in the number of children in poverty. This occurred even in industrial countries such as the United States, and it had massive results in Africa, South and Southeast Asia, and parts of Latin America. The number of children dependent on activities in the street – begging, prostitution, occasional unskilled labor, petty theft – increased in many places. Outright child labor went up for a time, as we have seen, in South and Southeast Asia – mainly in small production shops and other outlets where the cheapest possible labor was essential to stay afloat. The increase was 50 percent in the late 1990s in this huge region, not counting those in family employment in agriculture, defying the larger global trends. Even more widely, many poor families, pressed by debt, sold children into labor. Purchase of young women for the sex trade almost certainly increased, with some transported to centers of sexual tourism, such as Thailand, from original homes in Eastern Europe or elsewhere. Some families even sold body organs for transplants, with adolescents a particular target. Whatever its other benefits – and there were strong arguments in favor of its good overall results for rapidly-growing economies in places such as China and India – globalization dramatically worsened the struggle for survival for many children and their families.

Global consumerism was the final major facet of globalization, affecting values and behaviors alike, and quickly embracing many children. We have seen the increasing association of childhood with consumerism in the West and Japan; it was not surprising that the relationship spilled over into other societies. Lebanese teenagers, in the cities, began to attend Western movies fairly regularly in the 1920s and 1930s. Enthusiasm for baseball gained ground among Japanese and Latin American youth, and the passion for soccer spread still more widely. But the full explosion of global consumerism for children awaited the later twentieth century, with its new technologies and market opportunities. Young people began to patronize fast food restaurants, often to the dismay of their parents – which was, of course, one of the purposes of these new tastes. McDonald's and similar outlets became havens for youth in Korea, China, and elsewhere, a place to see and be seen, and often to indulge other interests such as dating and romantic love. Television shows such as *Sesame Street*, translated into most major languages, promoted new standards for children, and MTV and global rock tours offered a common youth musical language and generated literally global fan clubs. Dress for urban young people began to standardize in many places, often against adult and traditional patterns, usually around the ubiquitous blue jeans. Patronage of theme parks provided new standards for parents to demonstrate their economic success and love for their children in a single consumerist swoop: taking the kids to Orlando became a ritual for caring, successful Latin American parents. This was the context in which Disney figures and Barbie dolls became part of the global children's play kit. This was the context in which many Chinese youth stayed up until daybreak to watch a European soccer tournament half a world away. With some plausibility, certain observers began to contend that a global youth culture had come into being.

In 2000, a young American Peace Corps teacher was working in an eastern Russian village that had never seen an American before, and that had no computer or Internet connection. Despite their isolation, her students reported a very precise notion of who the most beautiful woman in the world was, and their choice was Britney Spears. In the same year an anthropologist, working in Madagascar on teenagers and youth in an urban slum, realized that her subjects had a very definite idea of the beauty products young women should seek: those that would make them look more like Britney Spears.

Around 2000 also, television reached some of the more remote Pacific Islands. Seeing the new images, many girls became discontented with their bodies and traditional standards of plumpness. Rates of anorexia and bulimia went up markedly.

Global consumerism for children favored relatively prosperous regions and families. By 2000, increases in childhood obesity began to be noticed among middle-class children in China and India, not just in the West. Sedentary occupations and leisure activities, along with food abundance, began to have global consequences. Youth parties in Iran or Pakistan that featured Western music, Western cigarettes, and Scotch whisky were clearly signs of elite status, even as they defied local religious customs. But relatively poor children were not entirely excluded, particularly in the cities. Their earnings might go in part to new consumer products – fashionable clothing and cosmetics, for example, for participants in the sex trade in Madagascar.

It is also vital to recognize that the global youth culture was not based entirely on Western sources. Japan and a few other countries became creative centers as well, based on trends that, as we have seen, began as early as the 1920s. Japan gained worldwide prominence in promoting cute images and products for young children, playing on, but also spurring, a new conception of infancy: the craze for the Hello Kitty series was one manifestation. During the 1990s, a global passion for the Pokémon characters was another sign of Japanese influence. Japan also began to take the lead in various styles and products for youth cool, and cool exports topped Japan's list, in terms of earnings, by 2003. Japanese styles provided leading models of youth culture for East Asia and even around the Middle East. Japanese animation and electronic devices for young people figured prominently around the world. *Wired* magazine began to feature products adopted by young Japanese women as harbingers of larger global trends.

Youth consumerism was not as homogeneous as many people imagined, even when it clearly caught on. A passion for American rap music meant something different to young people whose command of English was limited. Playing with Japanese games or toys – some of the fads like Pokémon had roots in specific Japanese culture that did not travel readily – offered different meanings as well, depending on context. This kind of blending is a common result of new cultural contacts, and it certainly limited an ability to define a single youth culture.

Efforts to blend did not always work, of course. By the early twenty-first century, as cities and consumer opportunities grew in some parts of Africa, parents were offered opportunities to buy strollers for their infants, an obvious translation of global standards. But much resistance developed because of longstanding African traditions of carrying infants close, even while working. Mothers were reluctant to abandon a valued contact, and one that could benefit the child's emotional development. In Kerala, a state in southern India, conservatives tried to adapt the growing enthusiasm for beauty pageants among teenage girls. Their solution: a pageant in which contestants would demonstrate their knowledge of the local language and cultural styles, including dance. The problem: the types of young women interested in participating in the pageants had inadequate grasp of customary lore, while most traditional girls still shunned the pageants. It was hard to find a real winner, and the effort at combining failed, at least in the short term.

There were, however, some shared features. From global consumerism, youth and, to a lesser extent, children in many regions gained a sense of separate identity and belonging. A young man in Hong Kong, asked why he patronized McDonald's, noted that he actually didn't like the food much, compared with Chinese fare, but he gloried in seeing and being seen in such a cosmopolitan place. Clearly, new styles gave young people an alternative to accepting full parental control; consumerism in this sense could be a real weapon in a quiet power struggle in which the balance shifted toward youth. Children often had an unprecedented edge in leading larger societies, including adult family members, toward greater consumer familiarity and competence (including computer literacy), a dramatic new role. At the same time, consumerism also affected adults' conceptions of childhood and their responsibilities as parents. At some point in the later twentieth century, parents in most places began to believe that providing goods and good times for kids was a vital part of their role, and experienced real guilt when their capacity seemed inadequate. There are hosts of symbolic and practical examples. By the 1980s, many Mexican parents began to convert to American-style Halloween, complete with candy for the kids, in contrast to the solemn religious festival that had long marked the celebration; parents in Istanbul began to buy Christmas presents for their children even though they were not Christian; and the Muslim holiday of Ramadan, a time of renunciation, began to alter through the purchase of gifts and cards for the young ones. Few institutions involving children could totally resist global consumerism, aside from the starkest poverty or the most remote rural locations.

Globalization by the early twenty-first century did not include actual global youth movements directed toward protest or agitation. During the late 1960s and early 1970s, ironically just before full-bore globalization, a hint of an international youth protest movement did emerge. Based particularly in Western Europe and the United States, but with some echoes in Eastern Europe and elsewhere, student risings attacked the Vietnam war, racism, the constraints of crowded schools and lack of mobility, and the trappings of consumer society that, the most vocal leaders felt, had snared their parents in superficial, meaningless lives. Student groups seized schools and, in Paris in 1968, mounted a near-revolution that gave them control of parts of the city for a time. Many observers contended that youth would replace the working class as the source of contemporary unrest, as the bearers of a humane conscience.

The prediction proved untrue. Western youth protest trailed off after 1973, though a few violent groups persisted in Europe for another decade. The passing of the baby boom reduced school crowding; some reforms in university programs were introduced; and consumerism proved more attractive than repulsive to most young people. We have seen that young people often joined in unrest by the outset of the twenty-first century, but it was most commonly under regional banners, including religious movements, rather than global ones. Many young people did support global human rights campaigns, and even more were drawn to environmental causes, though participation came disproportionately from the industrial countries. Different traditions and circumstances, as well as different degrees of attraction to aspects of globalization, divided the world's youth, even as it experienced some common influences.

Globalization itself was divisive, as we have seen. Relatively affluent children, participating in new forms of consumerism, differed greatly from the children newly pressed into work roles in India or the street-savvy kids in Rio de Janeiro, even though they, too, might aspire to some consumer lures. Teenage skinheads in Britain or Germany, who fomented violence against racial minorities, shared with immigrant youth an interest in youth-based musical styles, but the styles clashed just as the gangs did, and there was no uniform result. And for many children and adults alike, globalization influenced, but did not transcend, local traditions of childhood. Lebanese parents might seek a Western-style education for their kids, and read a few modern childrearing manuals, but they did not really want their children to accept Western levels of individualism over more traditional family obligations. The worlds of children remained diverse.

Globalization also had a complex relationship with the modern model of childhood, quite apart from the fact that its influence was incomplete in many areas. New streams of migration introduced more families to schooling and much of the other apparatus of modern childhood, though racism and unequal opportunities might limit the effect for some. Political globalization worked unambiguously toward the modern model: the international agencies wanted better health, lower birth rates, legal protections for children, less or no work, and heightened access to schooling. Unfortunately, of all the strands of globalization, the political arm was weakest in terms of actual impact. And economic globalization, in its results for many children, reduced the availability of the modern model for children in the streets or those formally employed, making it harder to win much time for schooling and, in some cases, complicating health conditions as well. Consumerism, finally, was compatible with the modern model for those children who saw consumerism as a source of pleasure along with schooling; it could have some individualistic implications compatible with the modern model as well, and it also promoted other modern features such as peer groups and age-graded activities. But consumerism could also distract from schooling and might prove irrelevant to the central features of the modern model.

Some observers argued, in fact, that globalization was setting the framework for childhood in many parts of Africa, at the expense of the modern model. Growing unemployment made many youth more marginal and reduced the relevance of schooling. Youth who could earn money, such as female prostitutes serving wealthy clients, often devoted their profits to consumerism, which did not, however, reverse their marginalization in the wider society. Youth in these circumstances did not emerge as a protected category with education its primary ultimate function. Marginalization was not a pattern that embraced all Africans, as eagerness for education persisted, with more aspirants for secondary schooling than there were places available; and the zeal for education often related to a commitment to reduce birth rates as well – in other words, the modern model in an African incarnation. But for many, in Africa and elsewhere, globalization could distract from the modern model or undermine it outright, generating a new set of factors at the dawn of the twenty-first century.

Finally, and more predictably, globalization could also encourage resistance in the name of tradition. Many young people rallied to threatened regional identities, even as they participated in some aspects of globalization. Many young women in the Middle East, for example, voluntarily returned to more traditional styles of dress around 2000, as a means of asserting their independence from foreign-dominated globalization and pressures for greater homogeneity.

Globalization, in sum, was a real force, adding to the factors prompting change in childhood in the years around 2000. Combining with the longstanding push toward the modern model in some cases, creating some additional common influences, globalization did not erase forms of diversity both old and new. The global village embraced many different types of childhood.

Further readings

Paula Fass, *Children of a New World: Society, Culture and Globalization* (New York: New York University Press, 2007); Rachel Christina, *Tend the Olive, Water the Vine: Globalization and the Negotiation of Early Childhood in Palestine* (Charlotte, NC: Information Age Publishing, 2009); Marilyn Fleer, Mariane Hedegaard and Jonathan Tudge, *World Yearbook of Education 2009: Childhood Studies and the Impact of Globalization: Policies and Practices at Global and Local Levels* (New York: Routledge, 2009); Heather Montgomery, *An Introduction to Childhood: Anthropological Perspectives on Children's Lives* (Chichester: John Wiley & Sons, 2008); B.S. Trask, *Globalization and Families: Accelerated Systemic Social Change* (New York: Springer Science+Business Media, LLC, 2009); Hugh Hindman, ed., *The World of Child Labor: An Historical and Regional Survey* (Armonk, NY: M.E. Sharpe, 2009).

See the special issue of the *Journal of Social History* (vol. 38: June 2005) on globalization and childhood. Nancy Scheper-Hughes and Carolyn Sargent, *Small Wars: The Cultural Politics of Childhood* (Berkeley: University of

California Press, 1998); Tracey Skelton and Gill Valentine, *Cool Places: Geographies of Global Youth Culture* (London: Routledge, 1998); United Nations Development Program, *Human Development Report* (Oxford: Oxford University Press, 1999); Tobias Hecht, *At Home in the Street: Street Children in Northeast Brazil* (Cambridge: Cambridge University Press, 1998); Jeremy Seabrook, *Children of Other Worlds: Exploitation in the Global Market* (London: Pluto Press, 2001); James Watson, ed., *Golden Arches East: McDonald's in East Asia* (Stanford, CA: Stanford University Press, 1998); Timothy Burke, *Lifebuoy Men, Lux Women: Commodification, Consumption and Cleanliness in Modern Zimbabwe* (London: Leicester University Press, 1996). See also United Nations Children's Fund, *The State of the World's Children 2002* (New York: UNICEF, 2002).

Chapter 13

The dilemma of children's happiness

Children's happiness has gained new attention, on a global level, in recent decades. Growing valuation of happiness for the young raises a number of interpretive problems, and can serve as a further introduction to the crucial analytical problems in the latest phase of world history. The happiness theme helps focus the discussion of changes between the contemporary period and the past, including the causes of change; it advances consideration of comparative issues amid the obvious importance, but also the limitations, of Western models; and, above all, it virtually compels further evaluation of the complex impact of new ideas on adults and children alike. There's a lot we don't know about happiness as a recent-historical aspect of childhood, but what we do know is provocative, and the additional questions we must ask are revealing as well.

The first point is striking, but needs some immediate cautions: with a few limited exceptions, traditional societies (certainly agricultural societies) did not systematically associate childhood with happiness. We have seen that, during the classical period, few of the adults who left written records of their lives looked back fondly on any aspect of their early years, except for an occasional nice word about their mother. Parents, for their part, felt no particular responsibility for making children happy. Making them obedient and diligent, yes; providing moral training, definitely; but happiness was not part of the equation. In some cases, as with Christian belief in original sin, particular cultural artifacts might expand the normal distance between thinking about childhood and contemplating happiness. Frequency of child death and the obvious need to make children work surely complicated any notions of happiness even more generally.

But the cautions are important. The fact that childhood was not equated with happiness does not mean that adults usually sought to make children unhappy. Some did (some do in modern societies), taking pleasure in children's suffering. But there's no reason to think most adults were deliberately abusive, and many took real pleasure in their children and in enjoyments that could be shared – despite the lack of an explicit happiness commitment. Furthermore, except under abuse, there's no reason to think that children themselves were necessarily particularly unhappy in traditional contexts. Surely they sometimes were, because of inferior status and work burdens in addition to the normal complexities of growing up. But children could often take pleasure in community festivals, and the extent to which they were left free to indulge in play, during non-work times, may actually have encouraged a certain amount of satisfaction. It's the *idea* of happiness that was lacking.

This situation began to change, in Western societies, in the eighteenth and nineteenth centuries – precisely the point at which attention to happiness began to gain ground in other aspects of the culture. The Enlightenment expanded a positive valuation of happiness – this would show up, for example, in the American Declaration of Independence, with its reference to pursuit of same, along with life and liberty. As older ideas of original sin began slowly to decline in some Christian groups, a door was opened to rethinking how children might be treated. Later on, with the demographic transition, the decline in children's death rates reduced a huge barrier to adult commitment to thinking of children in terms of more positive commitments, and attacks on traditional levels of child labor may have had the same effect.

Nevertheless, actual discussions of children in terms of happiness surfaced surprisingly slowly. There were some references in England, around 1800, but nothing very systematic. A few poems about infant joy, some intellectuals' comments about children's "freshness and wonder" barely suggested some new thinking. In the United States, references to children's happiness crop up during the nineteenth century, but with a target on traditional moral upbringing, more than happiness *per se* (though it was interesting that the word was used): a variety of advice-writers urged parents that only through morality could children gain happiness: thus (in a famous manual by Catharine Beecher) "children can be very early taught that their happiness both now and hereafter, depends on the formation of habits of submission, self-denial, and benevolence." Late in the nineteenth century, prescriptive literature increasingly mentioned the importance of cheerfulness in children, but while this was a new obligation in a society increasingly interested in pleasant human interactions, it was only a stepping-stone to a real association of childhood and happiness. The idea was that cheerful adults did best in life, so children should be handled in ways that would encourage this result.

Finally, by the 1920s, a full commitment to children's happiness, at least in principle, emerged, at least in the United States. Childrearing manuals began to be peppered with statements such as "Happiness is as essential as food if a child is to develop into normal manhood or womanhood" and "The purpose of bringing-up in all its phases should be to make the child as happy as possible;" and book titles included *How to Have Cheerful Kids* (1927) or *Child Training: The Pathway to Happiness* (1948). Even discipline should be reconsidered: better to let children get away with minor infractions than spoil their pleasure with a reprimand. The only question, in this growing American surge, was whether children were naturally happy, so that adults merely had to worry about not spoiling things, or whether there were challenges in children's nature that adults had to work against, in which case the new commitment spelled some additional work for parents and others. Considerable advice, for example, was now directed toward urging mothers and fathers to work hard to seem happy around their kids, to provide positive example and context – whether they felt like being happy or not. Even government policy might convert: by the 1950s, White House conferences on children turned from issues of physical health to broader concerns with happiness. And new organizations for young people, such as the Boy Scouts and the Campfire Girls, built happiness into their fundamental principles: the Campfire group, for example, simply urged "Be Happy" as their final directive.

More than rhetoric poured into the new happiness movement in places such as the United States. Having even very young children smile for photographs was an interesting implementation of the new campaign. A host of consumer practices, buying toys and entertainments for the young, obviously sought to fulfill happiness obligations. The Disney Company, born in the 1920s, took as its motto "make people happy," and sold lots of movie tickets to families expecting precisely this result for their offspring. During the Depression-infused 1930s, a child movie star, Shirley Temple, was billed as the Sunshine Girl. Psychologists urged the importance of childhood happiness, and many adults would be prodded to explain their problems by reference to unhappiness in their early years, implying that this could and should have been avoided. Perhaps most revealingly, in terms of capturing the new prescription, the song "Happy Birthday" (using a tune written in the 1890s) surfaced in the mid-1920s; initially used for shows and singing telegrams, over the next two decades the verse became a standard symbol for what children deserved on a newly special day.

The idea that children should be happy, then, is an innovation of recent history, initially in Western societies probably headed by the United States. The notion is so deeply embedded by now that some may be surprised by this fact, assuming that the whole concept is somehow natural. The contrast with more traditional ideas and practices makes it clear that real innovation is involved.

What caused the change? A number of factors conspired, but in fact it's not entirely easy to identify the most important spurs. We have seen that preconditions include a much lower death rate and the attacks on child labor (many of which, by the twentieth century, invoked happiness as a contrast to undesirable work burdens). Consumerism played a huge role, as companies of various sorts realized how much could be sold to parents as part of the fulfillment of happiness obligations. New beliefs about adulthood loomed large as well, in societies that increasingly assumed that cheerfulness was a sign of mental health and a precondition for economic success. Compensation for the drudgery of schooling may have figured in as well, as parents, aware of the importance of school success, sought to motivate or reward kids with pleasures outside the classroom, and as schools themselves increasingly tried to make learning "fun."

Do these factors add up to a sense that a turn toward happiness is an inherent part of the modern definition of childhood – or was it, rather, a product of a particular set of Western circumstances? The question is significant, the answer far more challenging.

What is clear is that, in recent decades, many Western notions have been adopted, or have more spontaneously developed, in a number of other societies, making children's happiness an increasingly global topic. Not surprisingly, change has particularly involved more affluent and urban groups, particularly in societies where overall living standards continue to lag; but the theme is significant even so, as the ideas and behaviors continue to gain ground.

Thus in the past 20 years or so the rapidly growing middle classes in India have explicitly moved toward greater interest in children's happiness. The website www.indiaparenting.com thus recommends "home-based birthday parties" with particular themes, adding that inviting a clown or a magician can help assure happiness. More generally, over 20 percent of parents in one Indian poll claim that children can and should be taught to be happy. The move away from an older view of childhood (after infancy) as a time of strict moral and religious training is considerable.

Similar patterns emerge in the Middle East, apart from the strictest Muslim groups. Dubai, in the United Arab Emirates, features a "Favourite Things Mother and Child" shopping mall advertising itself as a premier site for a birthday party: with clowns, cotton candy machines, a petting zoo, and other entertainment centers, the site bills itself as "the first choice for parents who are looking for that personal touch, excellent organization, and a truly memorable day for their children." Not surprisingly, a strongly competitive element enters into upper-class birthday celebrations. In Egypt also, lavish parties with decorations, singing, and dancing greet affluent children.

Latin American families have widely embraced the idea of children's happiness, and here too the extensive adoption of elaborate birthday parties is one indication. Special emphasis on the fifteenth birthday, the *Quinceanera*, picks up an older cultural tradition, but the larger idea of the importance of a happy family extends well beyond this. For some groups, signs that children are happy help demonstrate that parents are meeting their obligations even amid poverty.

Change is particularly striking in China, where birthdays were traditionally downplayed (except for the sixty-fifth, which obviously celebrated old age in contrast to childhood), or even served as occasions for children to bring humble gifts to their parents in gratitude. McDonald's, for example, rents out "party rooms" for the new focus on children themselves, with trappings very similar to those in the United States. Beyond celebration, parents increasingly report that disciplining children has become a stressful aspect of parents (in contrast to just fifteen years ago), because of the desire to share happiness instead.

All of this leads to the next question: how much of this is simply selective emulation of the West, which could turn out to be temporary, and how much responds to other changes in the circumstances of childhood?

A strong "westernization" element is undeniable. The Chinese parents most likely to talk in terms of children's happiness are those who have attended western-based workshops and conferences. Middle Eastern commitments to birthday parties come from social segments strongly influenced by Western consumer culture in other respects. On the other hand, westernization may not be the whole story. China's dramatic birthrate reduction has produced parents increasingly anxious about the wellbeing of their child, both because he or she is the only one they have, and because they worry that contemporary children are missing out on fulfilling social experiences that they themselves remember growing up in larger families. Happiness here may seem to compensate for greater loneliness. In Japan and Korea, as well as China, strong emphasis on the importance of school success has helped parents accept responsibility for providing happiness as a legitimate need outside the classroom, to reward but also to compensate. Western models, in other words, may provide some slogans and practices that meet new and genuine needs that are part of modern childhood more generally. Time will tell about the durability and wider dissemination of new ideas and practices.

One point is clear, which is a standard concomitant of mutual cultural influences: while Western experience promotes new interest in children's happiness in other societies, this interest is blended with local components as well. The spread of childhood happiness takes on varied comparative dimensions, even when a common theme of change is involved.

Thus the happiness theme in India merges with the much older tradition of extensive indulgence toward infants, showering love and attention in ways that many Westerners view as excessively permissive. What's new is the extension of happiness concerns beyond this early period, but the merger has distinctive elements. Middle Eastern and, to some extent, Chinese interest in children's happiness applies much more readily to boys than to girls, again reflecting older patterns. If only because the happiness impulse is newer in China, and partially foreign, discussions of the dangers of overindulgence are more extensive than in the contemporary West, and parents remain much more likely to be publicly critical of their children, particularly where school performance is concerned. Childhood happiness, in other words, is a real change, but it does not override local variants, reflecting a particular version of the local/global tension standard in the experience of globalization more generally.

The final question, applicable wherever happiness interests have accelerated, involves what the new emphasis means, for responsible adults and for children themselves. There's no doubt that the change has generated a range of consequences. Most obviously, for many adults involved, the pressure to provide toys and other consumer items for children has escalated steadily, supporting massive industries and redefining as least part of what it means to be a good parent. Shared pleasures can result, but also a sense of obligation and even guilt – when children's happiness does not seem adequate – that can complicate the appreciation of parenthood. Outright manipulation adds to the complexity, as many companies, including Disney, explicitly train sales personnel to convince both adult and child customers that they are having a happy time, whether or not this is the case; some observers worry that the artificiality of consumer happiness can dull the capacity to identify the real thing.

The big issue, of course, is whether children are happier now that they're expected to be. Some observers note that some of the drawbacks of childhood remain constant – lack of power, the stresses of growing up physically and mentally – so that all the happiness rhetoric imaginable cannot really have much impact. Others would add that specifically modern features, such as school tensions or lack of spontaneous play time, may actually make the attainment of happiness more difficult. The fact is that measuring happiness across historical time is virtually impossible, and judgments about childhood may be particularly challenging.

The narrower question involves the impact of the happiness push itself. On the one hand, many adults really do try harder to please children, and to avoid children's discomfort, than their counterparts did in the past, and that may certainly have some effect. On the other hand, the happiness culture itself generates drawbacks. It makes children more dependent on entertainment, readier to declare boredom. It encourages parents, at least in some societies, to think of relationships with their offspring in excessively consumerist terms, buying lots of stuff but stepping back from deeper emotional contact. Above all, for children themselves, the new expectations of happiness undoubtedly make it more difficult to express or acknowledge sadness or disappointment, some of which arguably goes with the territory of childhood anywhere, anytime. A sad child now makes adults feel guilty, which in turn can encourage the child to conceal, which in turn can lead to outright depression that might otherwise have been avoided. Childhood depression is undeniably on the rise. Some of this simply involves new levels of diagnosis – the whole concept of depression entered psychiatrists' diagnostic manual little more than a half-century ago. But some may be quite real, triggered by new modern pressures on children, but also the ironic constraints generated by happiness goals themselves.

The rise of happiness commitments as a tentative aspect of the globalization of childhood is a complex topic. Its analysis must embrace the drawbacks of explicit attention to happiness as well as apparent advantages. It must recognize the difficulty of comparing present with past, beyond surface rhetoric. It obviously has to incorporate some subtle issues of regional comparison.

And any analysis must acknowledge the huge, and in some ways increasing, gaps among childhoods in contemporary history. Happiness rhetoric has little or no applicability to the millions of children who have been caught up in warfare or civil conflict, or who are exposed to new levels of disease or labor exploitation. Even in affluent societies such as the United States, where poor children get some glimpses of the consumerist version of children's happiness through TV shows and commercials, growing gaps in income and even food adequacy challenge at least the most widely shared notions of happiness.

The inquiry into new ideas of happiness is a legitimate topic, but it calls attention to stark divisions in the ways childhood is defined and experienced.

The rise of a dramatically new approach to childhood, with happiness front and center, is an important development in the recent history of children and those who care for them. It places contrasts between modern and traditional contexts in sharper relief, and invites further analysis of the causes of change. It focuses attention, as well, on comparative issues – on the force of Western example; on other modern factors encouraging attention to happiness; and also on diverse cultural reactions and combinations as happiness is integrated with existing approaches to childhood. The big question, where the new ideas have surfaced coherently at all, of how happiness changes the actual experience of parents and children, is surely complex, requiring probes beneath the surface of pervasive rhetoric. And the whole process is not only recent, but ongoing: we cannot yet know how extensively Asian or Latin American societies will integrate the happiness approach, and there are certainly culture critics in the West who urge reconsideration, particularly against purely consumerist interpretations of modern goals for children.

Further reading

Carl Nightingale, *On the Edge: A History of Poor Black Children and their American Dreams* (New York: Basic Books, 1993); Douglas A. Riley, *Depressed Child: A Parent's Guide for Rescuing Kids* (Lanham, MD: Taylor Trade Publishing, 2001); Jeffrey A. Miller, *The Childhood Depression Sourcebook* (Lincolnwood, IL: NTC/Contemporary Publishing Group, 1999); Nicholas White, *A Brief History of Happiness* (Malden, MA: Blackwell Publishing, 2006); Darrin M. McMahon, *Happiness: A History* (New York: Atlantic Monthly Press, 2006); Daniel Nettle, *Happiness: The Science Behind Your*

Smile (Oxford, UK: Oxford University Press, 2005); Gary Cross, *Kids' Stuff: Toys and the Changing World of American Childhood* (Cambridge, MA: Harvard University Press, 1997). See also Peter N. Stearns, "Defining Happy Childhoods: Assessing a Recent Change," in *Journal of the History of Childhood and Youth*, 3(2): 2010: 165–86; Christina Kotchemidova, "From Good Cheer to 'Drive By Smiling': A Social History of Cheerfulness," *Journal of Social History* 39: 2005, 5–38.

Chapter 14

Conclusion

Childhoods from past toward future

Here's an important and tantalizing debate, applying to childhood the kind of discussion that models of modernity have provoked in other aspects of contemporary life. For many children still in the labor force, rather than primarily focused on schooling, key experiences resemble what children in Western Europe, the United States, and Japan encountered a century or a century and a half ago. Traditional family economies are eroding, if only because of rapid urbanization and the incapability of rural families to provide. In this context, a good bit of children's work becomes novel, even though the fact of child labor is not; and this sometimes involves increased exploitation and new vulnerabilities. Many girls in India or Africa are today working as domestic servants in the cities, just as in Paris or New York in the 1850s; some are also sexually exploited on the job, as in the West before. Street trades, begging, and petty crime draw many children, as in Charles Dickens' London. In the West and Japan, of course, conditions later changed, after this long and often painful transition; the modern model came largely to predominate even for most children in the lower classes, though it brought its own problems. Will further economic development and protective legislation, including pressures by global standards, move the poorer children of India or East Africa, or their descendants, into the more standard model over the next decades (as the very recent trends of child labor curtailment suggest)? Or are local traditions or permanent economic inequalities, often worsened by the new effects of disease and war, going to sustain a durable division in childhood around the globe, not only by social class, but also by region?

Pulling together the strands of a global history of childhood is no easy task. This book emphasizes three major versions of childhood: hunting and gathering, agricultural, and modern. Childhood, in this argument, depends first and foremost on economic systems – and this is still true today, amid schooling and consumerism (children trained as consumers are vital to sustain this particular system). However, cultures and family structures enter in, which is why there is no *one* traditional agricultural childhood and, in addition to economic variables, no single modern childhood either. There are, nevertheless, two basic questions that spring from the world history of childhood, particularly the modern history, as we think about where childhood may head in the future.

Does what we've called the modern model of childhood, embellished by growing consumerism, describe the near future of childhood around the world, with an increasing number of societies moving closer to the model, while other societies extend its implications? (Another way to put this question: should we expect the frameworks of childhood to become more similar from one region to another over the next few decades?)

And question number 2: should we want this to happen?

Recent history, in its diverse implications for childhood, certainly complicates any predictive effort. Depending on place and social class, we have seen growing numbers of older children sold into what amounts to sexual slavery. From Africa, the most common image of children seems to involve their presence in refugee camps, fleeing ethnic or religious conflict, sometimes maimed in the process, with the bloated stomachs and empty eyes of the starving; or, in southern Africa, lying on beds as AIDS victims, the disease contracted from parents at birth. Contrast this with the overbooked teenagers in the suburbs of the United States or Western Europe, cramming for exams that will determine college entrance, the day apart from school parceled out among so many activities that it will take some later years, in early adulthood, to regain a sense of spontaneity. Or, with overloaded, fashion-conscious California-style "valley girls," or Japanese teenagers trying to figure out the latest must-have good. Or, in yet another place, with the older children volunteering as suicide bombers, with the encouragement not only of local militants, but often of proud parents as well. It seems impossible to fix on a single pattern of childhood.

There is the contemporary reality of child soldiers, not only in Africa but in parts of Southeast Asia, armed with weapons more deadly than children have ever possessed before. Reality, in this case, is complicated by the fact that, as we have seen, child soldiers used to form a significant part of many armies. While global outrage at use of child soldiers may be quite appropriate, particularly in light of the guns involved, it also reflects some new standards.

Quite recently, experts have begun to worry that huge gaps in economic standards and political instability are jeopardizing one of the most precious parts of the modern model of childhood, the decline of death rates. During the 1990s, death rates worsened or stagnated in over a third of all sub-Saharan African countries, while in war-torn Iraq, 10 percent of all children were now dying before five years of age (double the 1990 rate). More generally, malnutrition and AIDS were the worst villains in the slowing of gains in terms of global averages.

Current childhoods are deeply divided by values, by affluence or poverty, by political chaos or relative stability. An anthropologist recently captured one aspect of diversity through the image of the fenced-in school, seemingly a common symbol of modern childhood virtually anywhere. But in Africa, the fence is designed largely to help keep children out who want schooling, who see it as a key to their future, but for whom there are simply not enough places given the limited resources available. On the other hand, in the United States, the fence is partly intended to keep students in, who find school a boring trap, a site of bullying and social tension that seems unrelated to any meaningful future.

The kaleidoscope of childhoods in the contemporary world offers almost endless variety, with dramatically different sets of opportunities and sorrows. Yet without denying this aspect of reality, there is also a reality of some overriding trends. The trends may seem familiar, but they constitute real change for many of the societies involved, and they do largely point to the applicability of the modern model.

There was no country, not even the most impoverished and disease-afflicted, where infant and early child mortality had not continued to decline during the last third of the twentieth century, despite recent stagnation and valid new concerns. Sierra Leone, with the world's worst rate in 1998, with 316 children per 1000 dying before age five, nevertheless had experienced a 20 percent drop since 1960, along with a doubling of female literacy and a 50 percent increase in male literacy between 1980 and 1995. The world's poorest countries collectively, with 282 children per 1000 dying before age five in 1960, had seen rates drop to 172, while the world as a whole dropped from 193 to 86 – a truly astonishing rate of change by any historical standard. The rise in literacy rates, though less dramatic, showed similar movement, reflecting the increased presence of schooling in global child-hoods. It was certainly appropriate to note the huge gaps between rich countries and poor, and the equally huge differences in childhood experience that these gaps reflected; but the directions of change were widely shared, at least into the early twenty-first century.

Table 14.1 Infant mortality by world region, 1950–2000

| Region | Infant mortality rate (deaths before age one per 1000 births) | | |
	1950–55*	1980–85*	2000
World	156	78	54
Africa	192	112	87
Asia	181	82	51
Europe	62	15	11
Oceania	67	31	24
Northern America	29	11	7
Latin America and the Caribbean	125	63	32

*Probability of dying before age one.
Source: *Mortality1988*, table A.2; US Census Bureau International Data Base 2000, www.census.gov/ipc/www/idb.

Any world history with a strong modern focus faces the inevitable tension of balancing regional and global characteristics, and this is obviously true of childhood. Shared overall patterns coexist with sharp differences. Growing numbers of people and governments are agreeing that the principal focus of childhood should be schooling, not work – the global statistics for the past two decades bear this out clearly. Despite deeply troubling pockets of disease, hunger, and strife, it seems plausible to predict that the school–work balance will continue to shift in favor of education – but plausibility is not certainty, which is one reason why scholars often object to the presentation of models of modernity. Not only are many societies still too poor to afford widespread access to education, but also significant groups remain who are not yet convinced that schooling makes any sense.

Kailash Satyarthi, a lifelong crusader against child labor in India and a successful mobilizer of world opinion, tells a story about his own childhood that dramatizes the problem. He went to school regularly in the town of Vidisha (and ultimately would graduate from university), but he always saw a cobbler sitting with his son outside the school, cleaning and repairing shoes. He could not understand why the man didn't let his boy join him in class, and when he finally summoned up the courage to ask, the answer was straightforward: "Young man, my father was a cobbler and my grandfather before him, and no one before you has ever asked me that question. We were born to work, and so was my son." Obviously, the answer did not satisfy Satyarthi, who went on in adulthood to chair the Global March Against Child Labor, the South Asian Coalition on Child Servitude, and the Global Campaign for Education, winning both Indian and international support in the process and rescuing as many as 66,000 children from work in manufacturing, domestic service, and circus performance. But the clash of values should not be ignored, nor the fact that child labor until very recently continued to increase on Satyarthi's home turf, despite reform efforts.

The questions involve social class as well as geography, for the debate over making the transition to the more modern model of childhood has been immensely complicated by variations in outlook and resources within individual societies. In 2004, entertainer Bill Cosby openly berated many African-American parents and children for, among other things, not taking school seriously, including the training it offered in language and manners – they attended, but they did not really buy into the model. What most British working-class parents mean by an educational commitment for their children differs markedly from the more gung-ho devotion of their middle-class counterparts, another version of the divide within apparently modern societies. And while both groups maintain birth rates far below traditional levels, their average family sizes still vary in ways that suggest different attitudes toward children and toward parental responsibilities. It is vital to note the common surface trends, including birth rate reductions and transitions toward schooling, while going beneath the surface as well.

Furthermore, the modern model of childhood – quite apart from variations in meanings and huge differences in stages of change from one part of the world to the next – is only part of the story. It says nothing, even under the heading of schooling, about whether children are encouraged to think of themselves as individuals, or are urged to find their identity in family or religion. It says nothing about learning styles and their impact, between memorized rote lessons (quite successful for certain purposes) or a commitment to often chaotic self-expression and assurances for self-esteem. Even exposure to common aspects of global consumerism or a rhetoric of happiness hardly assures a similar basic experience or outlook.

In 1994, an American teenager residing with his family in Singapore committed an act of vandalism, spray-painting parked cars. He was arrested and sentenced to a caning, with 30 blows to be administered across his bottom. The incident provoked a furor in the United States and other parts of the West: the punishment itself seemed barbaric, and the offense seemed trivial. The whole episode occurred at a time when several East Asian leaders were emphasizing their commitment to community values and discipline, as against excessive Western individualism and sloppy permissiveness, and of course the arguments about the American offender seemed to dramatize precisely these divisions. Here were two clearly modern, successful societies pitted against each other when it came to defining key standards for childhood. There is simply no escaping the messy need to recognize the mixture of common patterns that move childhood away from traditional bases, and sweeping diversities regarding the deeper meanings of childhood. The boy was caned, not seriously damaged according to accounts at the time, but he quickly left the city-state to get back to Michigan.

Assessing childhood in world history involves more than the characteristic local–global complexity: it also requires some qualitative evaluation of the modern experience, both for historical and for comparative purposes. Granting that what is modern can be variously handled – between working class and middle class, or between East Asia and the West – surely these diversities pale before the achievement of modernity itself. Remember the crudely pioneering historians of childhood, a generation ago, who couldn't help but note the improvements of modernity over the constraints on childhood in the past. The same temptation surely applies to current comparisons: how can we fail to agree that childhoods are better in societies that have moved more fully toward modernity than to those in which childhood is more vulnerable to stark poverty and disease? There is no way to escape some confrontation with value judgments on this particular historical subject.

Who could want, to take the most obvious apparent gain, to go back to a situation in which 30 percent or more of all children would die within two years of birth, in which virtually no family could escape the experience of at least one child's death? We can grant some interesting medical–ethical issues concerning the particular Western (especially American) devotion to keeping some children alive at great expense and with uncertain prospects for a healthy adulthood, but surely the society that has successfully cast off traditional fatalism about children's survival has made undeniable gains.

But this is not the whole modern package, of course, and some of the other components are clearly more open to debate – not about returning to the past, which is an improbable quest, but about recognizing that something other than pure progress describes the relationship of present to past, or of the more modern societies to those still grappling with transition. It is vital to remember some of the strengths and clarities of more traditional, agricultural childhood as laid out in the early chapters of this book.

Indeed, judging by polling results, many American parents, if they could articulate their historical model, would probably prefer more complex alternatives from the outset. They might not want to go back to ancient Rome, though more obedience might sound nice, but they definitely don't associate recent trends with unbridled progress. They would grant the improvement of modernity over certain agricultural traditions, with lower death rates, fewer crowded families, and schooling instead of some of the physical hardships and indignities of traditional work. But they might be inclined to argue that once modernity was achieved – say, early in the twentieth century – actual American childhood began to slide downhill. Still modern, it became too undisciplined, too self-centered, too disrespectful, too removed from family obligation – even apart from the debatable absorptions of rising consumerism. This might be why every American poll since the 1930s sees childless parents happier than those with children, and why parents who defined themselves as modern – a steadily growing group – indicated more concern about children and their own responsibilities than did self-identified traditionalists. Why else would "modern" parents tend to argue that the "good old days" were better for children (they probably meant an idealized nineteenth century, not really premodern good days) while expressing nostalgia for "more traditional standards of family life and responsibility." Without taking a parental approach exclusively, and while noting that 90 percent of American parents, while griping a lot, say they would choose to have children were they to do it all over again, there are some drawbacks to modernity that deserve comment, as against a blithely optimistic historical view.

There are two kinds of uncomfortable facts, though neither set is surprising. First, converting to some version of modern childhood does not remove all the problems that attended more traditional patterns. Take just one example: Abuse does not cease. It may be more clearly identified and attacked, as governments take a more active role; but there's a plausible argument that government monitoring does not match the kind of controls over abuse offered by tight-knit customary villages or neighborhoods. A historian of colonial America, well versed in childhood, notes how rare cases of child abuse were in New England, compared with more modern times. He admits that some punishments accepted then might be regarded as abusive today, and he certainly acknowledges the possibility of faulty records. But he argues that it was actually harder to conceal abuse in conventional villages than is the case today, which makes the absence of the kind of abuse crises encountered in more modern periods all the more impressive. Abuse, in other words, may have gotten worse; it certainly has not ended. Changes in definitions of abuse may not have kept pace with the problem.

The second set of facts involves issues that seem to attach distinctively to modernity itself. Declining birth rates have drawbacks, quite apart from transitional periods when parents are confused about proper targets and also have to adjust to the decline of sibling care. In contemporary India and China, birth control combined with customary preferences for boys has led to practices that create a considerable surplus of young men reaching sexual maturity – several million more young men than young women, in each giant nation. Lots of men are, as a result, going to have trouble finding normal outlets and satisfactions, and the situation could produce wider social tensions as well. This is a particularly dramatic instance, and it's always easier to identify problems in societies other than one's own.

Downsides of modern childhood go beyond distinctive implementations in distant parts of the world. Closer to home, the decline of close sibling relations certainly makes it easier for children to be lonely. New gaps between adulthood and childhood create new barriers of understanding. While lots of adults in traditional societies such as classical Rome once lamented the decline of youth – reflecting more about their own ageing than about actual youth – there is no precedent for the anxieties and divisions that surround modern adolescence. Psychological depression among children has almost certainly increased, granting that comparison with the past is difficult, and that we have become more attuned to the problem and so more likely to perceive it. Attention deficit disorder is another new and growing malady, though particularly widely identified in the United States, where patience with "overactive" children may have worn thin. Japan has its own categories. Early in the twenty-first century, several thousand Japanese schoolchildren suffered from a malady called *hikikomari*, an inability easily to leave home and function normally. In the West and Japan alike, youth suicides went up: 22 percent in 2003 alone, in Japan. Changes in family life, including greater marital instability, plus pressures associated with schooling and with finding identity and meaning, create a context for rising problems in these categories, in all the advanced industrial societies. We have seen that the push toward happiness may itself have directly counterproductive psychological effects on many children. Also troubling, in these same affluent societies, are acts of gruesome violence by children under 12, infrequent but dramatic and apparently on the rise. Eating problems have increased even more definably, ranging from the severity of anorexia nervosa to the more common, if less dramatic, escalation of childhood obesity. Given the changes in food availability and work and leisure patterns for young people, modern societies have not figured out the proper means to regulate children's eating habits, and the results are getting worse.

The point in all this is not to claim some dramatic deterioration of child-hood from the past, but to note that change has brought drawbacks as well as gain, along with some outright continuity added in, where patterns didn't change one way or the other. And this complex package is worth grasping, not just for the sake of historical accuracy, but as a means of helping modern societies, and societies moving toward the modern model, more clearly to identify areas that need attention, rather than celebrating pro-gressive triumphs alone. We may well hope that more and more societies will make the turn to low birth and death rates and to schooling rather than demanding work; but we should strive for more besides, to palliate some of the common problems associated with modern childhood. Quite properly, to take the now-familiar example, the World Health Organization has moved in recent years to seek new means of combating excess weight in children, along with its established historical mission against hunger and infant mortality. There is more to dealing with the issues of contemporary global childhood than pushing the modern agenda alone.

Many people are deeply committed to helping children; Kailash Satyarthi is one example, as are the many dedicated relief workers dealing with children in refugee camps around the world. It is legitimate, however, to raise two concerns about the attention available for children today, without claiming that, on a global basis, we face some unprecedented crisis. The first concern involves the tendency of most international movements to assume the validity of modern standards of childhood and urge that the rest of the world catch up. This approach minimizes the drawbacks of the modern model itself, while encouraging a patronizing tone towards the more tra-ditional societies, which may not produce a constructive response. The approach is undeniably humanitarian in intent, but charity does not always enhance mutual understanding. And at the same time, some of the problems in the more modern societies risk winning insufficient notice. The second concern, noted in Chapter 11, springs from the declining importance of childhood itself in the societies where the modern model has gone farthest – precisely the societies that still take the lead in modern global pronouncements. Increasing numbers of families either have no children, or have aged past the stage of active parenting. A provocative book by Muriel Jolivet describes Japan, admittedly with some exaggeration, as the first "childless" society; a British study of contemporary modern marriage, Young and Willmott's *The Symmetrical Family*, describes the fulfillment of contemporary relationships where both spouses work and jointly enjoy rewarding consumerism – and children are not mentioned at all. For increasing numbers of people in influential societies, in other words, most children at home and abroad are "other" – someone else's responsibility, neither seen nor thought about very often. They are poor, inner-city or remote rural, or immigrant, or foreign; they do not provide active, daily encounters in societies that steadily become less child-centered. Factors of this sort warrant attention, for contemporary children's issues are quite real and far more complicated than some well meaning rights pronouncements manage to convey.

Change, in the meantime, continues. The impact on children of new diseases such as AIDS; and new patterns of violence among children, whether youthful suicide bombers, or kids in Britain or the United States who turn guns on each other, mark new issues in the history of childhood in the late twentieth and early twenty-first centuries.

Implications of the further implementation of the modern model cause change as well. Many observers note a global trend toward the expansion of childhood or pre-adulthood, whether because of economic dislocations that prolong youth dependency, or the extension of educational requirements, or both. Lower birth rates also explain why parents, however reluctantly, can accept this expansion as well. China makes a new commitment to send 15 percent of its huge population to university, in the relevant age groups, a decision that will keep millions out of the labor force for a more extended period. American families note the number of college graduates who return to the family home for a period of post-adolescence youth, while they experiment with careers or maybe take on a bit more education. A Harvard admissions officer argues that a period of post-college youth is becoming psychologically essential as well, given the hothouse pace of successful childhood itself. Reasons for the extension of childhood may vary, and the phenomenon is not yet firmly established as a durable trend, but it seems to be cropping up in several different settings around the world.

Gender differences among children decline, though this is still fiercely disputed in some societies. Declining birth rates mean that a growing number of families have only a son or two, or a daughter or two – and those with only daughters inevitably pay more attention to girls than their traditional counterparts once did, even in places such as China. Education continues to equalize: from Iran to the United States, 55–60 percent of all university students are women. Some observers even argue that, with their greater interest in education and their ability to take advantage of jobs in the global economy that sometimes marginalize male youth, young women are beginning to reap distinctive benefits from modern childhood, compared with their male counterparts. Not enough to rectify traditional overall gender inequality yet, but sufficient to bear watching.

Recurrent change in childhood is not a modern monopoly. Childhood changed massively in the conversion from hunting and gathering to agriculture. Later shifts in social organization and religious beliefs brought more modest alterations, but significant ones. The advent of modern ideas and conditions for childhood, spread by imitation, by international pressure, and by the sheer requirements of trying to build industrial economies and modern states, heightened the pace of change once again – always amid great variety. The shifts are fundamental and they are still, in historical terms, very recent, even in the societies that pioneered the first versions of modern childhood. It is small wonder that difficult adjustments continue; that adults and children continue to debate what childhood should entail, whether explicitly or implicitly; and that further change is inescapable. The beauty of the history of childhood, for all its complexities and debates, is that it provides a roadmap of where this human experience is coming from, as it barrels through the present on its way from past to future.

References

Michael Young and Peter Willmott, *The Symmetrical Family* (New York: Pantheon, 1973).

Mitsukuri Shuhei, "On Education," in William Braisted, transl., *Meiroku Zasshi: Journal of the Japanese Enlightenment* (Tokyo: University of Tokyo Press, 1976), 106.

Muriel Jolivet, *Japan, A Childless Society?* (New York: Routledge, 1997).

Paula Fass, ed., *Encyclopedia of the History of Childhood*, 3 vols (New York: Macmillan, 2004).

Philippe Ariès, *Centuries of Childhood: A Social History of Family Life* (New York: McGraw-Hill, 1962).

Steven Mintz, *Huck's Raft: A History Of American Childhood* (Cambridge, MA: Harvard University Press, 2004).

Index